PIPE FITTINGS

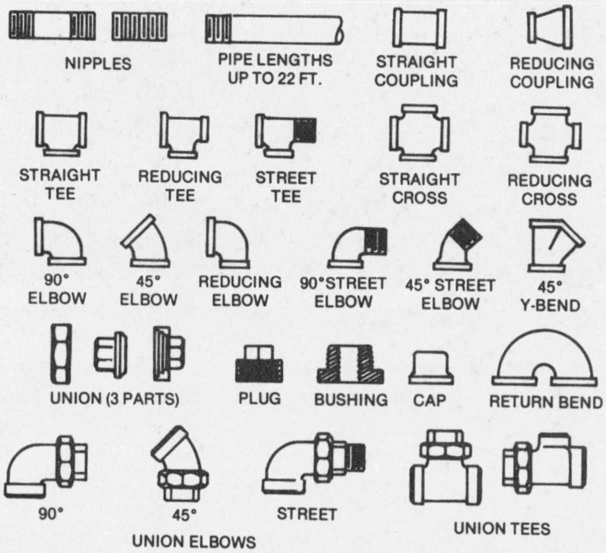

Here are the common steel pipe fittings. Nipples are simply short lengths of pipe threaded on both ends. Reducing fittings join two different sizes of pipe.

Compression fittings of the flared-tube type are the easiest for the novice to handle when working with copper tubing.

STANDARD STEEL PIPE (All Dimensions in Inches)					
Nominal Size	Outside Diameter	Inside Diameter	Nominal Size	Outside Diameter	Inside Diameter
1/8	0.405	0.269	1	1.315	1.049
1/4	0.540	0.364	1 1/4	1.660	1.380
3/8	0.675	0.493	1 1/2	1.900	1.610
1/2	0.840	0.622	2	2.375	2.067
3/4	1.050	0.824	2 1/2	2.875	2.469

SQUARE MEASURE

144 sq in = 1 sq ft
9 sq ft = 1 sq yd
272.25 sq ft = 1 sq rod
160 sq rods = 1 acre

VOLUME MEASURE

1728 cu in = 1 cu ft
27 cu ft = 1 cu yd

MEASURES OF CAPACITY

1 cup = 8 fl oz
2 cups = 1 pint
2 pints = 1 quart
4 quarts = 1 gallon
2 gallons = 1 peck
4 pecks = 1 bushel

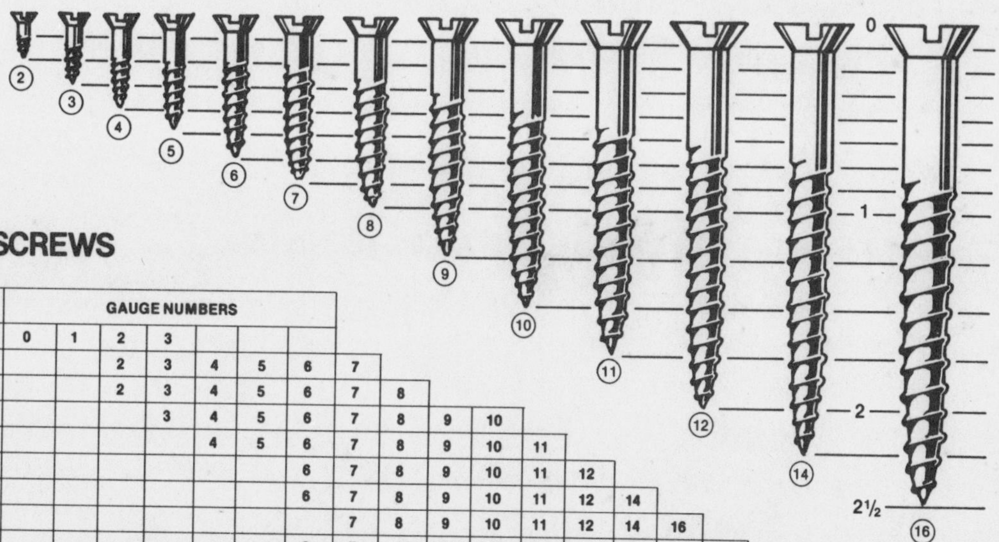

WOOD SCREWS

LENGTH	GAUGE NUMBERS																
1/4 INCH	0	1	2	3													
3/8 INCH			2	3	4	5	6	7									
1/2 INCH			2	3	4	5	6	7	8								
5/8 INCH				3	4	5	6	7	8	9	10						
3/4 INCH					4	5	6	7	8	9	10	11					
7/8 INCH							6	7	8	9	10	11	12				
1 INCH							6	7	8	9	10	11	12	14			
1 1/4 INCH								7	8	9	10	11	12	14	16		
1 1/2 INCH							6	7	8	9	10	11	12	14	16	18	
1 3/4 INCH									8	9	10	11	12	14	16	18	20	
2 INCH									8	9	10	11	12	14	16	18	20	
2 1/4 INCH										9	10	11	12	14	16	18	20	
2 1/2 INCH													12	14	16	18	20	
2 3/4 INCH														14	16	18	20	
3 INCH															16	18	20	
3 1/2 INCH																18	20	24
4 INCH																18	20	24

WHEN YOU BUY SCREWS, SPECIFY (1) LENGTH, (2) GAUGE NUMBER, (3) TYPE OF HEAD—FLAT, ROUND, OR OVAL, (4) MATERIAL—STEEL, BRASS, BRONZE, ETC., (5) FINISH—BRIGHT, STEEL BLUED, CADMIUM, NICKEL, OR CHROMIUM PLATED.

In this volume . . .

HERE'S AN ELEGANT electric serving cart—a plug-in warmer under a lift-up top that keeps side dishes piping hot. See plans on page 2570.

"HEAR THOSE BIRDS, old friend? Be ready, because they'll be here soon." It's a thrill only a hunter can know. But everything depends upon the scattergun he holds. Check how to select a shotgun, page 2674.

THERE'S UNTOLD EXCITEMENT in soaring high against the sky, pivoting, then plunging down through the soft snow. But only if you take care of your skis. See page 2698.

THE ARTICLE OFFERS advice from the experts, for all types of skis, on the best ways to wax, transport, store, file edges and repair gouges.

IN THE SILENCE of the depths are some of nature's most beautiful creatures, and you can capture them on film. But first you must learn scuba. See page 2692.

YOU SHOULD always dive with a buddy and wear a flotation vest in case of emergency.

YOUR FIRST GLIDE through a coral-filled world will thrill you with a feeling of flying.

BUILD AN EARLY AMERICAN server. It's great for storage and has the handsome antique look of a beautifully handcrafted piece. Find the plans on page 2564.

BELOW YOU SEE a complete sewing center, with built-in sewing machine, storage, and a generous cutting table. On page 2586 you'll find this sewing center and others. Make one soon!

Popular Mechanics

do-it-yourself encyclopedia

in 20 volumes

a complete how-to guide for the homeowner, the hobbyist—
and anyone who enjoys working with mind and hands!

All about:

home maintenance
home-improvement projects
wall paneling
burglary and fire protection
furniture projects
finishing and refinishing furniture
outdoor living
home remodeling
solutions to home problems
challenging woodworking projects
hobbies and handicrafts
model making
weekend projects
workshop shortcuts and techniques
hand-tool skills
power-tool know-how
shop-made tools
car repairs
car maintenance
appliance repair
boating
hunting
fishing
camping
photography projects
radio, TV and electronics know-how
clever hints and tips
projects just for fun

volume 17

ISBN 0-87851-082-6
Library of Congress Catalog Number 77 84920

MANUFACTURED IN THE UNITED STATES OF AMERICA

contents

VOLUME 17

DRAWER SLIDES on single glide mounted on shelf center. Cabinet sides are let into the blind dadoes in top.

An early American server

This handsome period piece features 'trackless' bypassing doors that are flush when they're closed. It is great for storage and has an old-world antique look

By HARRY WICKS

SEE ALSO

Cupboards, china . . . Drawers . . . Dry sinks . . . Gossip benches . . . Serving carts

THIS VERSION of an early American server is a handsome piece of furniture that offers well-organized storage space and occupies little floor area. It has the look of old-world craftsmanship.

Easy to build with power tools, the cabinet offers these advantages:

- Plaques ''carved'' of plastic look, and can be worked, like real wood.

HOW THE HARDWARE WORKS . . .

SLIDING DOORS bypass with the left-hand door (facing the cabinet) always remaining in front, no matter which door is moved. Bottom view of doors (left) shows a groove needed for the track that goes on the left door. A plunger (below, left) and guide pin (not visible) are only hardware in the cabinet bottom. Left door slides on the pin, corner brace acts as a stop. Bottom view shows shelf bottom and hardware mounted in cabinet on doors. Glide on shelf is for the drawer.

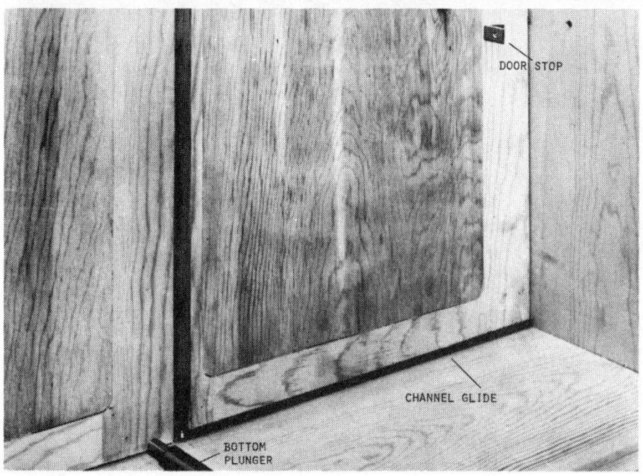

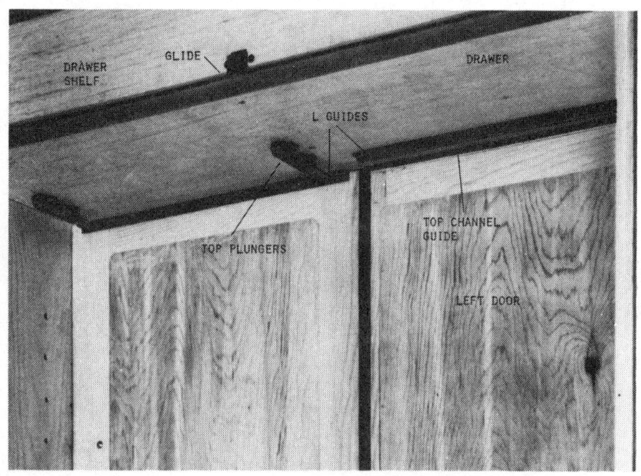

• Hardware for bypassing doors is concealed (there's no bottom track to clean out) and places the doors in a flush position when they are closed.

In building the prototype, we made sure that all door stiles and rails would reveal 2 in. (in closed position). Thus, you'll notice in the drawing that these sizes vary because of the bevel cuts and the cabinet stiles and rails.

The cabinet. To start, cut all pieces to size. They'll make quite a pile, so label each piece lightly with a soft pencil for easy identification later. Make certain that you kerf the underside of the drawer shelf before you go farther. This kerf is needed for the top rail and, should you forget it, would be a time-consuming task by hand after the cabinet is assembled.

It is good practice to tack the pieces together temporarily, using diagonal braces on the back to keep it in square. When satisfied with cabinet fit, you can assemble the drawer and doors using the cabinet for final determination of their measurements.

The drawer is simply a box made of ½-in. pine. Because it is shallow, ⅛-in. hardboard is adequate for the bottom, which is let into dadoes. The false drawer front is ¾-in. pine, and with the saw blade set as shown on page 2569, the raised panel is quickly made. Bevel ends first, then cut the lengths.

The doors are a little trickier, mostly because of the varying stile and rail widths. You may find it easiest to lay out both doors on the workbench and, after marking, shiplapping one stile or rail at a time. The ¼-in. plywood panels are let into a rabbet; the decorative plaques, glued to the fronts, are of molded plastic. Because the hardware will not permit a door thickness greater than ¾ in. (or the doors won't bypass), these had to be reduced in thickness. The plaques are attached with adhesive.

The hardware. You pay a slight price—in labor—for the beauty this hardware offers. It *is* harder to install than conventional sliding-door hardware and will likely call for a little trial-and-error fitting. The hardware package has a template. However, I found that once the cabinet was completely finished (varnished), a

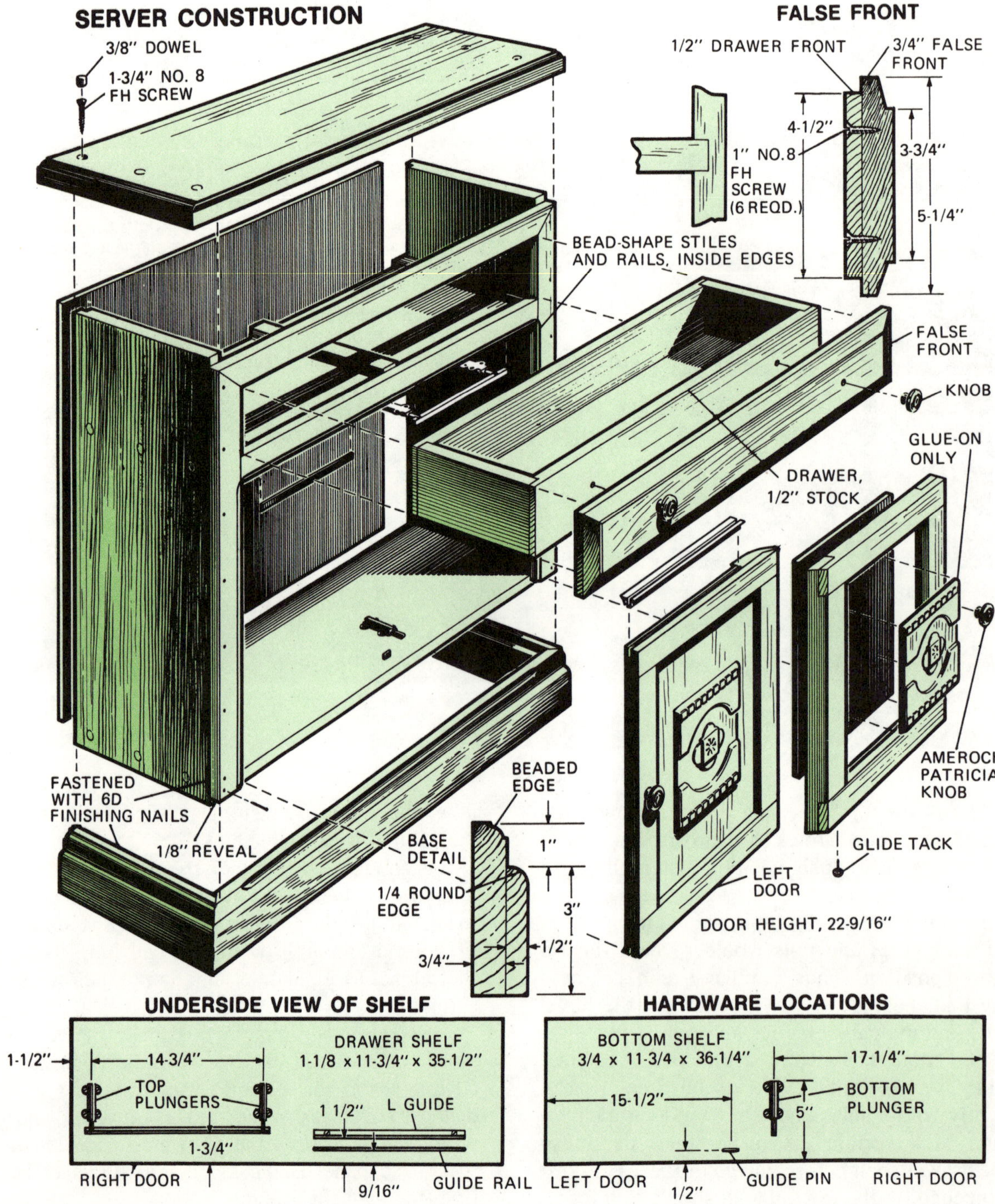

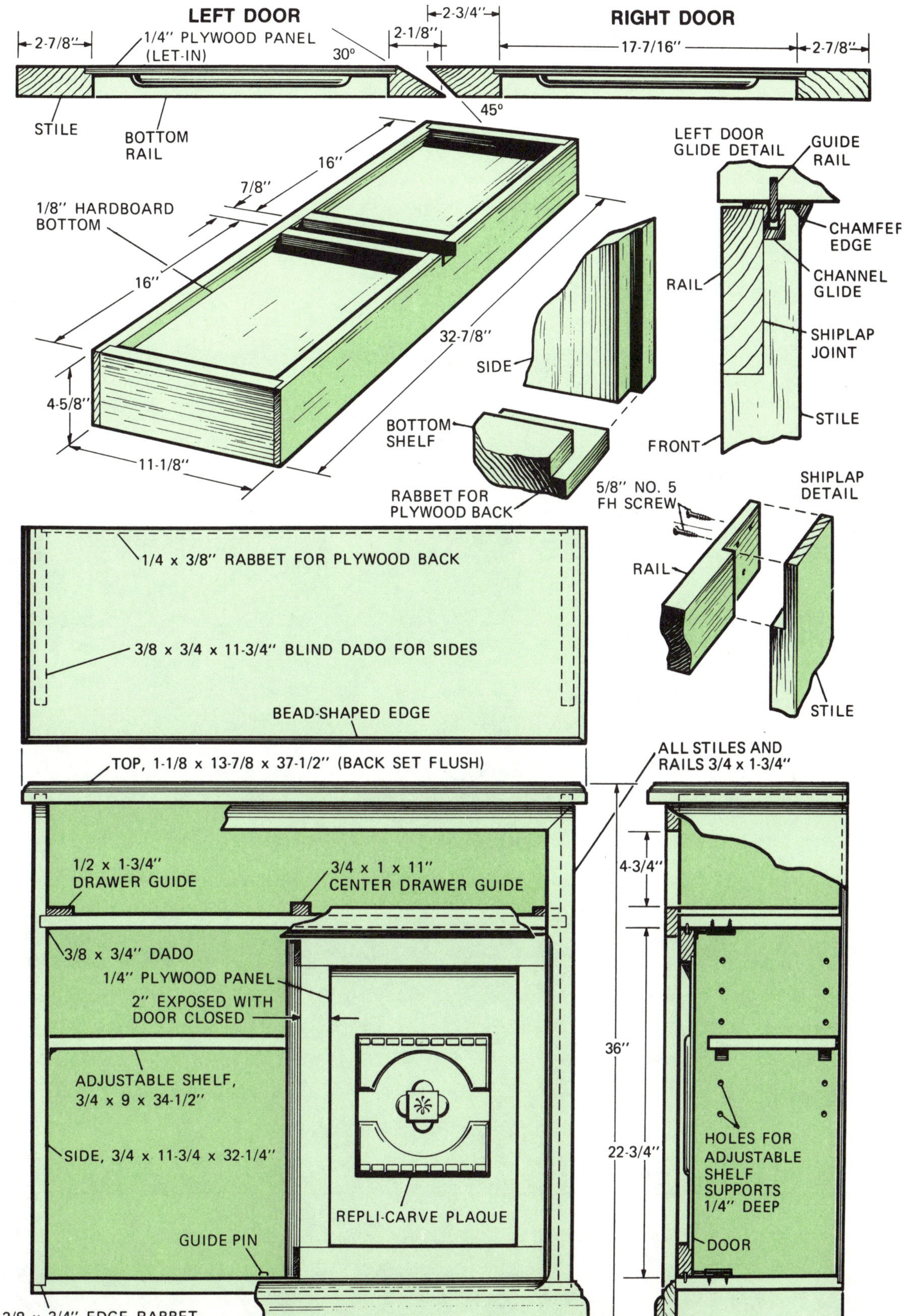

Technical Art by Fred Wolff

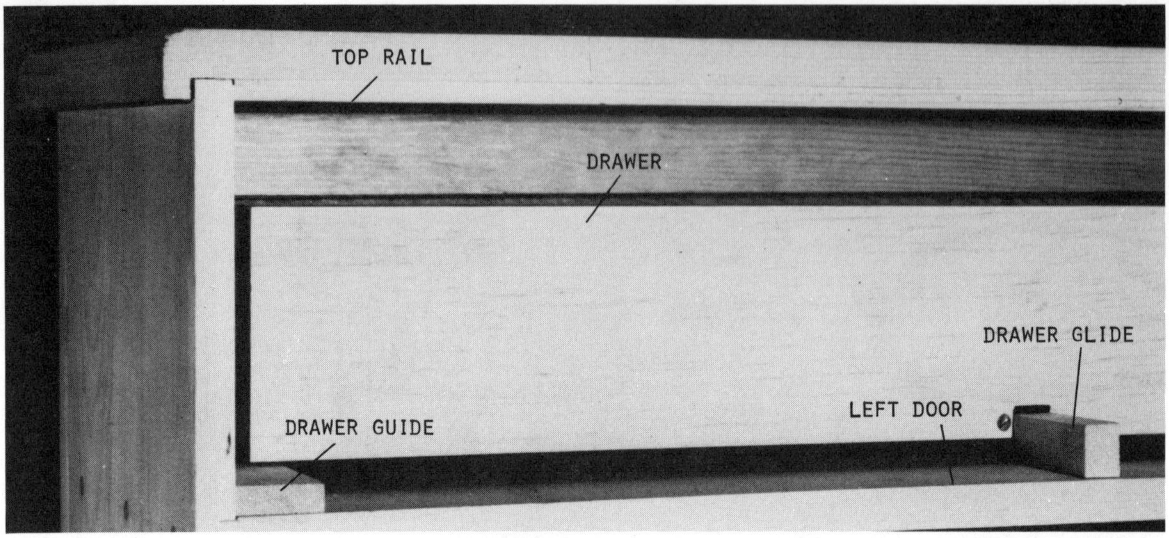

CUSTOMIZING THE PLAQUES

CUT DOWN the plaques to assure that door thickness will not exceed ¾ in. You can start by trimming four sides (right).

TRIM DECORATIVE nubs (below, left) so doors will bypass easily. When doors are in place, use belt sander to remove high spots.

PLAQUES, before and after trimming (below, right). Views of finished cabinet show that trimming doesn't hurt appearance.

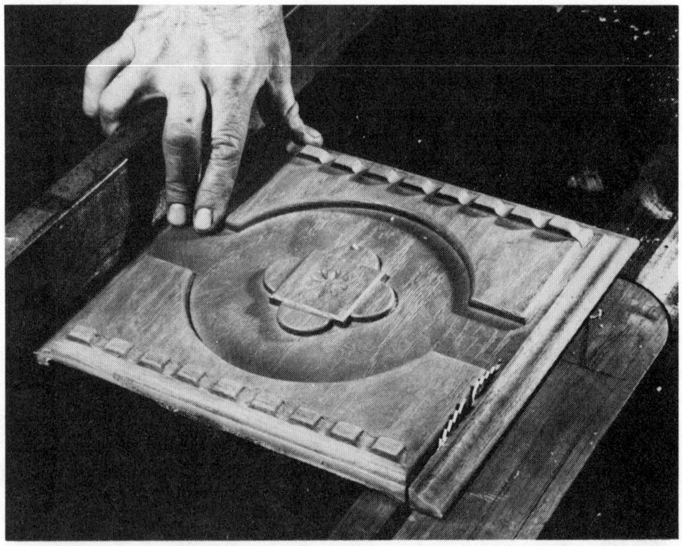

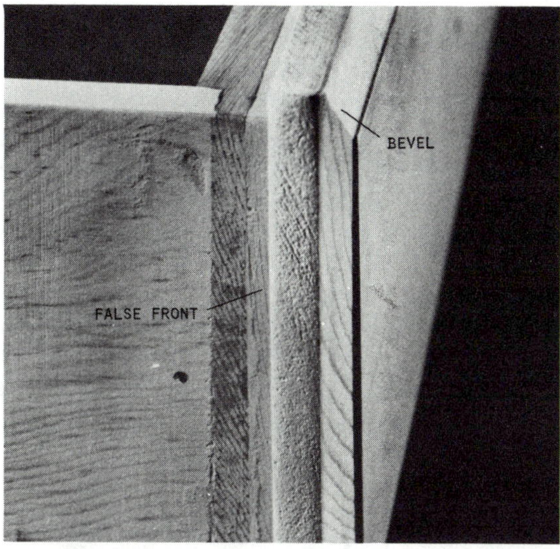

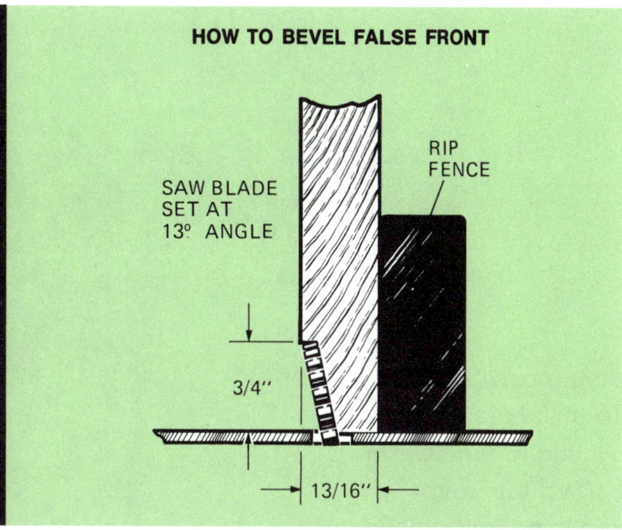

RAISED-PANEL effect is easily accomplished on a table saw; false front is then glued to the drawer.

quick blast of spray silicone made the doors bypass effortlessly.

Assembly. The cabinet top and sides are assembled using screws and dowel plugs. All other assembly is accomplished with well-set finishing nails. The holes can be filled, but for an antique look, they were not on the server shown.

Finish. After thorough sanding, wipe the server with a tack cloth and apply oil stain. Wipe off excess stain and let dry overnight. Next day, antique the server using a tube of burnt umber and a rag to darken those areas that are dark on actual antiques. Use the rag to blend all dark spots into adjacent stain.

Coat the plaques with red enamel, allow to dry and antique the same way as before using a flat black enamel.

Finally, give the entire piece three coats of varnish. You can, if desired, let the final coat cure for three or four weeks and then apply Butcher's Wax.

MATERIALS USED IN PROJECT

If not available locally, write to manufacturers for buying information.

Hardware: Bara Industries, Inc., Box 935, Somerville, NJ 08876.

Plaques: Emco Repli-Carve, Box 864, New York Ave., Des Moines, IA 50304.

Finish: Pecan oil stain and Heirloom semigloss varnish, McCloskey Varnish Co., 7600 State Rd., Philadelphia, PA 19136.

HARDWARE for the pair of sliding doors is shown below. It is also available for four-door cabinets.

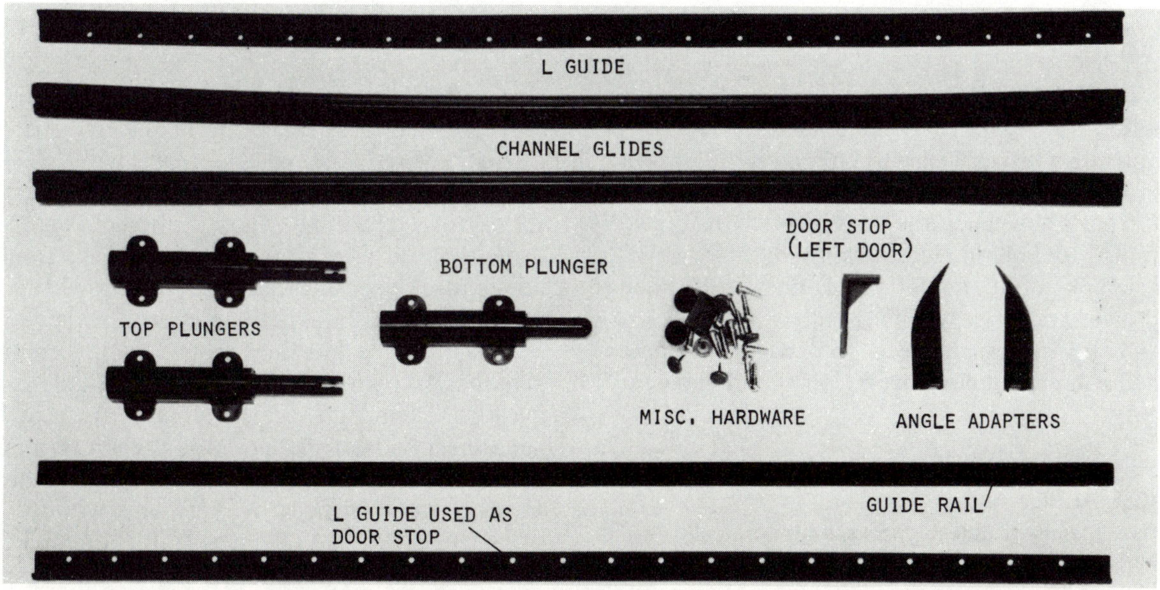

This serving cart features a durable plastic laminate top. A plug-in food warmer under a lift-up top keeps side dishes piping hot and flavor perfect when you entertain

By WAYNE C. LECKEY

Build an electric serving cart

IF YOU MAKE the mistake of showing your wife this elegant early American serving cart, you might just as well start building it. She won't give you a moment's peace until you do.

That's how much she'll love its rich fruitwood finish, its built-in electric warming tray, its retractable cord, its felt-lined silver and linen drawer and its easy-rolling ball casters.

You'll need such special tools as a wood lathe and router, but don't worry about being an expert at finishing. Its slick finish is a decorative laminate—you just cement it on and that's it.

We covered the original cart with Consoweld's Colonial cherry and used solid cherry for the turned legs and exposed edges of the top, drop leaves, drawer fronts, lower shelf and front crossrails. These surfaces were later stained and finished to closely match the cherry laminate.

First turn the four legs from 1⅞-in. turning squares. To turn all four alike, make a full-size cardboard template to mark off the round and square sections of the leg. Mount each turning between centers so the top of the leg is at the headstock end of the lathe. This way, with a bit in the tailstock, you'll be able to bore holes dead-center in the ends of the legs for casters.

SEE ALSO
Dining tables . . . Kitchen accessories . . . Mobile furniture . . . Servers

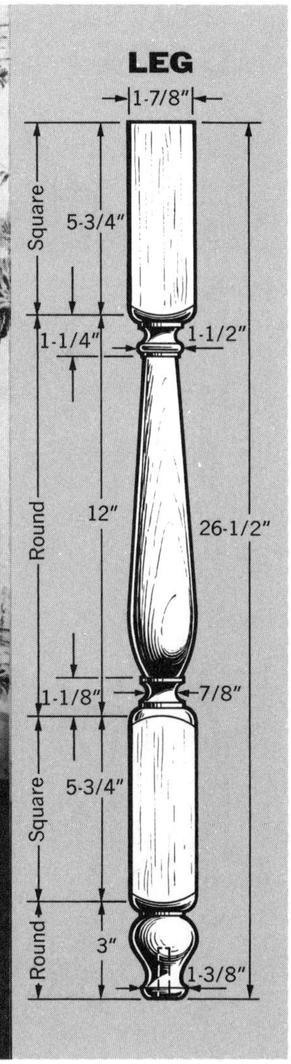

Take caliper readings directly from the template.

Next cut the four end aprons. The two top ones are 5¼ in. wide; the two bottom ones are 4⅜ in. Cover the aprons with laminate before you trim them to size and bore the dowel holes. The upper aprons are kept even with the tops of the legs and 3/16 in. in from the face. The lower aprons are ¾ in. from being centered on the square portion of the leg to allow for the bottom shelf which rests on them. Now dowel and glue the aprons to the legs. Cover and cut the top and bottom back aprons to size and bore for dowels. They're 26¼ in. long and the same widths as the end aprons, set in the same amount and cut from fir plywood.

The recessed front apron is built up as shown in section A-A. Top and bottom rails of cherry are glued and nailed to a center piece of ½-in. fir plywood. Then a filler block of cherry is glued to the front to divide the recessed apron exactly in half. The ends are bored for dowels as before to align with holes in the legs. The top surface of the top rail is later covered with laminate so the lid will be flush with the rest when closed.

Cut the lower crossrail 26¼ in. long from cherry and bore for dowels. Now glue the parts to the end assemblies. Do this at one time, preferably with clamps. Keep the assembly square.

While the glue is drying, make the recessed shelf for the Salton warming tray (Detail A). It consists of a ¾-in. fir-plywood panel with a hole in it to fit the flanged tray. Two ¾-in.-square

SERVING CART

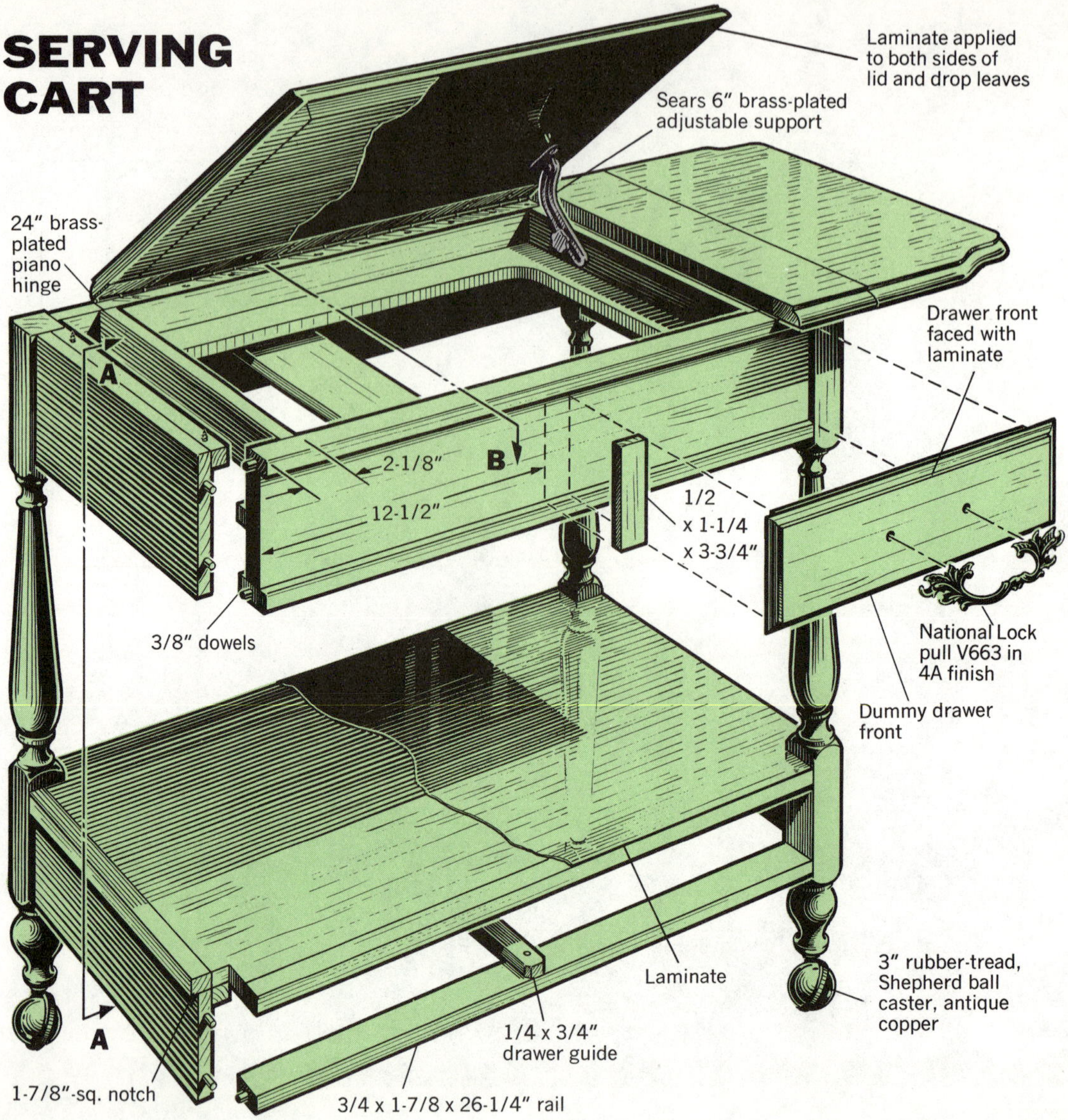

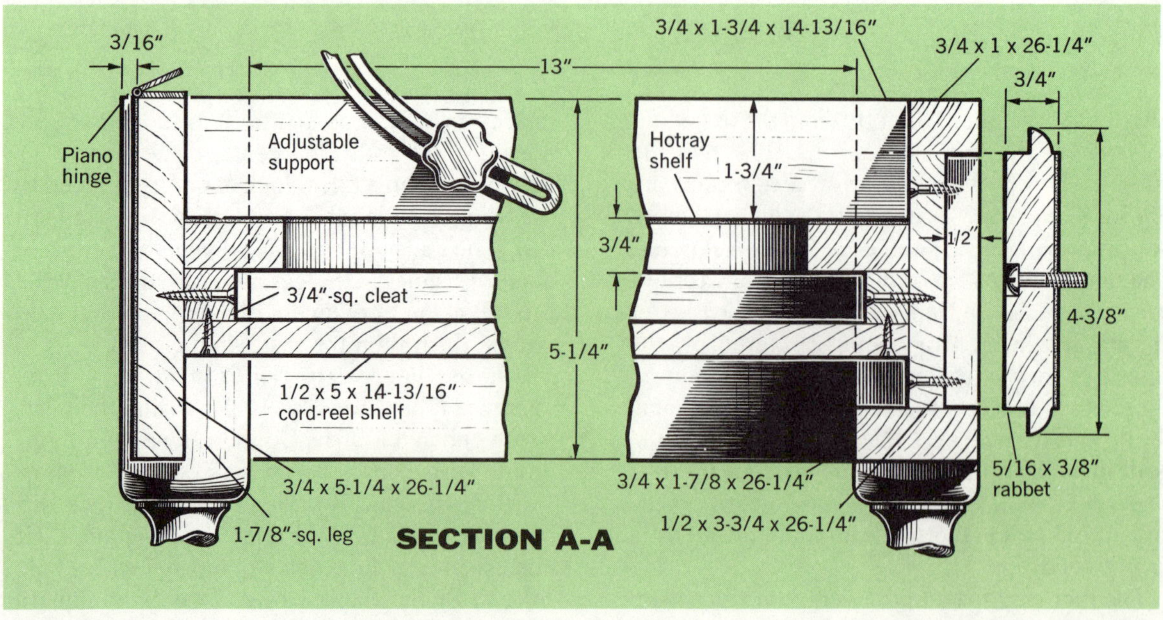

SECTION A-A

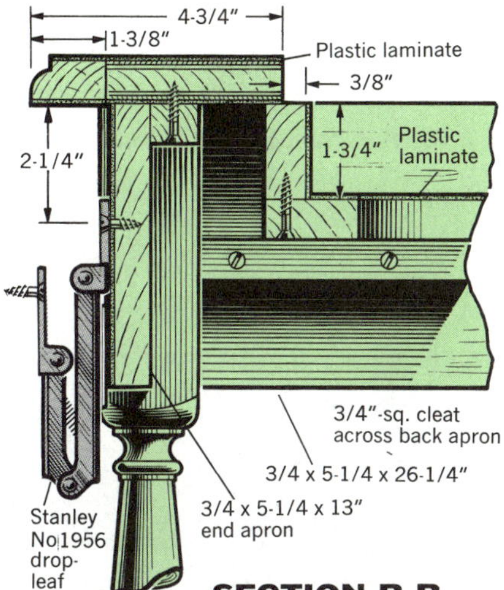

SECTION B-B

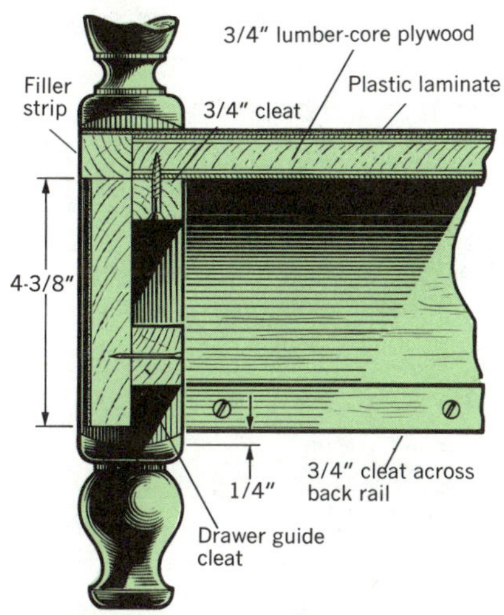

cleats are glued to the front and back edges, and two ¾ x 1¾-in. members are glued on edge at the ends. (Here it's wise to check the 14$^{13}/_{16}$-in. dimension against the actual inside width of the cart.)

Since the tray shelf is also faced with laminate, it's easier to cover it before it's installed. We covered the shelf top and inside surfaces of the ends with yellow laminate. After installing it, we added 1¾-in.-wide strips of the laminate to exposed parts of the aprons. The ½ x 5-in. cross-member, screwed to the shelf cleats, supports the self-winding cord reel.

To make the bottom shelf, glue ¾ x 1-in. strips of cherry to the edges of a plywood center panel, notch the corners for legs and cover the top with laminate. Attach the completed shelf to the cart with screws through cleats glued to the end aprons. (Study section B-B.)

Make the lid, top and drop-leaf parts essentially the same way, but make the edge pieces 1½ in. wide and miter the corners. Note that the narrow top sections are banded only on three edges. Both top and bottom surfaces of the five top parts are covered with laminate, then the edges are shaped. Use a standard drop-leaf cutter and its mate to shape the hinged edges. The other edges can be shaped with less of a shoulder or even with a different-shaped cutter. Mortise the drop-leaf table hinges flush with the laminate. Be sure the barrels of the hinges are centered exactly on the shoulder of the shaped edge.

Attach the narrow top sections to the cart with cleats and screws from below and let them overhang the ends 1⅜ in. The lid should fit between

UNDERSIDE view of drop leaf shows bracket which holds leaf up. It's surface-mounted with four screws.

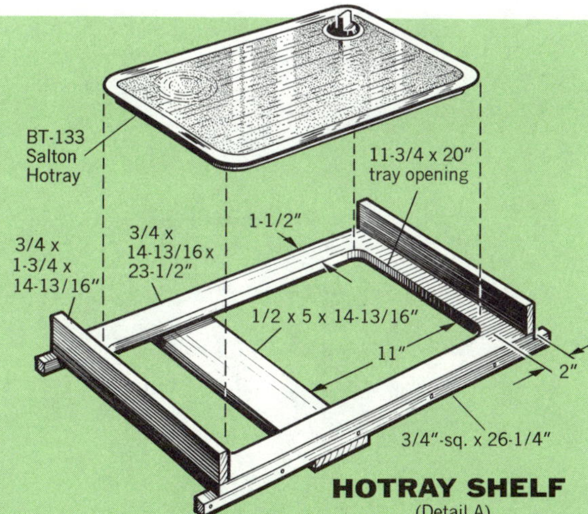

HOTRAY SHELF
(Detail A)

the two with $^{1}/_{16}$-in. clearance at each side. It's hinged at the back with a piano hinge mortised flush with the laminate. The lid should overhang front and back ¾ in. Adding an adjustable support like the one shown completes the lid. Fit the drop leaves with surface-mounted, spring-loaded brackets.

The drawers complete the job. The two upper ones are dummies, of course; they're actually made and attached before laminate is applied to the inside of the tray shelf. The fronts are pieces of cherry, rabbeted around the back, faced with laminate and shaped. Attach the pulls before you screw the fronts in place.

Make the front of the bottom drawer as just described, and the rest is typical drawer assembly (see construction details, below). Attach a grooved guide to the bottom to ride on a rail screwed to the front crossrail and to a cleat added to the back apron. Note in section B-B how drawer rubrails are nailed to the end aprons.

Wire the plug-in Acopian cord reel to a junction box mounted on the tray bottom. Use wire suited for 167° F., and be sure the tray is properly grounded.

A RETRACTABLE REEL, which holds 6 ft. of cord, is wired to the junction box that comes with the tray.

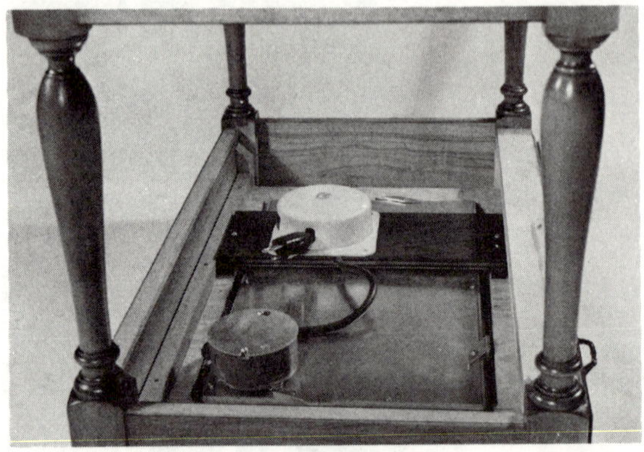

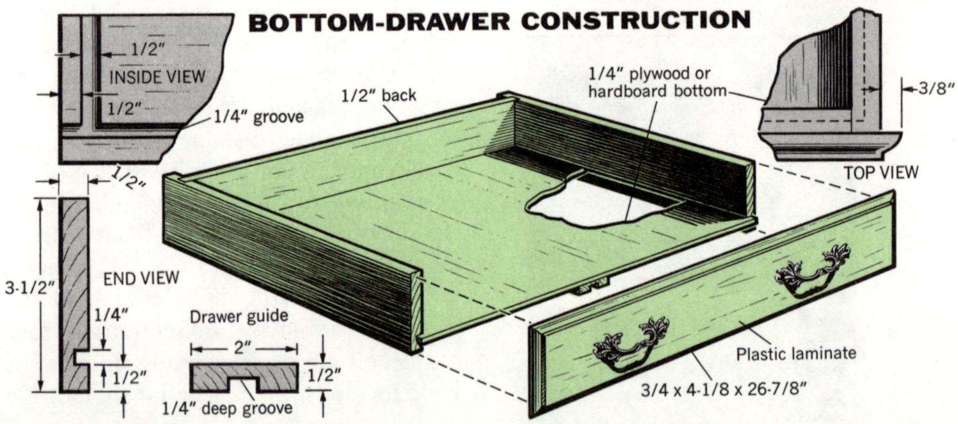

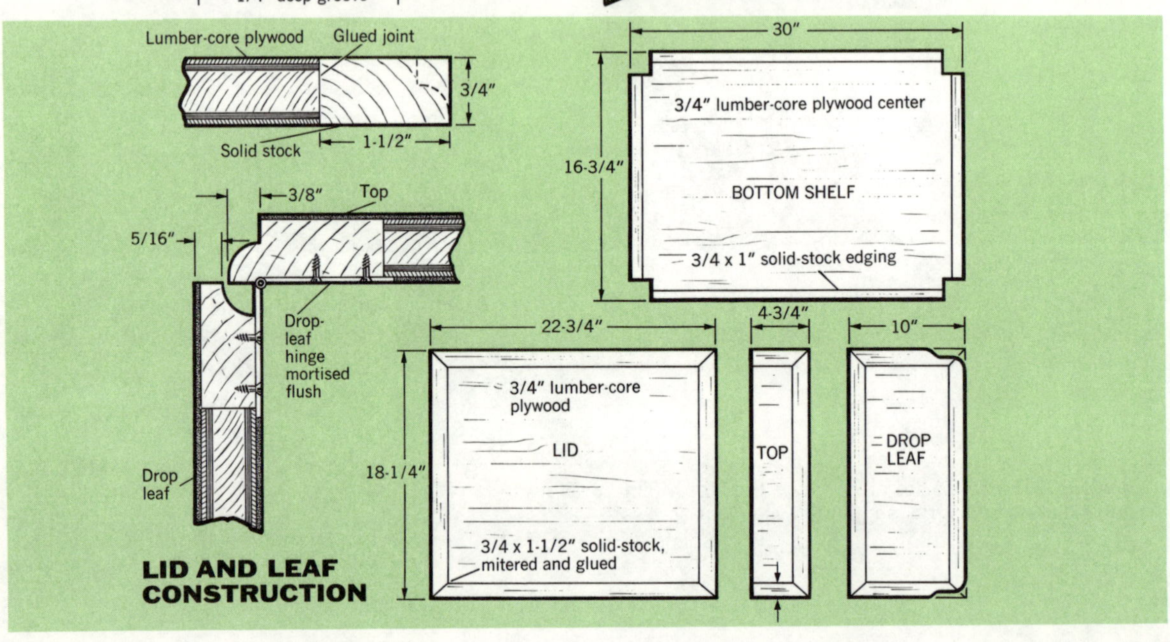

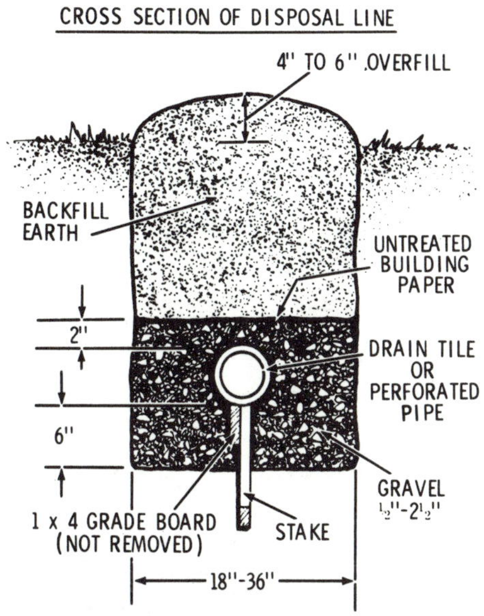

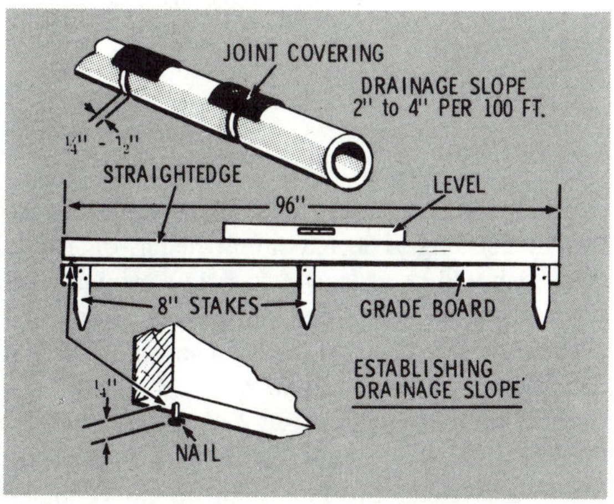

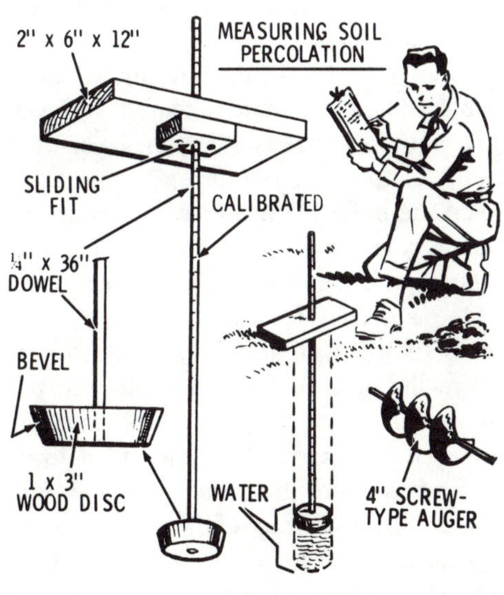

Have a trouble-free septic system

Knowing how the system operates, how and why its design is determined, aren't difficult. But they're the first steps in keeping it running well

TROUBLE-FREE OPERATION of a septic-tank disposal system depends, first of all, on good design, adequate size and proper installation. Of equal importance is the volume of waste discharged into the system, and how often the tank is inspected and emptied.

Most communities require strict compliance with local ordinances in granting a permit for a disposal system and approving its installation. Therefore, when planning one, first acquaint yourself fully with local regulations.

How system works. In a typical septic-tank disposal system, waste entering the tank decomposes in liquid that normally fills the tank up to the outlet. Part of the waste settles to the bottom forming sludge, and part of it floats on the liquid forming scum. Only the clear liquid, called "effluent," should pass through the outlet. The purpose of a septic tank is to condition the effluent for absorption in the soil. When sewage enters the tank, an equal volume of the effluent passes into the disposal lines to soak into the earth within about 36 in. from the surface. Disease-producing bacteria in the effluent are eliminated here.

Location requirements. The septic tank and disposal field must be located at safe distances

SEE ALSO
Bathrooms . . . Bathtubs . . . Drains . . . Garbage disposers . . . Plastic pipe . . . Plumbing

septic system, continued

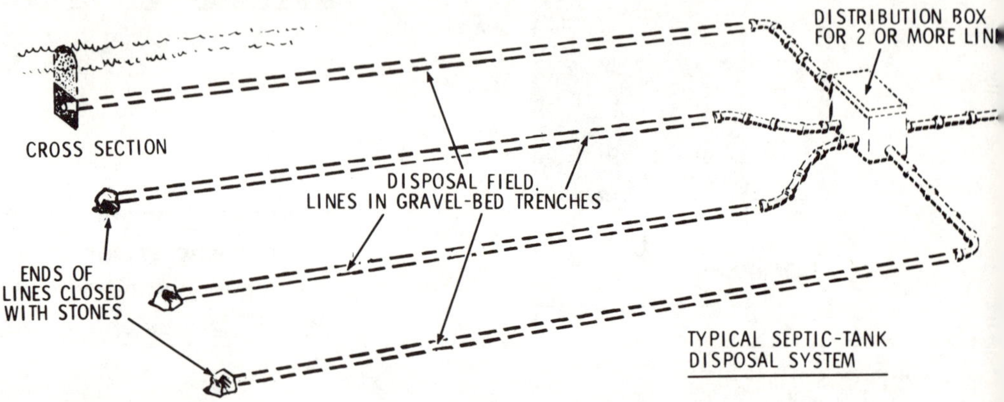

TABLE A
RECOMMENDED SIZE OF DISPOSAL-FIELD TRENCHES

PERCOLATION RATE — (MIN. WATER FALLS 1")	LINEAL FEET OF TRENCH PER BEDROOM			
	WIDTH 18" DEPTH 19"-30"	WIDTH 24" DEPTH 19"-30"	WIDTH 30" DEPTH 19"-30"	WIDTH 36" DEPTH 24"-36"
2 OR LESS	57	43	34	28
3	67	50	40	33
4	77	58	46	38
5	84	63	50	42
10	110	83	66	55
15	127	95	76	63
30	167	125	100	83
60	220	165	132	110

OVER 60—NOT SUITABLE FOR DISPOSAL TRENCHES.
NOTE—MINIMUM TRENCH LENGTH IS FOR 2 BEDROOMS.

TABLE B
DISTANCE BETWEEN TRENCHES

TRENCH WIDTH	FEET DISTANCE BETWEEN CENTERLINES
12" TO 18"	6'
18" TO 24"	6½'
24" TO 30"	7'
30" TO 36"	7½'

from sources of water supply. In general, the distance should not be less than 50 ft. for the septic tank and 100 ft. for the disposal field. Both should be on the downhill side of the water supply source, since ground pollution moves in the same direction as ground water.

A septic tank should be at least 5 ft. from any building. The disposal field should be located in an open area at least 10 ft. from buildings; about 15 ft. from property lines; about the same from trees and dense shrubbery (to avoid root troubles); and 25 ft. from streams or lakes.

Neither septic tank nor disposal field should be located in a swampy area or one subject to frequent flooding. The maximum height of ground water should be at least 4 ft. below ground level. Rock strata and other impervious formations should be at least 4½ ft. below disposal lines. You can check for all of this with a 2-in. earth auger fitted with extensions.

Soil porosity. When planning a septic-tank disposal system, the first thing to do is to test soil porosity. Use a 4-in. soil auger to make 6 or 8 holes about as deep as the disposal trenches are to be, space them uniformly over the selected site. Scrape the sides and bottoms of the holes with a knife to eliminate smeared surfaces and remove loose earth. Place a 2-in. layer of gravel or coarse sand on the bottom.

Keep the holes filled with water overnight and make percolation tests 24 hrs. after water was first put into the holes. (The percolation rate is the time required for water to drop 1 in.) If water is still present, adjust its depth to 6 in. and measure the drop in level over 30-min. periods, using the last check to figure the percolation rate. If there is no water in the hole, fill it to a 6-in. depth and measure the drop at 30-min. intervals over a period of 4 hrs., refilling as necessary and using the last check. In soils where the first 6 in. of water seeps away in less than 30 min., measure the drop every 10 min. over a period of 1 hr. and use the last check. Refer to Table A for the needed length of the disposal field per bedroom

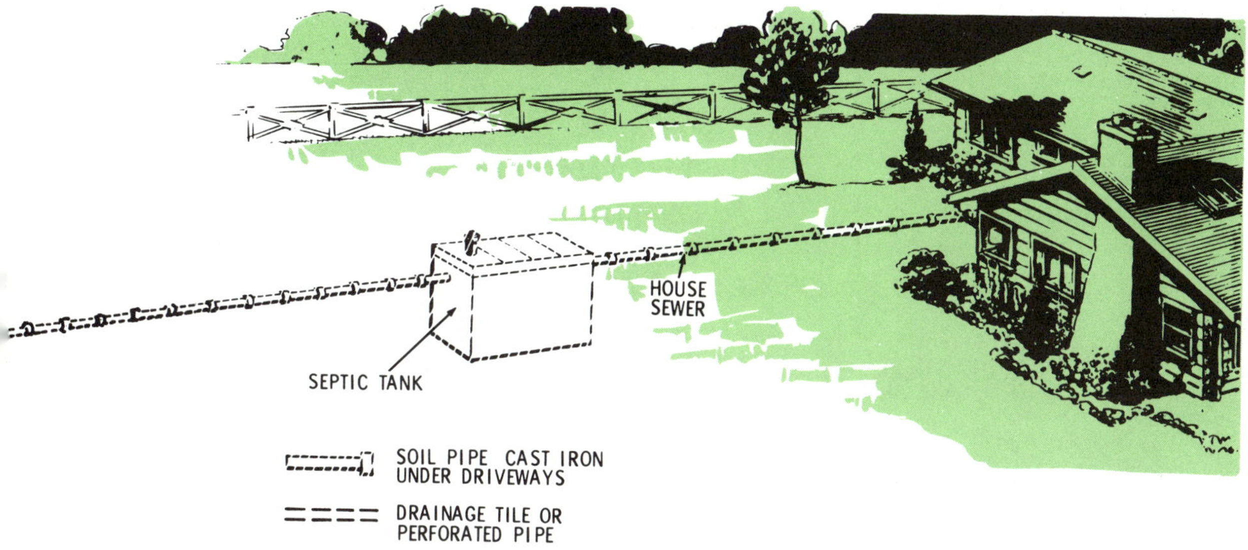

in the dwelling it is to serve. If the soil has a percolation rate slower than 1 in. in 60 min., it is not suitable for a disposal field. In such cases the local health authority should be consulted for recommendations.

Disposal field. Most disposal fields consist of trenches in which drain tile or perforated, nonmetallic pipe is laid in gravel. Only this type of disposal area will be discussed here. Trenches should not be less than 18 in. nor more than 36 in. in either depth or width. The depth is influenced by septic-tank outlet and ground slope.

A single line should not exceed 100 ft. in length. Parallel lines should be spaced as in Table B. If there are two or more lines, a distribution box is needed to control the flow uniformly. It may be prefabricated or cast in concrete on the site. The outlets are at equal level just above the bottom. The cover should be removable, sealed and at least 8 in. below ground level. The pipe line from the septic tank to the distribution box and also those from the distribution box to the separate disposal lines should be soil pipe with leakproof joints. A gravel bed under this pipe is unnecessary but the pipe should have the same drainage slope as the disposal lines.

After the trenches are dug, 1 x 4 grade boards on which pointed stakes are nailed are located centrally in the trenches. The upper edge should be about 6 in. above the trench bottom and should have a drainage slope of ¼ in. per 8 lin. ft. The bottoms of the trenches are raked to a depth of 1 in. to eliminate smeared and compacted earth which interferes with absorption. Gravel or crushed stone (½ in. to 2½-in.) is laid on the bottom up to the top edge of the grade boards, which remain in place.

Next, 4-in. drain tile, or perforated pipe with holes down, is placed centrally on the boards while more gravel is added on either side and on top, enough to cover the pipe to a depth of at least 2 in. Joints between drainage tile should be open from ¼ in. to ½ in., and the top of each joint is covered with a piece of asphalt-impregnated paper or a sheet-metal cover. After the gravel is smoothed, it is covered with untreated building paper, or with a 2-in. layer of straw or hay. When refilling the trench, pile up a mound of earth 4 in. to 6 in. high to allow for settling, so no depression will form along the trench line.

For sloping grades the disposal lines are laid at right angles to the direction of the slope if it is straight. Otherwise, the lines follow the ground contour. *A driveway should not be laid over any portion of the disposal field.* Drainage tile may be crushed by the weight of heavy vehicles. If the disposal field is on one side of a driveway and the septic tank on the other, the two should be connected with cast-iron pipe.

Septic tank: This may be a prefabricated steel tank suitably coated to prevent rusting; a prefabricated concrete tank having reinforced walls

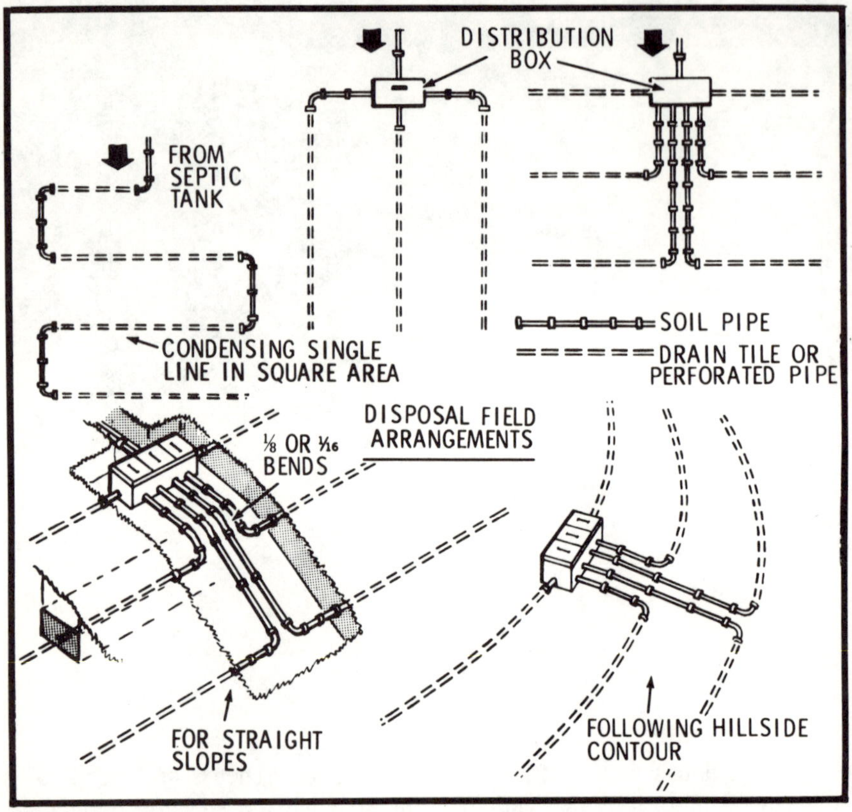

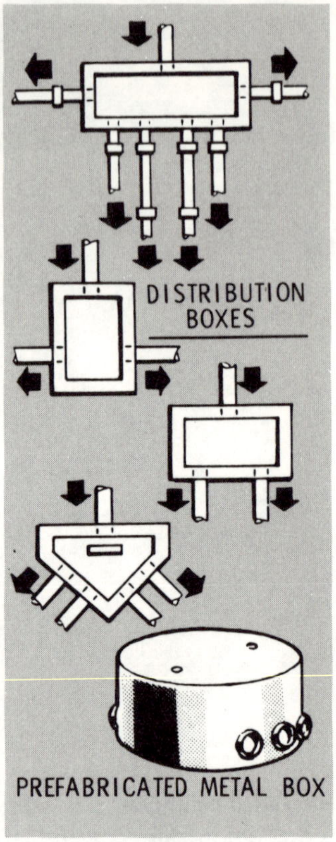

septic system, continued

WHEN A SEPTIC TANK is cast on the site, the walls and bottom should be at least 6 in. thick and reinforced. Also, the inner surfaces must be completely waterproofed.

not less than 2½ in. thick; a concrete tank, cast on the site, having 6-in. reinforced walls and bottom; or a tank made of concrete blocks. The inside surfaces of the latter two should have a ¼-in.-thick coating of 1:2 portland cement-sand plaster, or other effective waterproofing.

Table C gives the required capacities of septic tanks based on the number of bedrooms. (The capacity of a tank is the volume below the liquid level.) These capacities allow for the disposal from garbage grinders, automatic washers and other common household appliances. It is best to have a tank that exceeds requirements, however, as fewer cleanings then will be necessary, which reduces maintenance cost.

A septic tank must be watertight. Cover slabs of 3-in. reinforced concrete are sealed with asphalt mastic or cement mortar to prevent the entrance of water or escape of gas. No vent is needed on the tank as the soil-pipe stack of the house serves this purpose.

The shape of a septic tank, whether square, rectangular or cylindrical, is of little importance. The top of the closed tank should come at least

8 in. below ground level. The outlet is provided with a tee, elbow or baffle extending below the liquid surface a distance of about 40 percent of its depth, for tanks having vertical sides, and about 35 percent for cylindrical tanks installed horizontally. For the former, the distance from the inside of the top to the liquid surface should be about 20 percent of the liquid depth, and for the latter this distance should be about 15 percent. The inlet should be at least 1 in. above the liquid surface, and preferably 3 in. A tee or baffle is provided to extend about 6 in. below the liquid surface to assure minimum disturbance from entering sewage. The upper end of the tee or baffle should be about 1 in. below the tank top to permit gas in the tank to escape through the house stack.

A single-compartment tank will give entirely satisfactory results, although a two-compartment tank (or two tanks connected) will be slightly more efficient. If a disposal system becomes too small to meet increased requirements, a second tank can be added and the size of the disposal field increased. The depth of the house sewer is determined after a septic tank has been installed. This pipe should have a cleanout opening at the house.

TABLE C
RECOMMENDED SIZE FOR SEPTIC TANKS

INCLUDES ALLOWANCE FOR GARBAGE GRINDER, AUTOMATIC WASHERS AND OTHER APPLIANCES

NUMBER OF BEDROOMS	MINIMUM CAPACITY (GALS.)	RECTANGULAR TANK SIZE (FT)			
		WIDTH INSIDE	LENGTH INSIDE	DEPTH INSIDE	LIQUID DEPTH
2 OR LESS	750	3½	7½	5	4
3	900	3½	8	5½	4½
4	1,000	4	8	5½	4½
5	1,250	4	9	5½	4½

(1 CU. FT. VOLUME EQUALS 7.48 GALS.)

Maintenance: When first put into operation a septic tank does not require an additive such as yeast to start fermentation, although this may accelerate it. Septic-tank systems in constant use seldom freeze. Where winter temperatures are exceptionally low, protection can be provided with an adequate layer of straw, hay or snow. When the system is out of service for a period of time it is more susceptible to freezing. Clogging of disposal lines by roots occurs mostly in lines not having enough gravel under them. Usually the roots concentrate in the gravel.

Soaps, detergents, bleaches, drain cleaners,

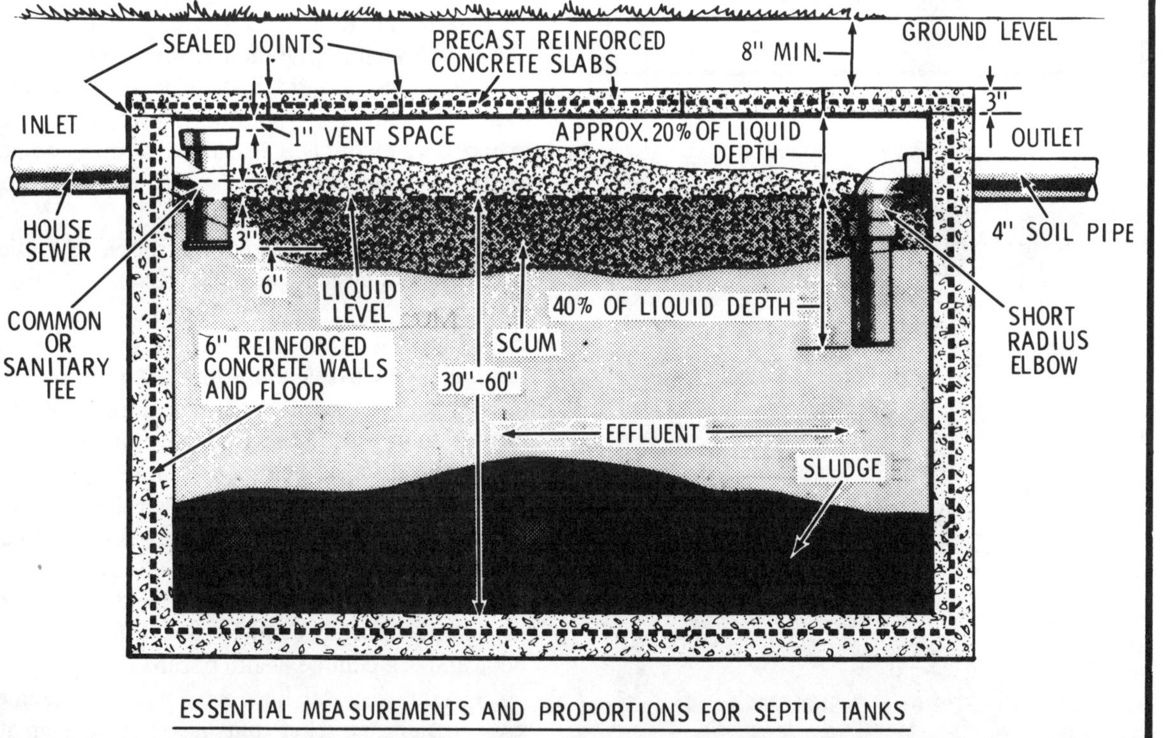

ESSENTIAL MEASUREMENTS AND PROPORTIONS FOR SEPTIC TANKS

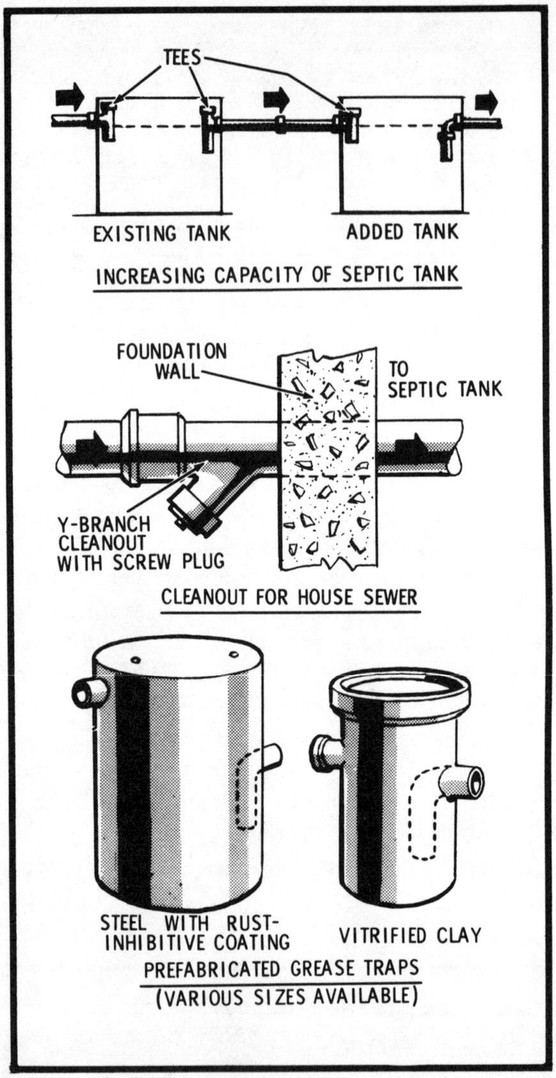

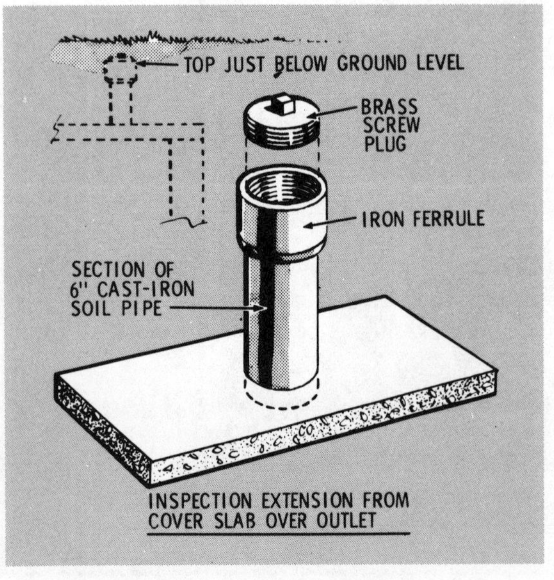

disinfectants, fat, oil, grease, the discharge of a garbage grinder and of other common household appliances connected to the plumbing system—none of these will, in normal amounts, have any adverse effects on septic-tank disposal systems of the sizes given in the tables. Waste brines from water softeners also are not harmful in a septic tank, but they may shorten the life of the disposal field.

Chemicals not normally used in homes may cause trouble, so it is unwise to risk their disposal in a septic-tank system. These include chemicals used for photography or other hobbies and workshop activities. Substances not likely to decompose easily in a septic tank (toilet-paper substitutes, paper towels, newspapers, rags, etc.) should be disposed of elsewhere. Another thing to avoid is the introduction of large volumes of water, such as the drainage from roofs.

Where an excess of oil, fat and grease is anticipated, it is best to provide a grease trap. The grease is skimmed off the surface frequently so that only clear fluid will pass into the septic tank. With such an installation the discharge of a garbage grinder must not be passed into the grease trap but directly to the septic tank.

Many products, some containing enzymes, are being sold for the purpose of improving operation of septic tanks and to prevent or cure troubles. As far as is known, none of these products has proved of value in properly controlled tests, according to the U.S. Dept. of Health, Education and Welfare. Drain and septic-tank cleaners containing sodium hydroxide or potassium hydroxide should not be used too frequently nor in excessive amounts. (The above findings do not apply to chemicals designed to maintain soil porosity in disposal fields.)

The predominant reasons for trouble in septic-tank disposal systems are: (1) Lack of consideration for the percolation rate of the soil when installing a system; (2) level of ground water too high; (3) overloading the system with substances and chemicals that interfere with fermentation or reduce the absorptive quality of the soil in the disposal field; (4) failure to empty a septic tank when necessary, which allows solids to pass into the disposal field and clog it. When soil porosity of the disposal field is reduced for any of the above reasons the effluent can rise to the ground surface which causes an offensive odor and is a definite health hazard.

Flushing disposal lines with water sometimes gives temporary relief, but may not help at all. To remedy the condition in a disposal field of

TABLE D ALLOWABLE SLUDGE ACCUMULATION			
LIQUID CAPACITY OF TANK (GALLONS)	LIQUID DEPTH(FEET)		
	3	4	5
	DISTANCE FROM BOTTOM OF OUTLET TO TOP OF SLUDGE (INCHES)		
500	11	16	21
600	8	13	18
750	6	10	13
900	4	7	10
1,000	4	6	8

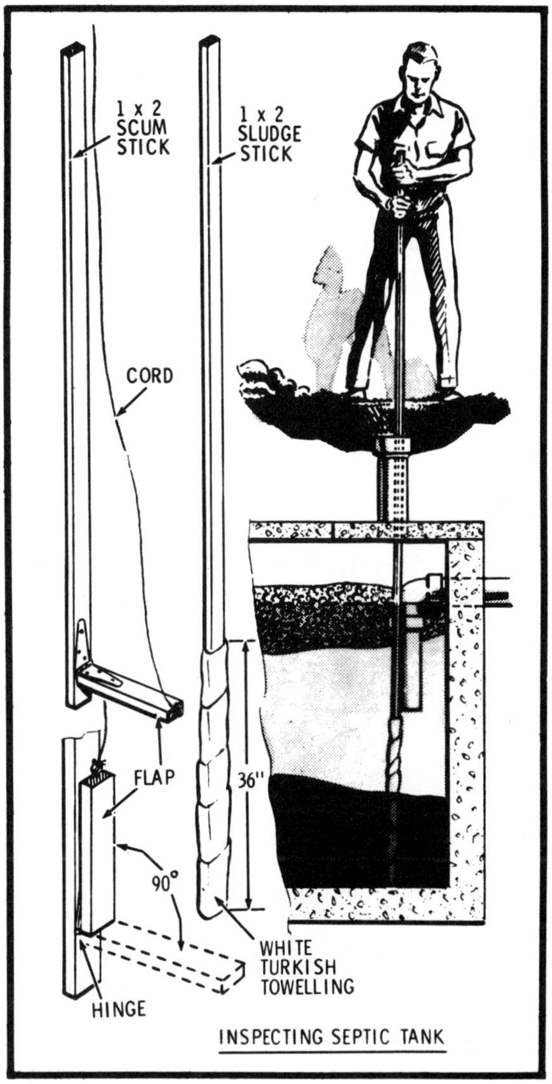

With two sticks you can measure accumulation of sludge to see if tank needs cleaning

adequate size, and one that originally had sufficient percolation rate, the soil porosity must be restored or a new disposal field provided.

Inspection and cleaning: Although constant fermentation decomposes much of the scum and sludge in a septic tank, inert solids gradually accumulate to the point where the tank must be emptied. This varies considerably according to load. Some tanks will require cleaning within three years. Others may not require cleaning for much longer periods. To be sure that solids in the tank will not pass into the disposal field and clog it, an annual inspection is recommended. This can be done by a septic-tank cleaning concern. For homeowners who prefer doing this themselves, much unnecessary work can be avoided by providing an inspection outlet on the cover slab over the tank outlet. After uncovering this, allow gas in the tank to disperse by ventilation before inspection.

Avoid breathing the gas or igniting a match near it since the gas is both asphyxiating and explosive. Use a stick with a hinged flap to force it through the scum layer near the outlet. Let the flap drop to a horizontal position and then pull the stick up until you feel resistance of the scum layer. Then mark the stick at the top of the inspection outlet. Next, lower it again and pull it up against the lower end of the outlet elbow, tee or baffle, again marking the stick. The difference between the marks is the distance of scum to the outlet.

To measure the sludge thickness, wrap the end of a stick with rough, white toweling and tack it in place. Insert this through the hole previously made in the scum, and push the stick to the tank bottom, turning it as you would an auger. After a few minutes pull it up slowly so some sludge will remain on the toweling and so indicate the sludge thickness.

The tank should be emptied when the lower surface of the scum is about 3 in. above the bottom of the outlet, and as soon as the sludge comes within the limits given in Table D. Usually, tank cleaning is done by means of a tank truck equipped with a pump. An emptied tank should not be washed or disinfected; some of the sludge should be left to resume fermentation.

Chairside sewing cabinet

If your wife likes to sew, she will love the convenience of this chairside companion. Made with ready-made legs of your choice and hardwood or hardwood-faced plywood, it is a beautiful project

HERE'S A PROJECT that is fun to make and is sure to please your wife. Construction is simplified by using ready-made legs that you can buy in many different shapes and merely screw in place.

While it will necessitate gluing up boards, you'll have a more handsome piece if you build it of solid stock—walnut, birch or cherry. Not only will you be able to shape the top and bottom edges as indicated, but you'll have no problem in finishing all edges. However, if you skip the shaping of the edges of the top and bottom members and leave them square, you can use hardwood-faced plywood and cover the exposed wood with glue-on-flexible wood tape.

Start with the two inner side members. These are alike but are made right and left-hand when you're running the dadoes on the inside for the

SEE ALSO
Drawers . . . Hobby centers . . . Joinery . . . Occasional tables . . . Sewing centers

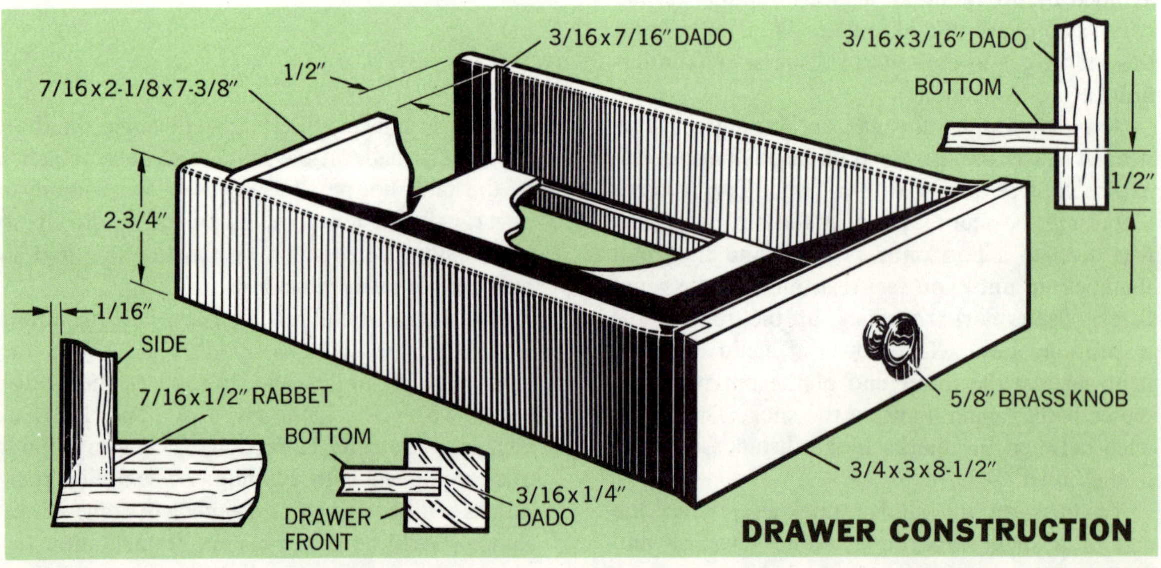

DRAWER CONSTRUCTION

WITHIN ITS THREE roomy drawers and swing-out spool racks, this handy cabinet will keep all sewing essentials in one convenient place.

two 3/16-in. drawer shelves. Notice that the ¼-in.-deep dadoes are stopped 1¼ in. from the front edges and then finished up by hand with a narrow chisel. If they're made with a router, you won't have to chisel them. Cut the upper dado 3 in. down from the top.

The back is the same height as the sides and is simply a plain, square-edge member. Before it can be nailed and glued to the sides, the two drawer shelves must be in place. Notice that the back member projects 1½ in. past the sides.

After gluing up stock to a width of 15½ in. cut the top and bottom members 16 in. long. They're shaped only along three sides, not the back. You'll notice that spring-loaded bullet catches are used to "lock" the swing-out spool doors, and you'll be smart if you bore the ¼-in. holes for them before you add the top and bottom members. The latter are kept flush with the back when you glue them.

Both side doors are alike but, again, they must be made right- and left-hand. The narrow fronts are joined to the sides with a miter-and-spline corner joint, after which three shelves, bored for rows of ⅛-in. dowels, are added. The upper shelf is located 1¾ in. down from the top and the lower one is positioned ⅛ in. up from the bottom. Each door is hinged to the back (see detail). Hinge them for 1/16-in. clearance top and bottom.

The detail shows how each drawer is made. You should actually fit them to their openings, leaving enough clearance all around for free slid-

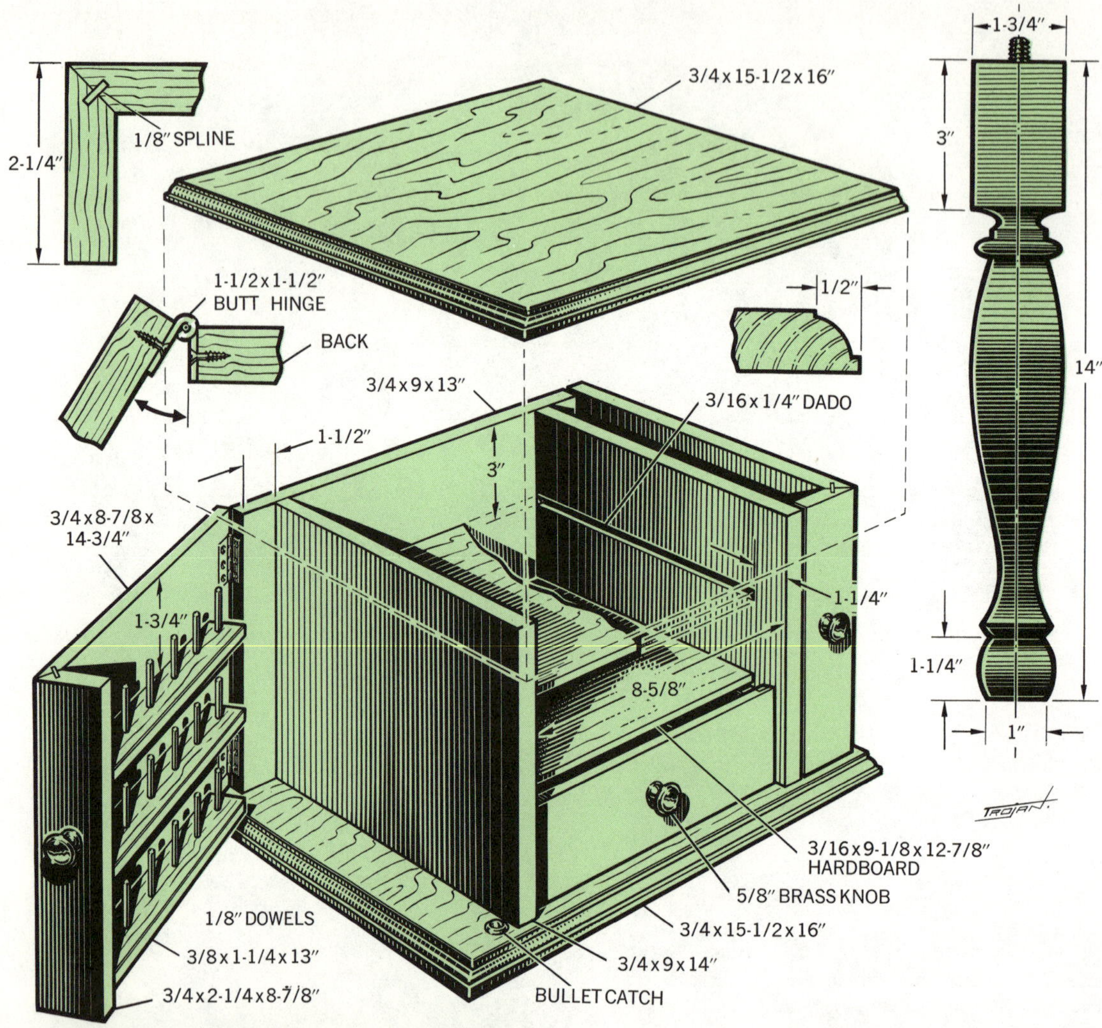

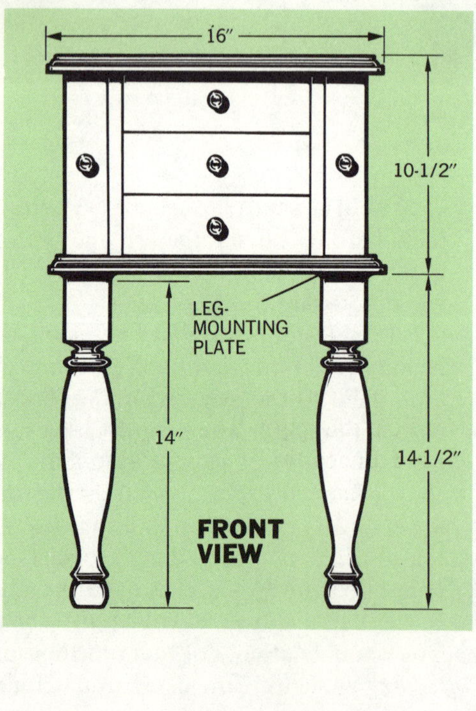

ing. The fronts are ¾-in. stock; sides and backs are ⅜-in. The fronts are also ⅛ in. higher than the sides to lap and conceal the drawer shelves. Notice that rabbeted ends of the drawer fronts have a slight inward bevel. This assures ample side clearance for the drawer itself without a sloppy fitting front. Notice, too, that the drawers set back in ¼ in. A thumbtack at each front corner of the lower opening will keep the bottom drawer from rubbing on the cabinet and marring its finish.

If you own a router or shaper, you can give the drawers a factory-made look by rounding the top edges of the side members. You would do this, of course, before the drawers are assembled and stop the cutter at a point where the side enters the rabbet. Your cabinet is completed when you add small brass knobs.

A cabinet for spools

By R. C. BARNES

THE SEAMSTRESS in your family will appreciate this wall cabinet for storing an easy-to-reach lineup of spools and bobbins. An 11x14-in. wooden picture frame, either purchased or made of molding, gives the project an attractive custom-cabinet look.

Edge-glue pieces for the front panel and cut bevels to create the raised panel. Cut spool holders and bore holes for dowel pegs using jig in photo. Cut parts (A, B, C), bore bobbin peg holes and assemble. Stain and finish with varnish.

MATERIALS LIST—SEWING CABINET

Key	Pcs.	Size and description (use)
A	2	¾ × 5 × 16½" basswood (side)
B	2	¾ × 5 × 12-⅞" basswood (top/bottom)
C	1	⅛ × 12-⅞ × 15-¾" plywood (back)
D	8	¾ × ⅝ × 9-⅞" basswood (front spool bar)
E	1	¾ × 11 × 14" basswood, two pieces edge-glued (front)
F	1	1-½ × 11 × 14" i.d. basswood (frame) with 1-¾"-wide members
G	158	3/16"-dia. × 1-¼" dowel (pegs)
H	8	¾ × ⅝ × 11-¼" basswood (back spool bar)

Misc.: 6, 1-¼" turn buttons; pr. 1-½" brass-plated cabinet hinges; 2 sawtooth picture hangers; magnetic door catch; 2d finishing nails, glue; light walnut or other stain, varnish.

HANDSOME wall-hung spool cabinet is built around an 11x14-in. picture frame. It holds 60 bobbins and 128 spools of thread. Smallest spools are kept on the cabinet door. Bobbins are stored two to a peg along the cabinet bottom. Jig (right) helps you bore holes perpendicular to face of the spool bar.

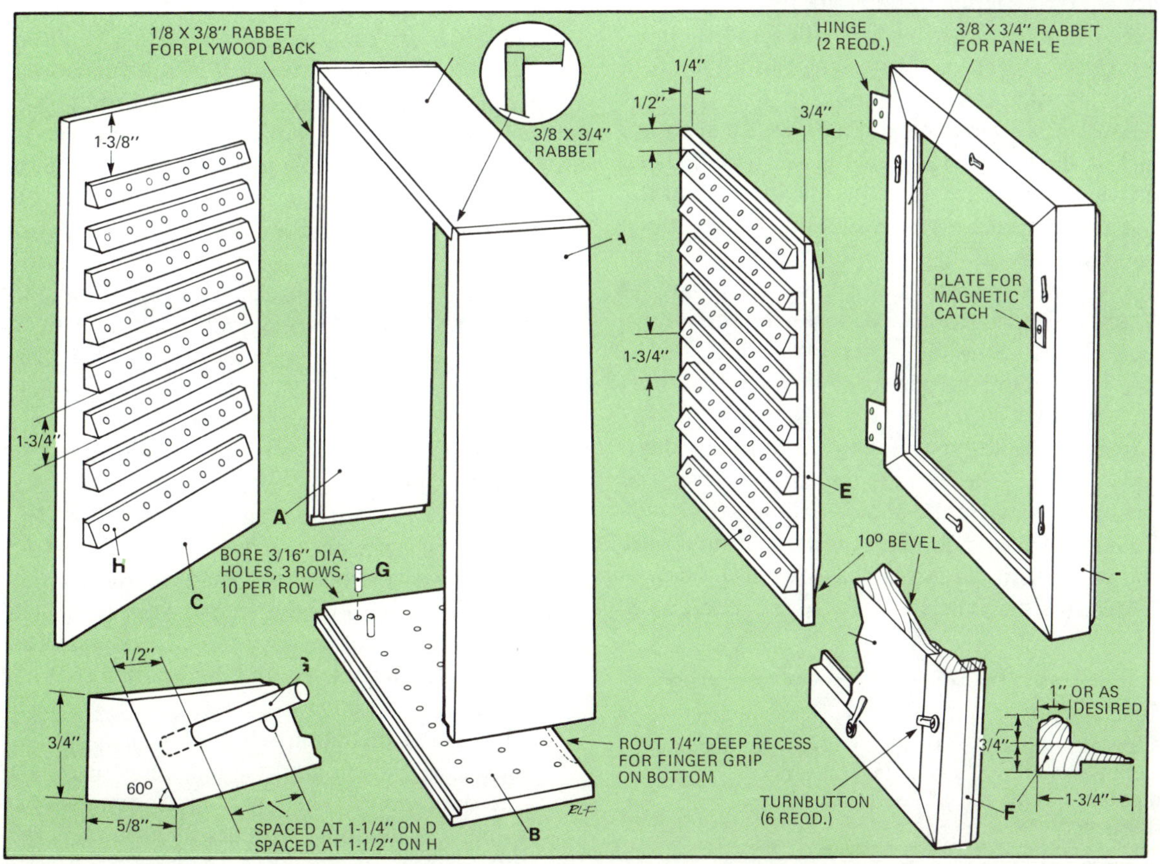

A sewing center for every taste and need

By WAYNE C. LECKEY

Every person who sews has a 'perfect' sewing center in mind. More often than not you will never find one on the market to fit all your needs. Here are four great centers with many interesting and functional features. If you want to go 'all-out' or if you're working with a limited amount of space and money, one of these should fit your needs

■ LIKE ANY HOBBY, sewing becomes more enjoyable and creates a lot less clutter when you have a work center where there's a place for everything and everything is in one convenient place.

We kept this thought in mind in designing these four highly functional sewing centers. Incorporated in each design you'll find a work counter for pattern cutting, shelves and roomy drawers for keeping fabrics, yarns and patterns handy and trays for pins, needles and threads. Two of the centers are designed to attach to a wall; all fold up in a minimum of space.

Most sewing-machine stands we've seen are just that—stands for sewing machines. They provide a place to store the machine when it's not in use and that's about all. Few, if any, offer a good-size worktable to spread out a pattern. There's little space to keep dress patterns handy. There's no space to stow your sewing and often a lack of tray space to hold countless little items. We've tried to give you these features that most stands lack.

Any portable-type sewing machine is adaptable to any of the four centers shown here. The machine shown in the photos is Singer's Golden *Touch & Sew,* and the counter cutouts were made to fit its particular base. While a cutout allows the machine to sit flush, this can be optional; the machine can simply sit on top of the counter. Plans and instructions for building all four of these sewing centers are shown on the following pages.

SEE ALSO

Cabinet furniture . . . Desks . . . Frames, picture . . . Hobby centers . . . Laminates, plastic . . . Modular furniture . . . Sewing cabinets . . . Study centers

The high-rise unit

■ EMPHASIZING convenience, this sewing center is built around three 1⅜-in. flush doors, one left intact and the others cut into sections. The boxlike case to which they are hinged and pivoted is divided into three compartments.

To make the case, cut two side members 13¼ x 84¾ in., then cut a ⅜ x ¾-in. rabbet in the top edges and ⅜ x ¾-in. dadoes 2¼ in. up from the bottom. The rabbets are for a 13 x 76-in. top member; the dadoes for a 13 x 76-in. bottom member. A ¼-in. plywood back laps the edges of top and bottom members, but fits in rabbets cut in the edges of the two side members. The two partitions, 13 x 81 in., are nailed in place through top and bottom members. The left partition is positioned 25¼ in. from the outside; the right one, 23¼ in.

Front edges of the case are faced with 1⅛ x 1½-in. trim pieces of pine, with a 3-in.-wide piece across the bottom. Details B and C in the drawings show how the trim is kept flush with inner faces of the two partitions. Casing nails are used to attach the trim, and the heads are set and puttied.

The left-hand compartment is fitted with a stock 22x80-in. flush door hinged with regular 3-in. door butts. The opening as dimensioned provides ⅛-in. door clearance all around. A rab-

THE ULTIMATE in sewing centers, this one opens up to offer maximum convenience. Standing 7 ft. tall, it features a closet for storing an iron and ironing board, a swing-down 28x64½-in. cutting board, a leg-free, pull-down sewing machine, a mirror door and more storage than you'll ever need. Three common interior doors are used for the front; the rest is chiefly plywood. When tipped on side, the cabinet will easily pass through any standard-height doorway.

the high-rise unit, continued

beted stop is on the full length of the door (see detail B); similar stops are on both right-hand doors; the upper stop being 29¾ in. long, the lower one 13⅞ in. The upper right compartment has a ¾-in. bottom 31½ in. down from the top, and a 1½-in. trim piece covers the edge.

The 28-in. center door is cut in two sections at a point 64½ in. from one end. Since interior doors are hollow, filler strips of solid wood must be inserted and glued in the cut ends. The 64½-in. section is the cutting board and is covered on the back with plastic laminate.

The 20-in. right-hand door is cut in three sections: 29¾, 34½ and 13⅞ in. The 34½-in. section is a swing-up sewing-machine counter. To provide a well for the base of the machine, the counter must be double-thick as shown in the detail, after which the top surface and the three exposed edges of the sandwich are covered with plastic laminate.

Modified mending plates and ¼-20 T-nuts are used to pivot the cutting board and machine counter. As shown, the plates are attached to the edges, 12½ in. from the far end in the case of the cutting board, 12⅞ in. for the counter. T-nuts are installed in 5/16-in. holes in the cabinet at points 29⅜ in. up from the bottom for the counter and 31¼ for the cutting table. Both sets of holes are

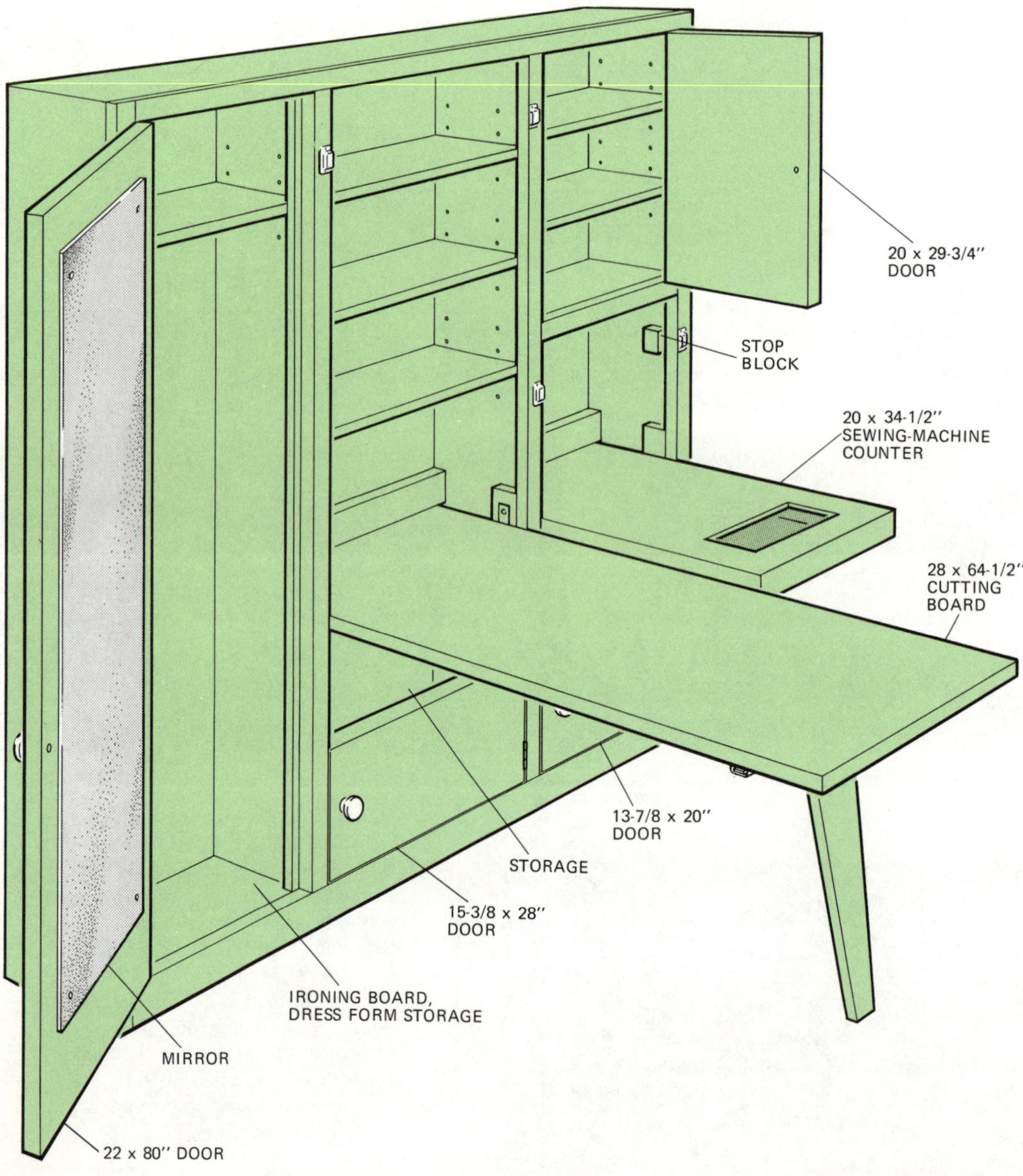

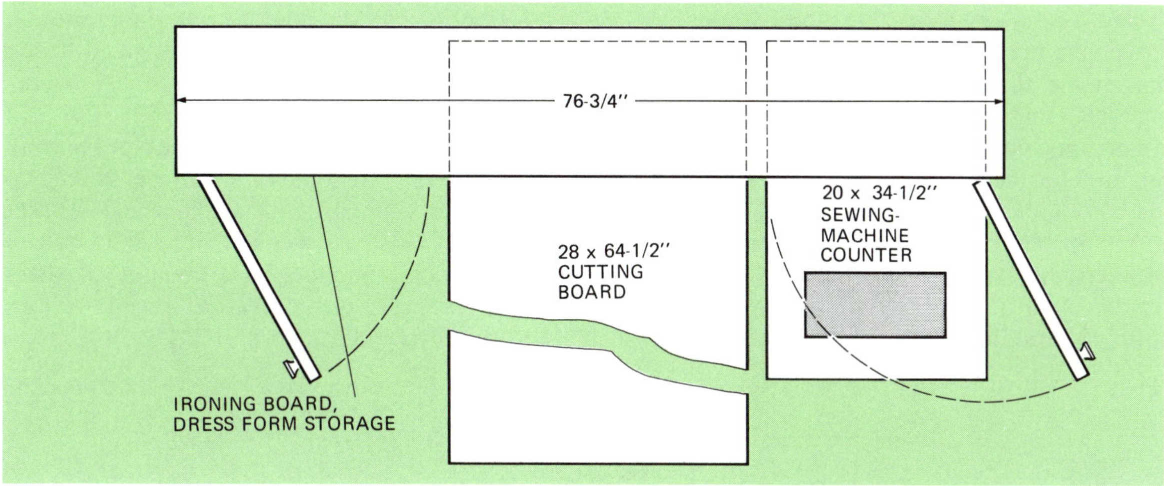
76-3/4"
20 x 34-1/2"
SEWING-
MACHINE
COUNTER
28 x 64-1/2"
CUTTING
BOARD
IRONING BOARD,
DRESS FORM STORAGE

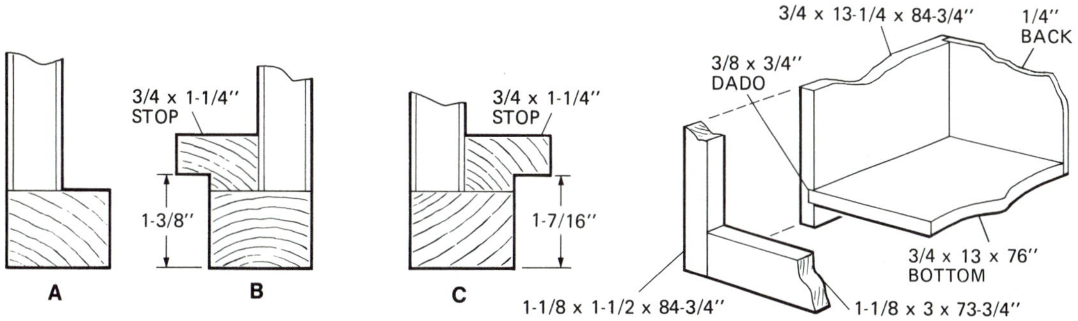
3/4 x 1-1/4"
STOP
1-3/8"
A
B
3/4 x 1-1/4"
STOP
1-7/16"
C
3/4 x 13-1/4 x 84-3/4"
1/4"
BACK
3/8 x 3/4"
DADO
3/4 x 13 x 76"
BOTTOM
1-1/8 x 1-1/2 x 84-3/4"
1-1/8 x 3 x 73-3/4"

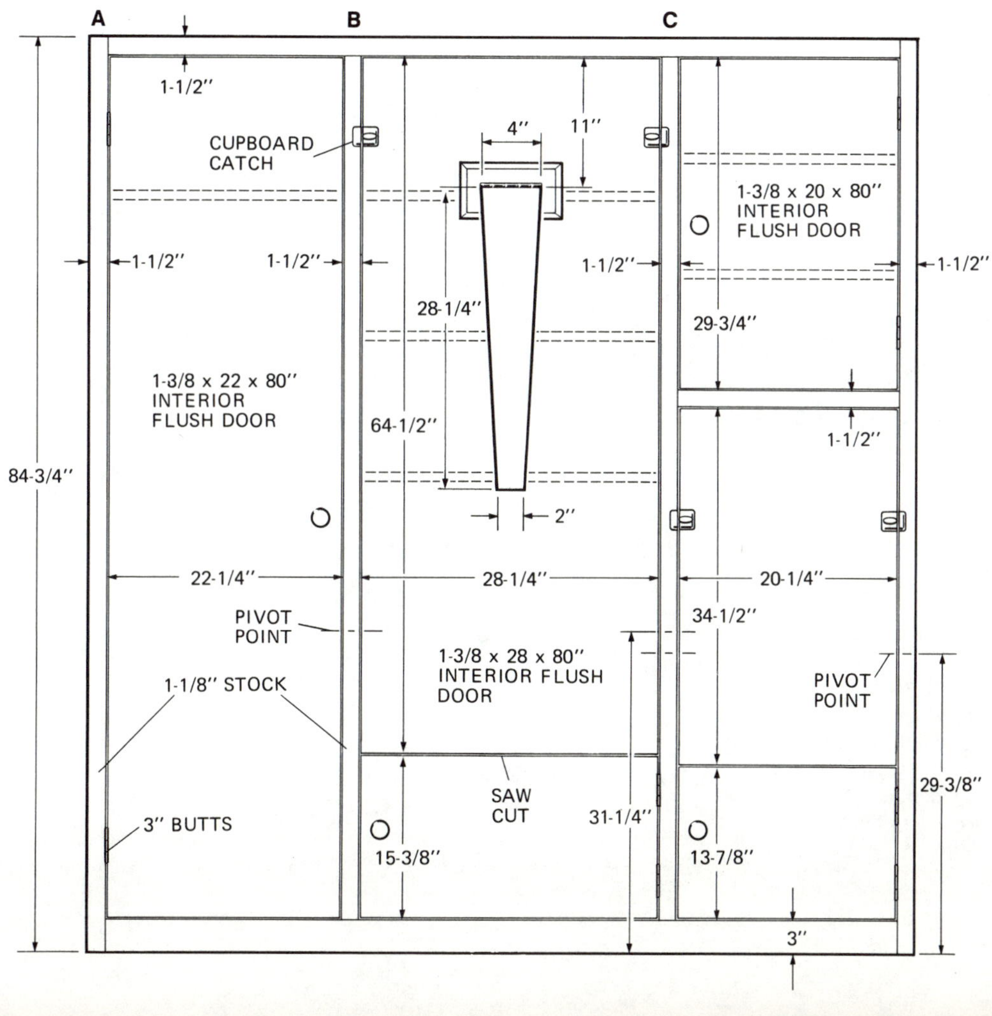
A
B
C
1-1/2"
CUPBOARD
CATCH
4"
11"
1-3/8 x 20 x 80"
INTERIOR
FLUSH DOOR
1-1/2"
1-1/2"
1-1/2"
1-1/2"
28-1/4"
29-3/4"
1-3/8 x 22 x 80"
INTERIOR
FLUSH DOOR
64-1/2"
1-1/2"
84-3/4"
2"
22-1/4"
28-1/4"
20-1/4"
PIVOT
POINT
34-1/2"
1-3/8 x 28 x 80"
INTERIOR FLUSH
DOOR
PIVOT
POINT
1-1/8" STOCK
SAW
CUT
29-3/8"
3" BUTTS
31-1/4"
15-3/8"
13-7/8"
3"

drilled 1¾ in. in from the edge. Roundhead stovebolts are turned through the T-nuts from the outside, through the pivot holes in the mending plates and on into holes in the edges of the counter and cutting board. Bolts 2½ in. long are required for the machine counter, 1 in. long for the cutting board.

A stop block across the back supports the counter in a level position when it's down, and regular cupboard catches are used to hold the cutting board and sewing-machine counter when up. Friction catches hold the four doors shut. A swing-down leg hinged to a block glued to the front of the cutting board supports it. All shelves are adjustable; more can be added.

The method used to hold the machine securely in the counter cutout so it can be swung up depends on your particular machine and its base. One way to fasten it would be to drill four small holes through the metal base; countersink them and drive nickel-plated oval-head wood screws into the plywood top.

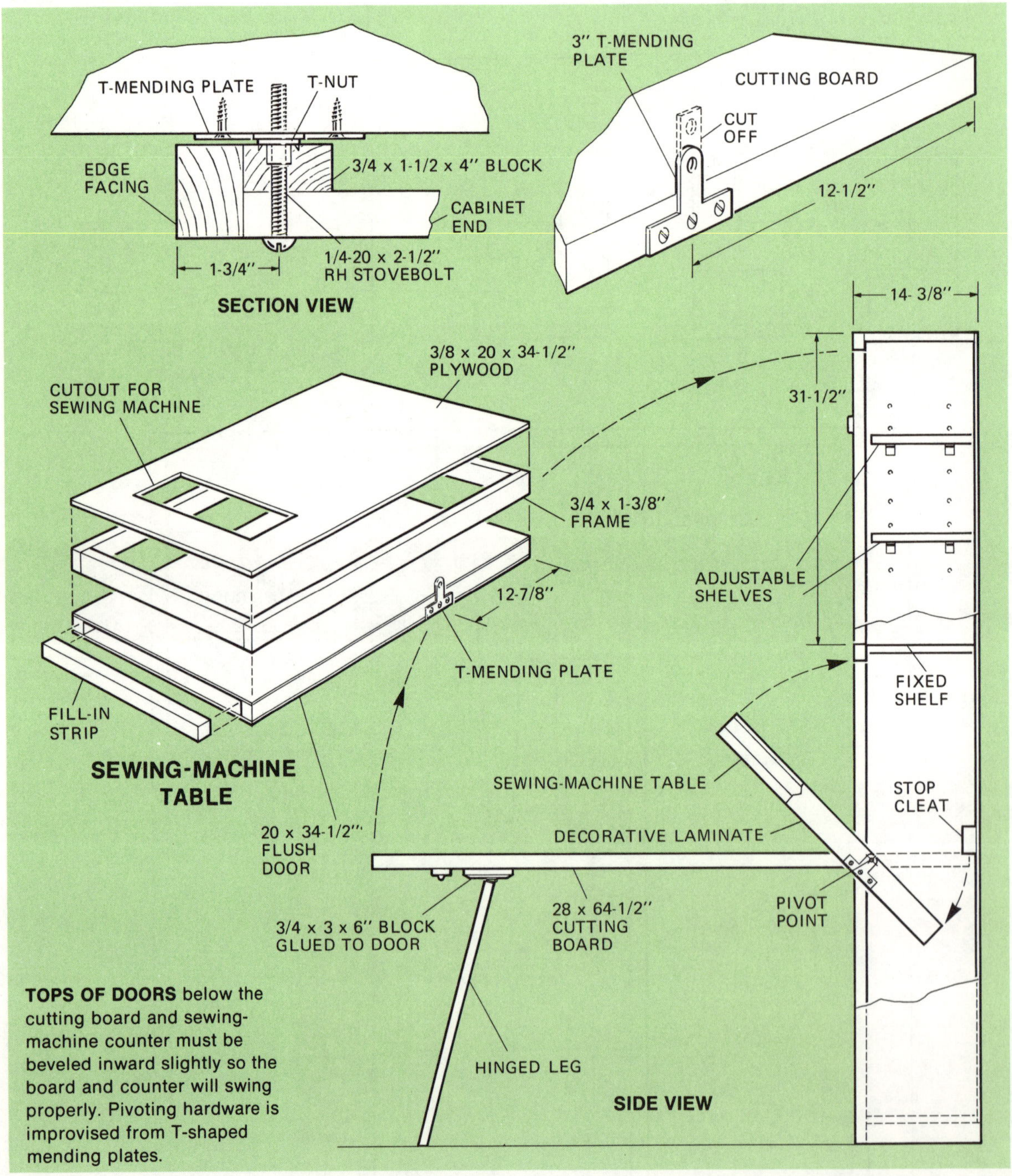

TOPS OF DOORS below the cutting board and sewing-machine counter must be beveled inward slightly so the board and counter will swing properly. Pivoting hardware is improvised from T-shaped mending plates.

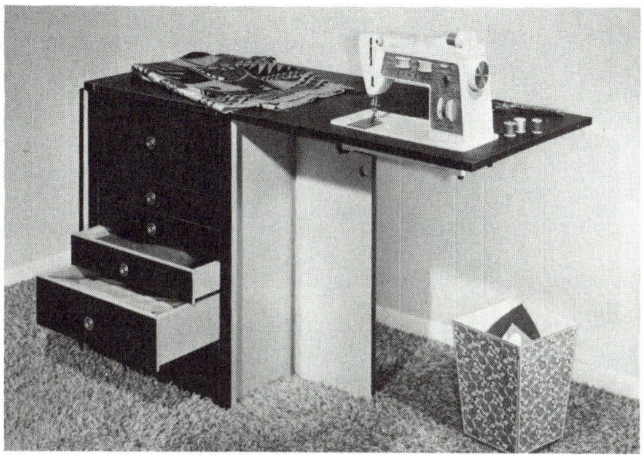

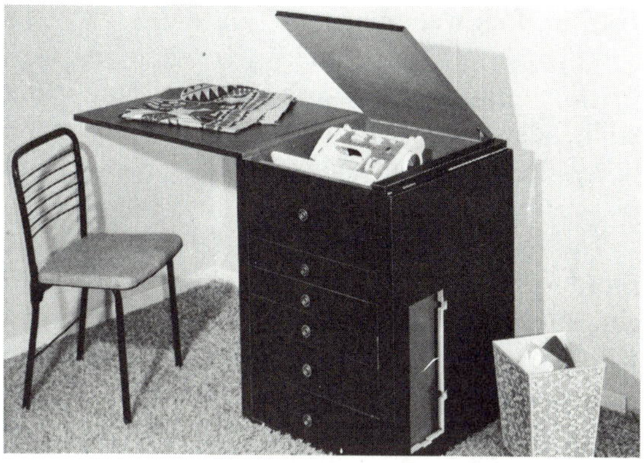

DROP LEAVES on island unit swing up to provide a whopping work surface nearly 84 in. long. Five center drawers offer storage space galore. Sewing machine fits in the cutout, stores in compartment under the hinged lid.

The island unit

IN CHECKING the construction details of this work center, you'll see that you can make the sides with 1/4 or 3/4-in. plywood. Begin by cutting the 3/4-in. back panel. It will be 22 3/4 in. or 23 1/4 in. wide, depending on the plywood thickness used for the sides. Where 1/4-in. plywood is used, run 3/8-in.-deep grooves along the two outer edges of the back 7/8 in. in from the edge. Next cut the two top rails and front pilasters—1 3/8 or 1 5/8 in., as the case may be—and run similar grooves in them 7/8 in. in from the edge.

A 3/4-in.-thick bottom nails to the back panel even with the bottom edge, and a second panel (1/2 in. thick) is installed 8 1/4 in. down from the top. The latter is 3/4 in. shorter, front to back, than the bottom one. If the sides are 1/4 in. thick, the bottom member has to be notched at the front corners to fit around the pilasters and be even with them. You'll notice the two top rails project 1/2 in. beyond the faces of the pilasters.

Start assembling the parts you have cut, nailing the bottom to the back first, then the 1/2-in.

COMPARTMENT under lid provides storage space for portable machine. Bin at rear is handy for filing patterns. Cutout in counter is optional; the machine can rest on top if you desire. Use friction-type lid support; it helps to hold up the lid when storing machine.

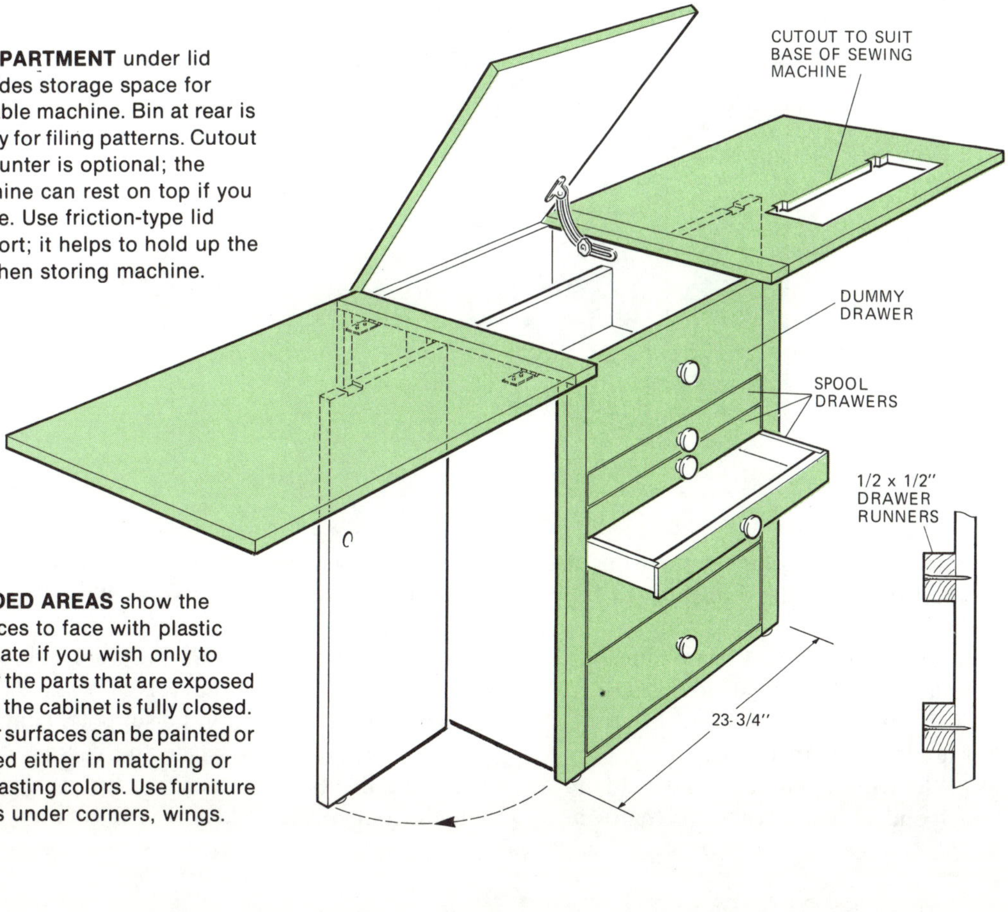

SHADED AREAS show the surfaces to face with plastic laminate if you wish only to cover the parts that are exposed when the cabinet is fully closed. Other surfaces can be painted or stained either in matching or contrasting colors. Use furniture glides under corners, wings.

bottom, followed in order by the sides, top rails and pilasters. If you plan to cover the parts with plastic laminate, you won't have to worry about nailheads showing. If not, you'll have to set and putty the nails that show in the top rails and pilasters.

The 8¾-in. dummy drawer front is cut and fitted next. Notice that it is held in place with glue blocks on the inside, and that it fits even with the bottom member. We found it easier to apply the plastic laminate to the face of it before gluing it in place. Notice how the laminate (see section B-B) is cut back 1/16 in. at each end to simulate normal drawer clearance. A 6-in.-wide partition, either 20 or 20½ in. long, as the case

END VIEW
(DROP LEAF REMOVED)

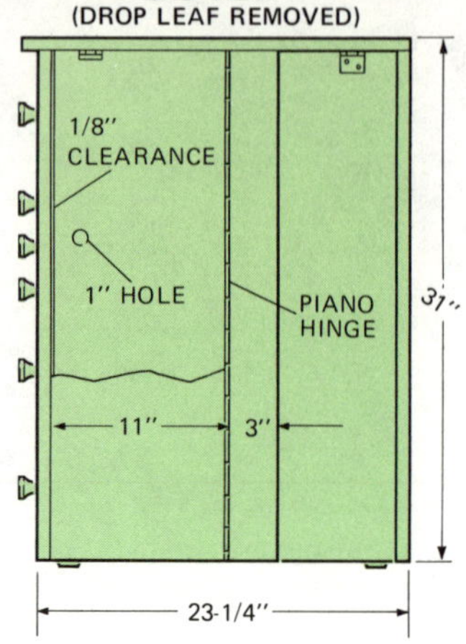

TOP VIEW

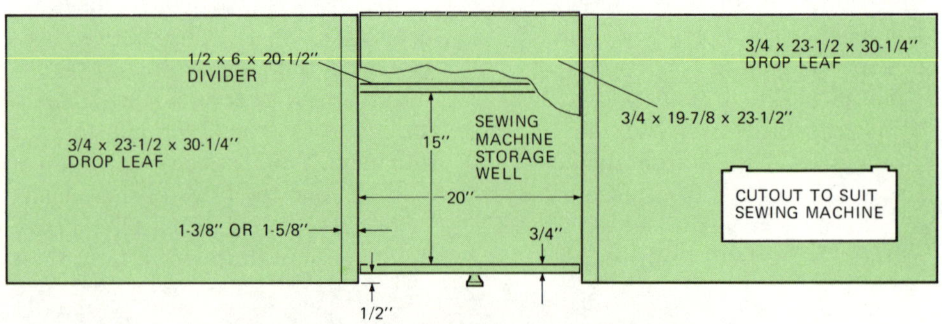

FRONT VIEW

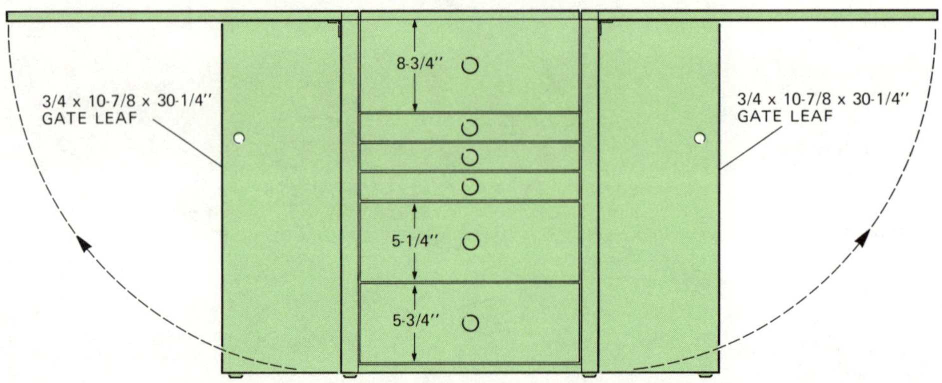

may be, is installed in the machine compartment 15 in. from the front and nailed in through the sides.

Supporting wings for drop leaves are hinged to ¾ x 3-in. vertical members, added to recessed sides of the cabinet 11 in. back from the front. Finger holes are made an inch or so in from the front edges of the wings, and a notch is made in the top of each one so that it will clear the front hinges. Allow a ⅛-in. space for clearance at the cabinet front so that the wings will swing out easily.

Cut the hinged top 19⅞ in. wide and use a piano hinge to attach it securely across the back. Complete it with a friction-lid support. Hinge the two drop leaves, then place the cabinet on its back and drive rubber-cushion furniture glides into the four corners and outer ends of the wings.

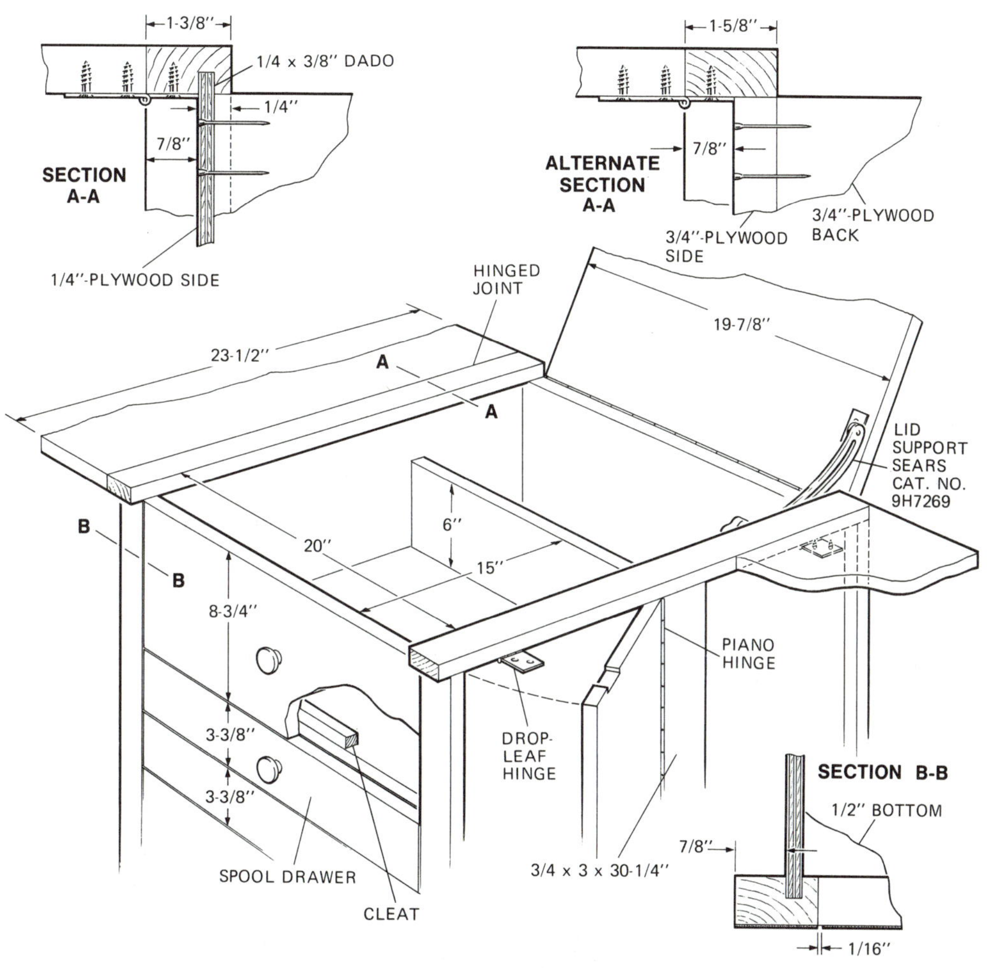

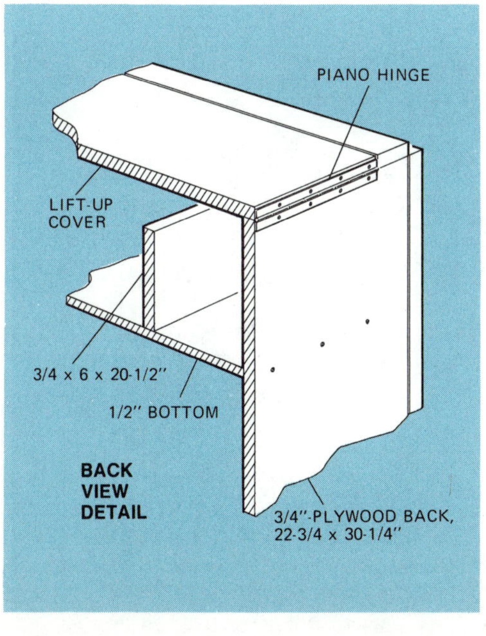

Cementing plastic laminate

1. Cut your laminate ⅛ in. oversize all around.
2. Surfaces to be bonded must be dry and clean.
3. Apply even coat of contact cement to both laminate and wood, using brush or spreader.
4. Let both surfaces dry before bonding (10-20 minutes normally). Surfaces will bond when adhesive will adhere but not transfer to brown wrapping paper if touched lightly. If cement becomes too dry (over 3 hours), apply another coat.
5. Bring surfaces in contact *exactly* where desired (cement bonds instantly on contact, so you can't shift the work later). Two overlapping pieces of kraft paper placed over cement will let you position the laminate without sticking. When laminate is where you want it, pull out one paper, press down the plastic, then pull out second paper.
6. Using rubber mallet or hammer and wood block, apply pressure all over surface for positive contact.
7. Trim laminate flush with work; use block plane and flat file or router and special laminate cutter.
8. Clean tools, brushes with contact-cement solvent.

The dual unit

■ SIMPLEST TO MAKE of the four sewing centers is a dual-unit center that appeals to the builder who wants to spend a minimum of time and money. Of its two individual units, one is attached to the wall to accommodate a portable sewing machine and the other is placed alongside. Together they offer the sewer convenience and storage galore.

Little more than a box fitted with a back and shelves, the drop-counter wall unit is practically a hammer and saw project. The ends and the top and bottom members are cut in pairs as are the four shelves. The top and bottom boards lap the end members, and the two long shelves butt between. To gain "headroom" for nailing the short divider in place, you should install the lower long shelf first, then the two short shelves and finally the upper one. Chains support the drop front; hooks and eyes hold it shut. Two 3-in. angle brackets across the top and bottom anchor the unit solidly to wall studs.

Although the base unit is twice as deep as the wall unit, construction is much the same. The top and bottom members lap the end members, and a divider forms compartments. One difference you'll notice in basic construction is the 1½-in. apron that's let in across the front at the top. This requires ¾ x 1½-in. notches cut before assembly.

The sit-down ironing board pivots on a single carriage bolt that passes through a hole in the second shelf and swings clear of the end when not in use. Two drawers with handholds are made to slide easily in the 12 and 22½-in. openings. Stock cabinet louvers are used for doors and trimmed to fit. They're hinged to fold, and held shut by magnetic catches.

The wall unit should be hung so that the drop front will level at about table height (30 in.) when open.

SEPARATE COMPARTMENT for the sewing machine provides a place to put it when you want to "clear the deck" and use the drop front for cutting a pattern. Shelves are made shallow to gain room for support chains behind front.

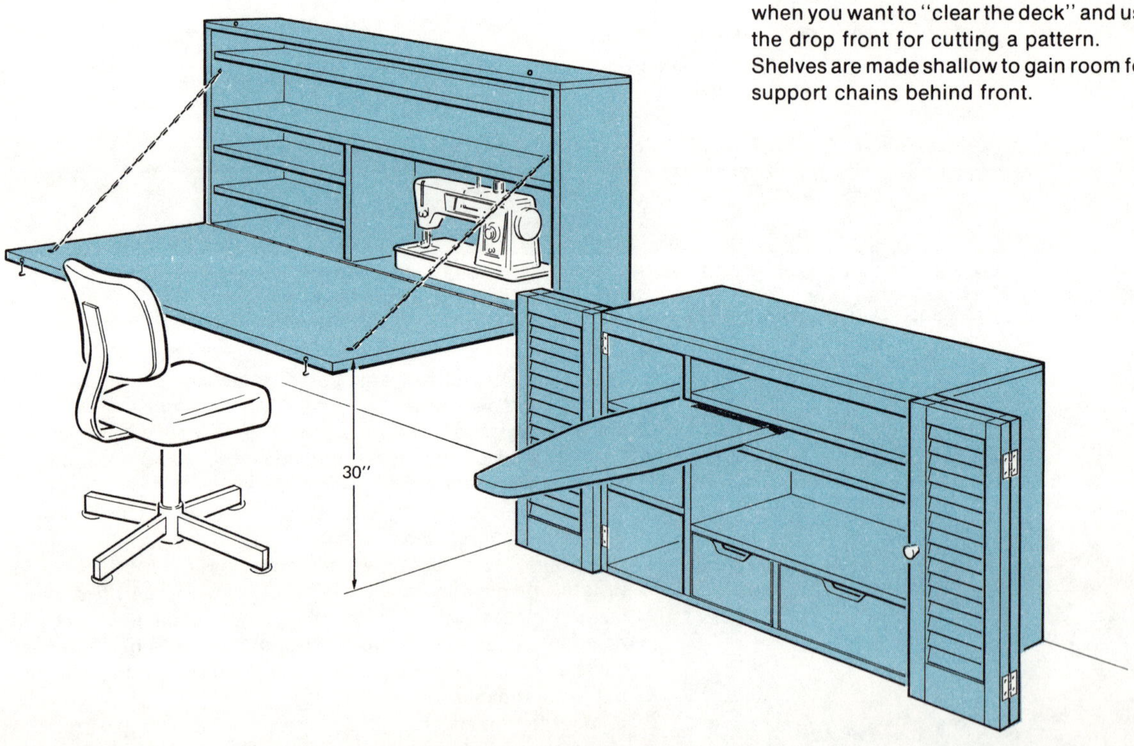

FURNITURE GLIDES attached to the four corners will raise the cabinet enough to provide clearance for the louver doors.

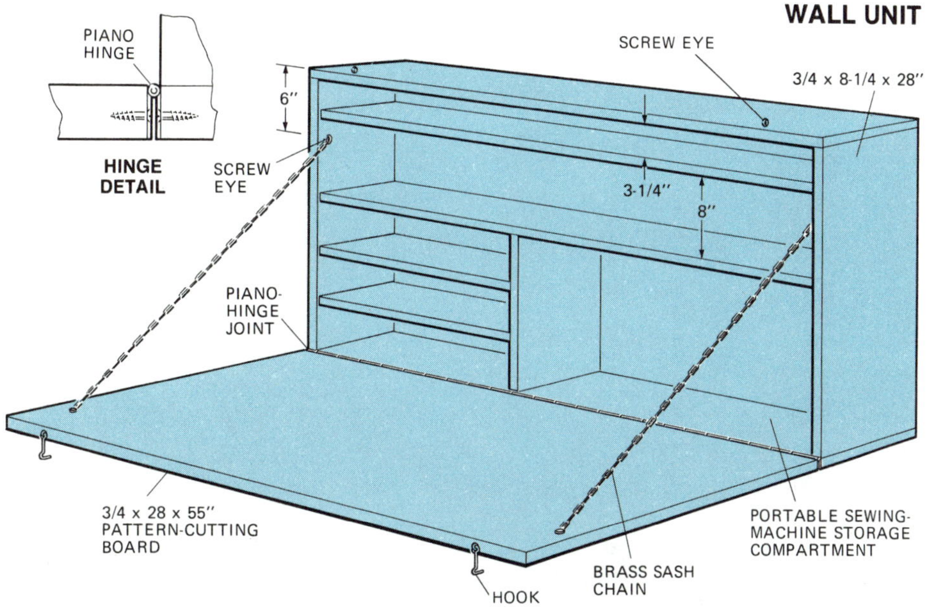

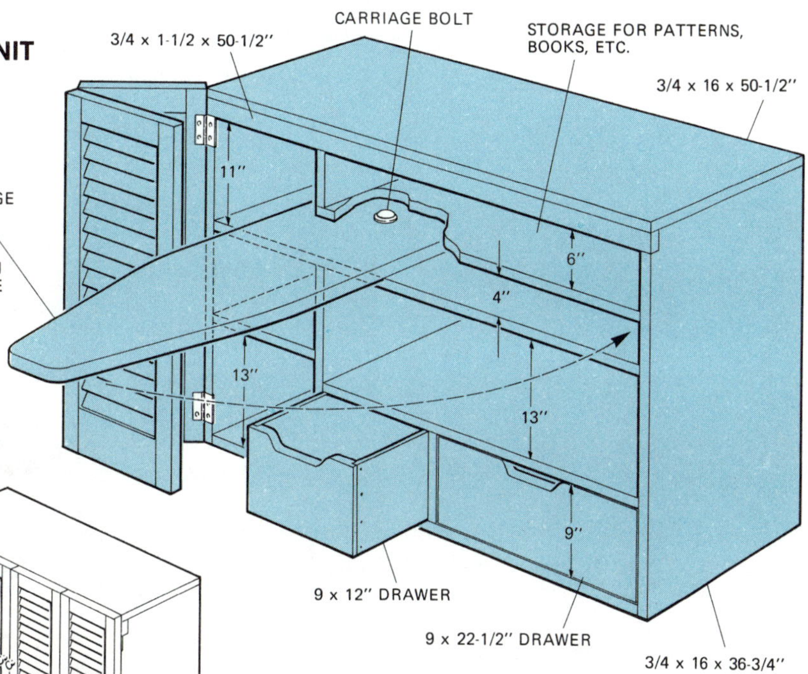

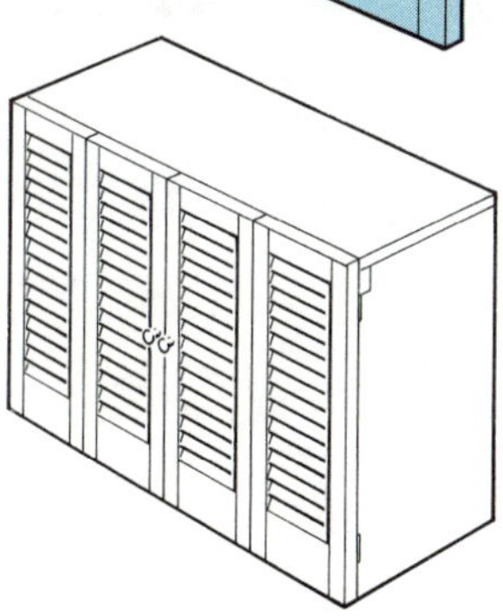

DECORATIVE louver doors that are hinged to bifold provide an attractive front to the base cabinet and permit full access when open.

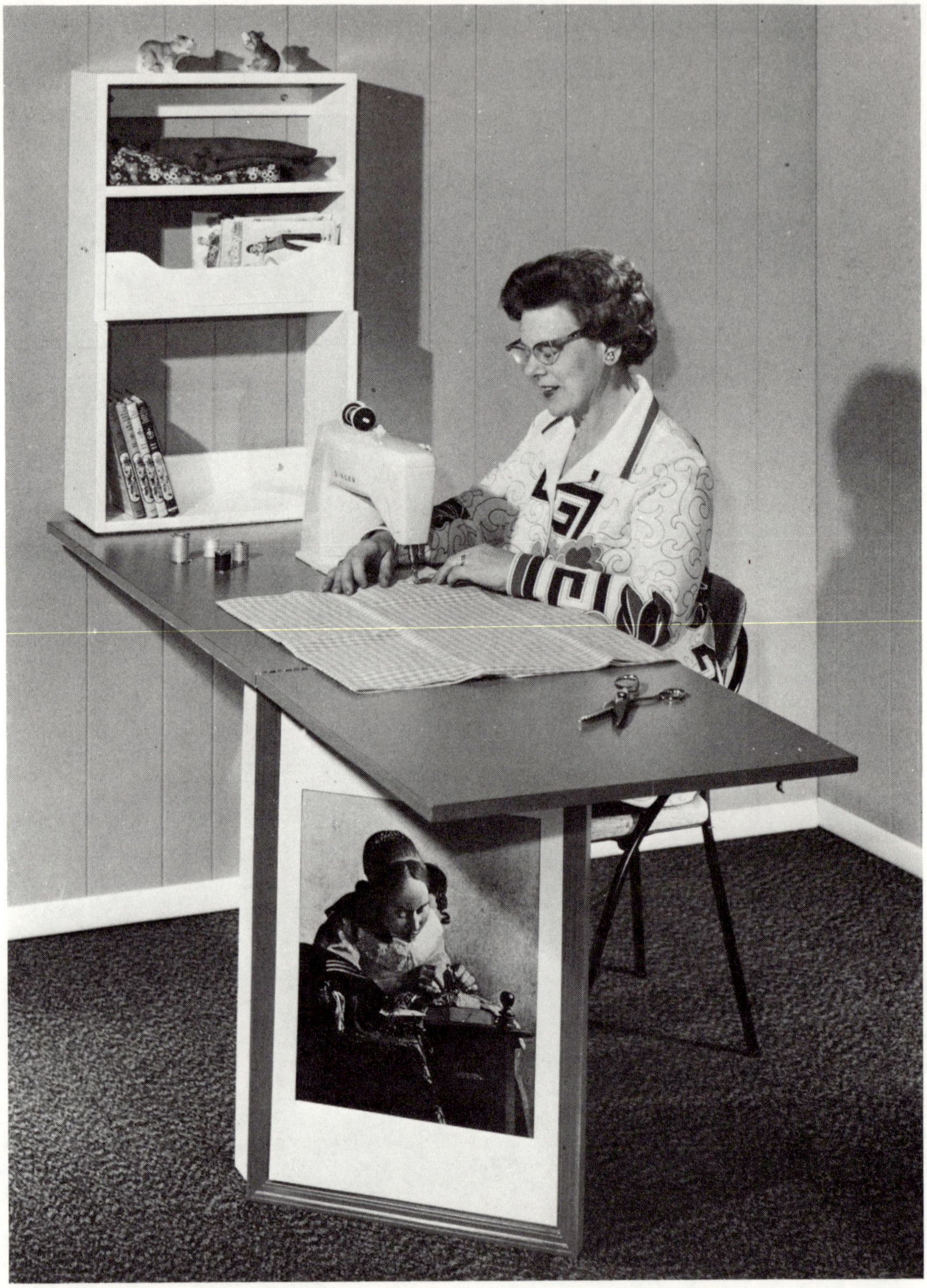

THIS SEWING CENTER, when open, extends to a king-size, 20x65-in. work counter. When swung up out of the way it is cleverly hidden behind a decorative wall plaque of your choice.

The dual-role unit

WHERE SPACE is limited and there just isn't room to have a sewing center in the way all the time, this one retracts against the wall to serve as a decorative plaque. When stored, it projects only 14 in. from the wall, leaving free floor space under it. Even when the sewing center is retracted you still can get at thread and other small items.

There are three parts: a cabinet bolted securely to a wall, a counter and cutting board hinged to the cabinet, and a swing-down cabinet-leg hinged to the outboard end of the cutting board for support. The leg has a picture-frame door that swings open to support a flip-over extension. When fully open, the cutting board measures some 65 in. long and 24 in. wide. The wall cabinet provides storage for the machine, and shelves above for sewing, patterns and what not. The cabinet-leg has shelves for odds and ends, and the back of the door has four handy trays for thread, buttons, thimbles and the like. The door front is made to look like a framed picture. Hooks and eyes keep the whole thing stored against the wall. When in use, the sewing machine is flush in a cutout in the cutting board.

Except for the two mounting cleats, the back of the wall cabinet is open. Each side is 9 x 32½ in. and is rabbeted top and bottom for 8 and 9-in.-wide members 19¼ in. long. Two 8-in.-wide shelves fit between in dadoes, the bottom one being placed 17 in. down from the top and even with the notched cutback.

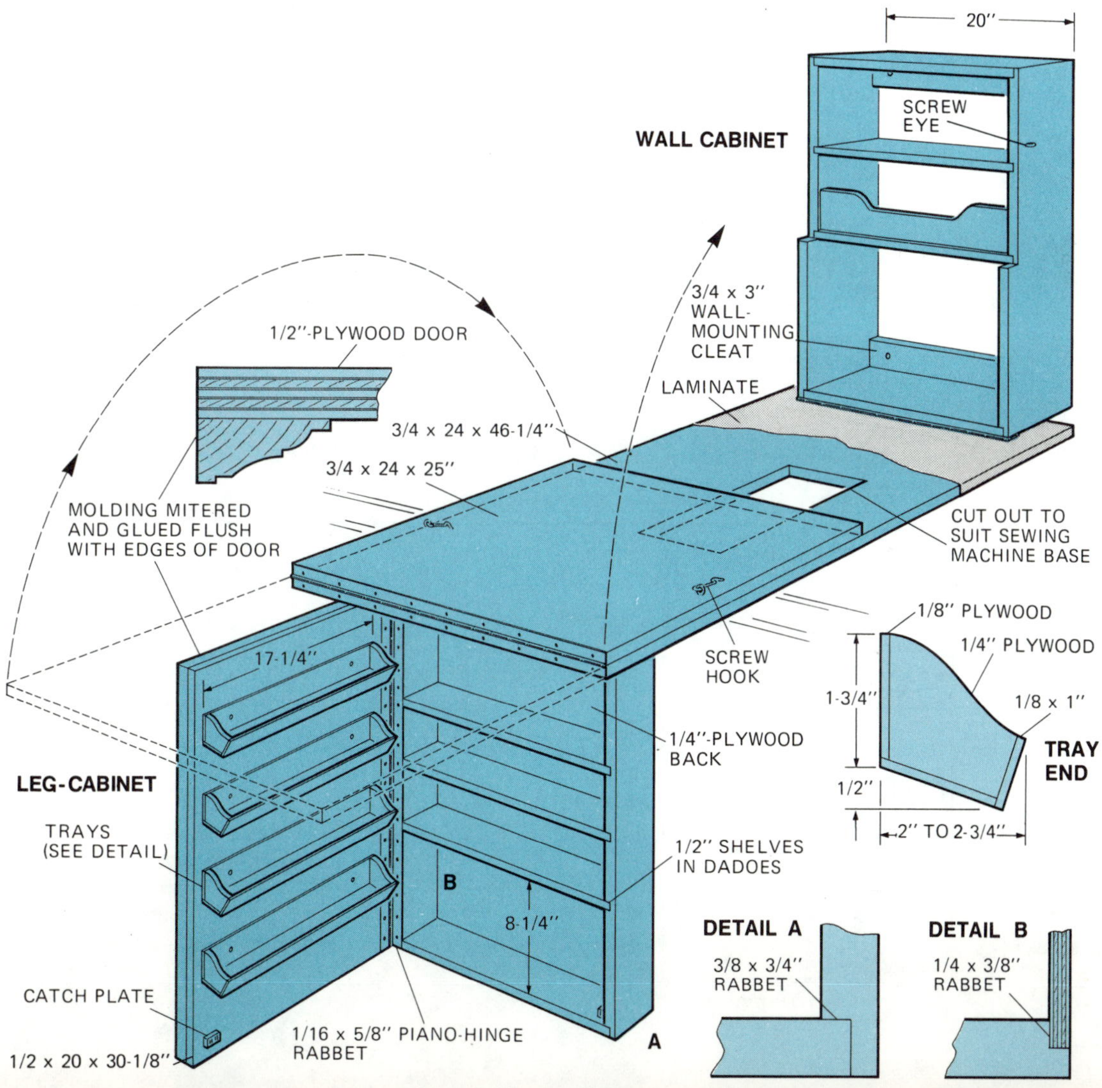

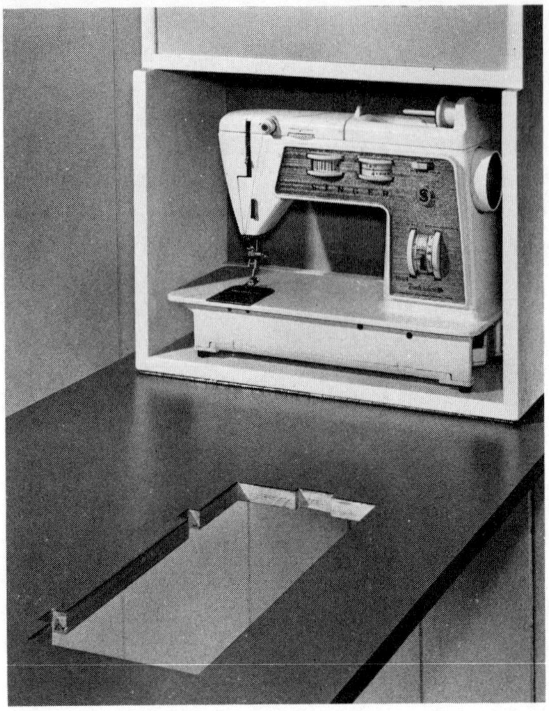

The cabinet-leg, 20 in. wide and 30¼ in. high, is made from 1x4 pine. Edges are rabbeted for a ¼-in. plywood back, side members are dadoed for ½-in. shelves, and 19¼-in. top and bottom members are housed in ⅜-in.-deep rabbets. The ½-in. plywood-panel door has a mitered frame of lumberyard molding glued to the front. Mat and picture are framed by simply gluing them to the plywood with rubber cement. Choose a painting or photograph which will look best if it is standing out a distance from the wall.

The framed door is attached with a piano hinge set in 1/16-in.-deep rabbets in both door and cabinet so there is no gap between the two when closed. The four spool trays vary in depth from 2 to 2¾ in., with bottom tray being the deepest. Ends are cut from ¼-in. wood, the rest from ⅛

SEWING MACHINE stows in base of open wall-hung cabinet when the sewer calls it a day and closes up shop.

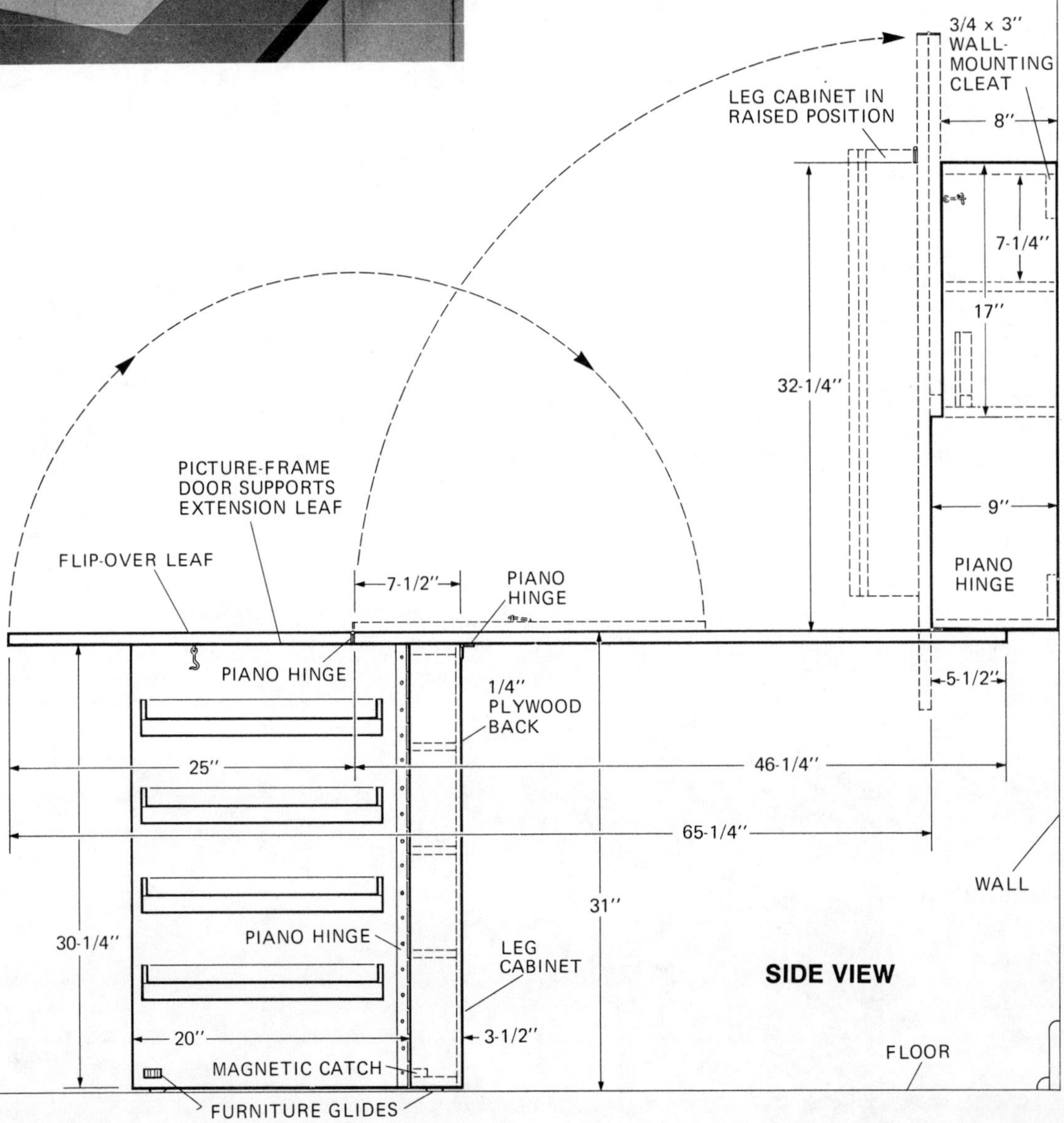

HINGED PICTURE FRAME provides access to thread and other items, even when the sewing center is stored.

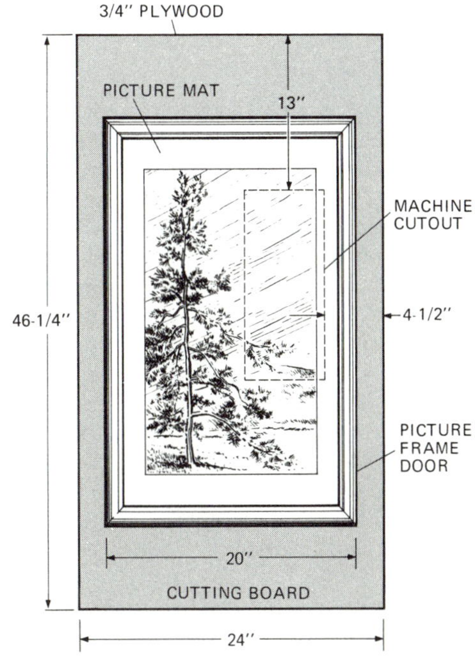

in. Each tray is fastened to the door, after painting, with small oval-head wood screws.

We banded the edges of the cutting board first with plastic laminate, then covered the top surface, before hinging the extension to the end with a 20-in. piano hinge. To assure that the extension aligns properly with the cutting board when it lies back on top of it, hold them with two C-clamps while you hinge them together. As shown in side-view drawing, the hinge point for the cabinet-leg at the outboard end of the cutting board is 7½ in. It's hinged to the wall cabinet 5½ in. from the end. Paint the cabinet to complement the decor of the room.

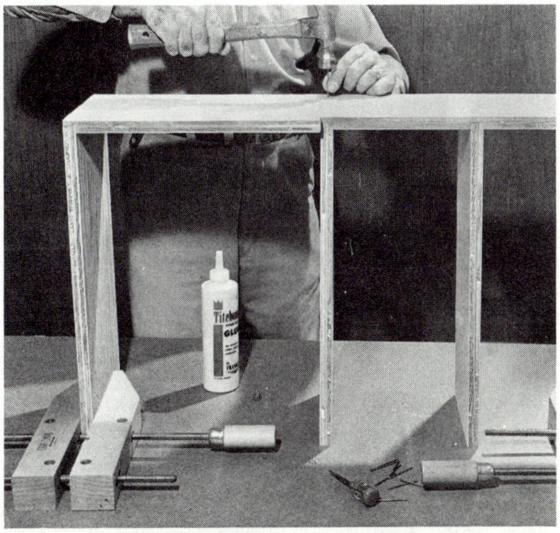

PAIR OF WOOD clamps is of great help for holding part of the wall cabinet during the first phase of assembly.

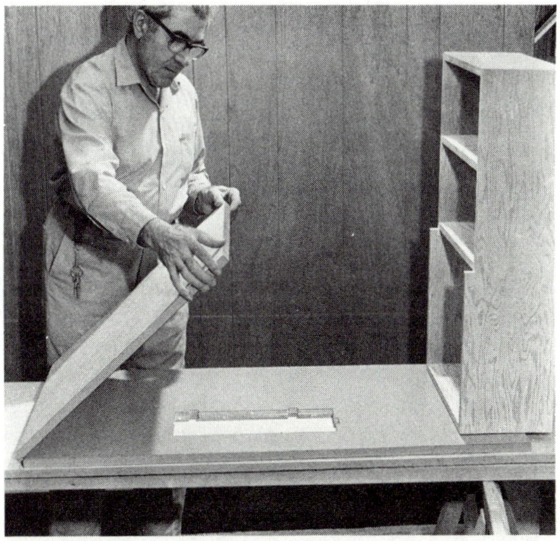

FLIP-OVER EXTENSION should align with edges of cutting board when it lies back on top for storage.

Slippery when wet

My concrete garage floor is extremely slippery and dangerous when wet. How can I correct this?—Harlan Gruber, Appleton, Wis.

A steel-trowel finish, such as that on your garage floor, is great when you're sweeping, but treacherous when wet. You have several alternatives. One is to use a concrete cleaner-etcher sold at Sears. This product etches the smooth surface, exposing more of the sand (aggregate) in the concrete. It won't harm the floor, but be sure you use safety equipment (including rubber gloves and goggles) and follow instructions on the container. Essentially, you scrub the diluted solution onto the floor, then hose it off.

Another product, also sold by Sears, is Safe Step, an extra-fine sand that is mixed with Sears Porch and Patio paint. It's available in several colors and is made for concrete surfaces. When applied, it produces a nonskid surface.

Kitchen ceiling crack

How do I repair an 8-foot-long crack in my drywall kitchen ceiling? We were thinking of using texture paint to hide the crack, but were worried about flaking because I'll be washing the ceiling often. Should we just cover it with tile?—Mrs. J. Stewart Wright, Wolf Point, Mont.

The crack may have been formed by shrinkage in your ceiling joists which has since subsided. First, retape the joint. Liberally apply joint compound to cover at least 1½ inches on each side of the crack. While the compound is still wet, embed the tape over the crack. Press the tape firmly into the compound with a taping knife and lightly draw off excess compound. When dry, sand lightly and apply a second coat. Draw off excess more firmly. Sand when dry and repeat. For the second and third coats, use a curved drywall trowel—it has a concave surface—which provides a slightly thicker buildup at the center and feathered edges. When dry, apply a coat of shellac to seal and you're ready to paint. Texture or sand-finish paints won't cover a crack that's not properly corrected. Many people find it easier to paint than wash a ceiling.

Tree root problem

A green ash tree stands 15 feet behind my house. It's about 40 feet tall and 2 feet in diameter. Do its roots pose a threat to my 8-inch poured concrete foundation?—William V. Fogler, St. Louis.

According to the Department of Agriculture, green ash grows well on home lawns and may reach up to 50 feet in height and 1½ feet in diameter. Your tree has apparently reached maturity. If your foundation shows no signs of cracking now, I'd say you have no problem.

A tree with horizontal root growth like the silver maple, however, is a serious threat to foundations and sewer lines. As with any large tree close to a house, have yours pruned of any dead wood which might fall on your home.

Film on shower-stall doors

After several years we have a soap film on shower-stall doors that seems to defy all efforts at removal. Every cleaner I've tried has failed. Have you a suggestion?—Carl Lampl, Tavares, Fla.

If it is, as you say, a soap film, then it should yield to any household cleaner containing a fine abrasive, such as "Soilax." The film might, however, be due to mineral content in the water—which may take a more active solvent, such as alcohol. You might also try a commercial glass cleaner. In any case, rub vigorously and rinse with water to get the original clarity.

Laying a brick walkway

I'd like to lay a brick walkway leading to our front door, but have no idea where to begin. What base should I use?—A.M. Walker, Northbrook, Ill.

The walkway can be laid on concrete or on sand and gravel. Bricks laid on concrete should be mortared with ⅜ to ½-in. joints depending on the brick size. On a sand and gravel base, lay the brick fairly snugly together and sweep enough sand in between the joints to fill them.

Your local dealer can help you estimate the amount of brick and other materials needed. You'd be wise to purchase SW-grade (severe weather) brick.

Remove screw anchors from wall?

I have purchased an older home with plastered walls. In two of the rooms there are several Molly-type screw anchors in the walls. How do you get 'em out?—Richard Olsen, Helena, Mont.

You don't, ordinarily, unless you can cut an opening in the plaster, which is hardly advisable, particularly if the plaster is over wire lath or a masonry base. However, by working carefully, you can drive the anchor into the plaster so that it is ¼ in. or so below the surface. Undercut the resulting hole a little and fill it with spackle. Mound the fill slightly and then sand it smooth after the spackle dries. Finish with a matching paint, and you'll have a smooth looking wall.

Ideas for sewing built-ins

BUILT-IN NEXT to the washer and the clothes bin, this tidy sewing center is handy for sewing a rip in Junior's jeans. After the mending is complete the washing machine is right there to throw the dirty clothes in. Behind the machine is a pegboard wall to hold scissors and other sewing essentials.

■ SINCE MENDING is often done in connection with washing clothes, a logical place for a sewing built-in is the laundry room. Complete with portable machine and a pegboard wall to hold patterns and sewing essentials, plus a clock and phone, the built-in sewing nook at left is an idea from Maytag that makes good sense.

Three flush doors supported by four two-drawer file cabinets placed along a wall make a complete sewing center (below, right). The file cabinets provide eight roomy storage drawers for yard goods and patterns galore, and the long counter gives all the room in the world to lay out and cut a pattern.

An unusual way to find space for a convenient sewing center is in a spare bedroom closet (below). Folding doors cover the opening when you close up shop for the day.

THIS SEWING built-in was once a spare bedroom closet. The machine counter should be 30 in. high to leave a kneehole. Shelves in the back hold sewing supplies and folding doors close to hide everything.

A QUICKIE to rig is this "built-in." The counter is made of three flush doors and is supported by common metal file cabinets. Kneeholes and chairs provide comfort at each of the sewing stations.

SEE ALSO

Built-ins . . . Closets . . . Hobby centers . . . Modular furniture . . . Mudrooms . . . Sewing cabinets . . . Study centers

Your router becomes a shaper

By WALTER E. BURTON

Build this cabinet for your router and you'll have an instant shaper for your shop. Here's how to do it

SEE ALSO

Molding cutters . . . Moldings . . . Motors, shop . . . Power-tool stands . . . Routers . . . Workbenches . . . Workshops

IF YOU TURN a portable router upside down, you have, essentially, a wood-working shaper. To do it, the inverted router must be supported in such a way that it can function as a shaper with work guides, guards and the like. This shop-built version was designed to accommodate a Millers Falls MF router, Model A, catalog No. 7200. But, where necessary, dimensions can be altered for your own router.

The router hangs suspended from the underside of the cabinet top so that it can be removed for conventional routing operations by unscrewing four nuts. The hinged top tilts upward for convenience in changing cutters and making adjustments—although you can make cutter-height settings by reaching into the cabinet.

The cabinet top is hinged to the rear panel. Centered on the top is a $\frac{1}{16}$ x 8 x 8-in. aluminum plate that rests in a recess so the plate surface and adjacent wood are in the same plane. The hole at plate center is approximately $1\frac{1}{8}$ in. in diameter. In the wood top, concentric with this

THE ROUTER cuts a recess in cabinet top to hold the plate against which router base is clamped.

BOTTOM OF the top panel shows the router clamped in place against the metal plate.

IN PARTIALLY assembled cabinet, the accessory drawer and vent openings for airflow are seen.

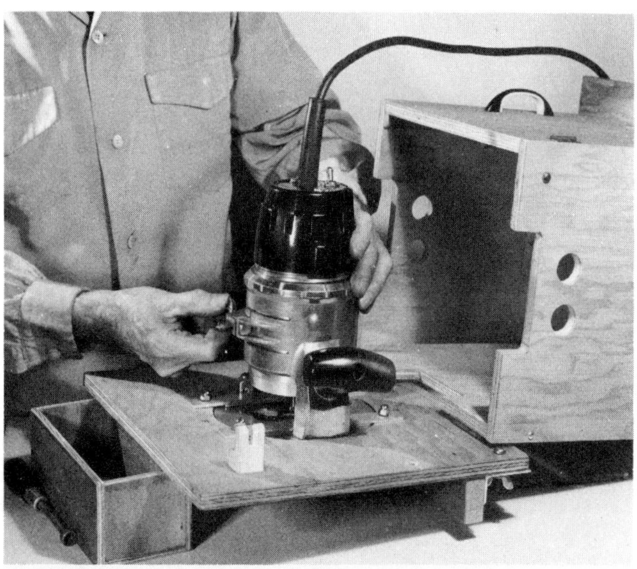

FOR INSTALLING or removing the router, the cabinet is flipped on its back and top panel swung open.

TO CHANGE cutters, the router is swung up and held by a dowel engaging sockets on the side panels.

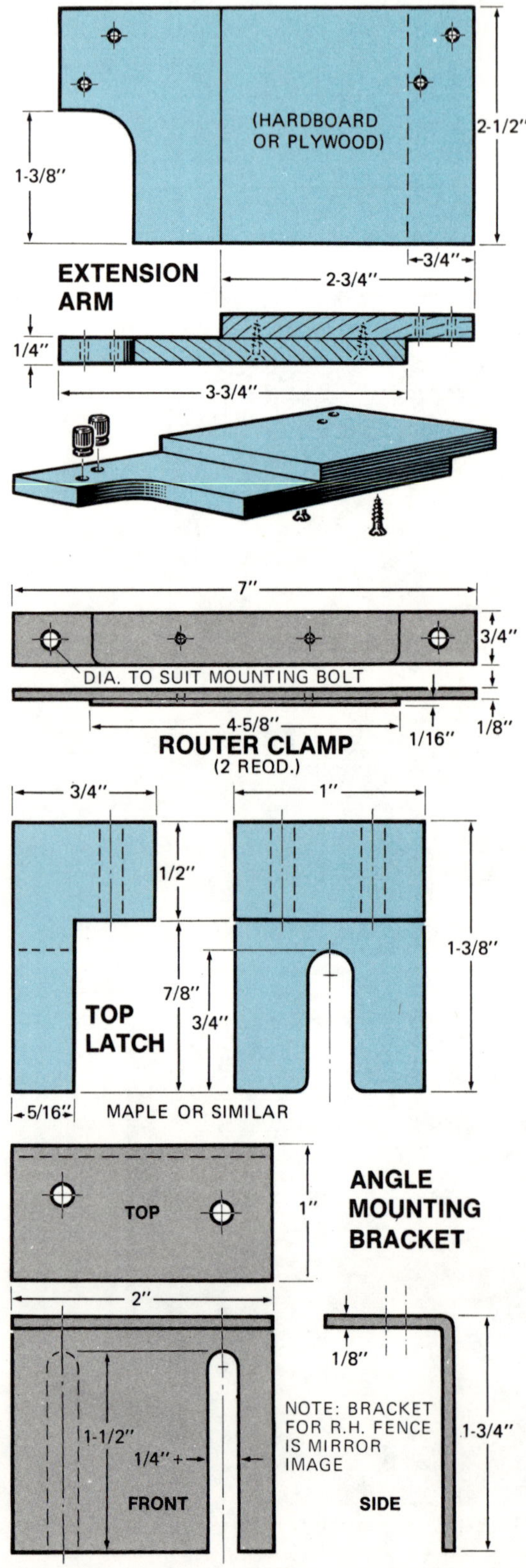

router becomes a shaper, continued

hole, is a 6-in.-dia. opening for the router base. Check your router's shoe diameter before cutting this circle.

You can form the 1/16-in.-deep recess by routing out most of the area with a straight bit. Leave an "island" in the center until last so the router shoe is supported. Then, remove the island with a router bit in a drill press. Next, jigsaw the 6-in. opening. Fasten the plate in its recess with two countersunk wood screws near the opposite corners.

To determine the center of the 1⅛-in. hole, insert a pointed cutter in the router and place the router base into its opening. The point where

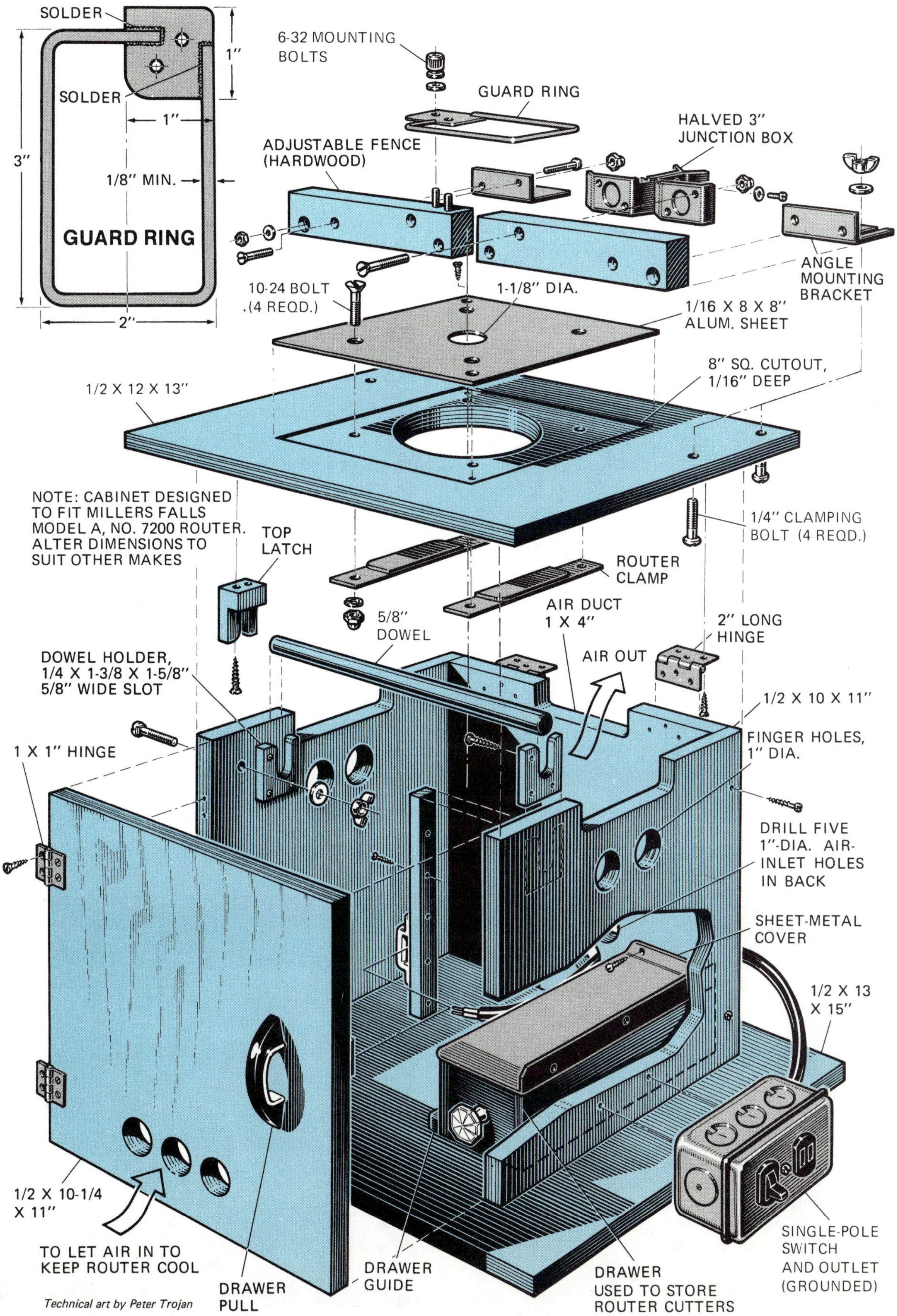

Technical art by Peter Trojan

the bit touches the metal plate is the center for the hole. Use two 2-in. butt hinges to join top to back panel. Although the router's weight will hold the top down, rigidity is increased by installing a simple wooden latch at the corner near the front panel hinge.

The router-mounting arrangement is dictated by router-base construction. For the tool shown, two 1/8 x 3/4 x 7-in. aluminum strips, with 1/16 x 3/4 x 4 5/8-in. pads (to compensate for difference in router base and wood thickness) riveted to them, worked fine. Four 10–24 bolts extend through these strips, through countersunk holes in the metal top insert and plywood and are secured to the cabinet top with nuts and washers.

The cabinet and cabinet-top sizes are not critical. The dimensions given provide adequate space, although the power cord must be curved sideways in order to clear the bottom at the usual cutter depth settings.

Since a router motor "breathes" by drawing air in at cord-end and discharging it around the cutter, it's a must to provide airflow holes in the box. These consist of 1x4-in. notches at top edges of the sidepieces and back panel and multiple 1-in. holes in the back and front panels. (The two 1-in. holes at the top of each side are primarily finger holes for carrying.) If the intake air seems to carry excessive dust and chips, it's a good idea to install some fine-mesh screen over the inlets. Chips should not be permitted to build up in the box; if the router is to be used for long periods, periodically check the motor to avoid overheating. If necessary, leave the door open.

INTERIOR VIEW shows the router in operating position. Original plastic shield was replaced by the ring type.

The hinged top can be raised to give better access to the router when you change cutters. The router is held in the tilted position by resting it on a piece of 5/8-in. dowel whose ends engage notched plywood pieces screwed to the inside surfaces of sidepieces.

The storage drawer is made of 1/4-in. plywood and is located in one corner of the cabinet. To keep it in position, glue a guide strip along the

MOUNTING clamps and center coupling, made from a halved 3-in. junction box, are attached to fence.

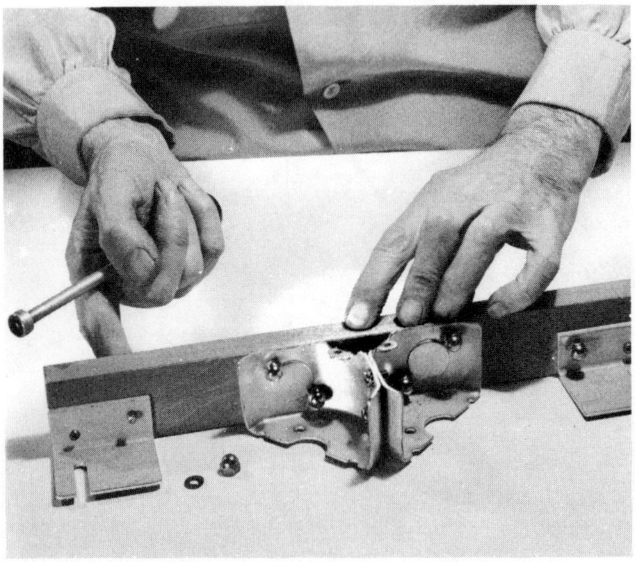

REAR OF guide fence is in position for straight work. Notice the ring-type guard in foreground.

bottom. A sheet-aluminum cover helps keep dirt out and the drawer in place. Inside, a wooden block drilled to receive cutter shanks holds stored cutters.

An adjustable fence guides straightedged work past the cutter. I used a piece of maple cut to the dimensions indicated. An angle mounting bracket was then fastened to each end with bolts.

An adjustable bracket assembly made from a 3-in. electrical junction box (sawed diagonally in two) is bolted to the fence center. A little hammering and filing will let you fit the box halves squarely with the surfaces at a right angle and parallel where they contact the wood. Three 8–32 bolts hold the two halves together; holes in one of them are slotted so the guide fence can be adjusted for cut depth when jointing.

After bolting the junction-box bracket assembly to the wooden strip, saw a section slightly over 1 in. wide from the center of the strip to provide space for the cutter. Normally, the fence is used with surfaces of both halves in the same plane, but they can be offset as desired—by loosening the bolts holding the junction-box halves together. The fence assembly is centered with respect to the cutter, and holes for the ¼-in. clamping bolts are located near edges of the cabinet top. A second set of holes is drilled near the back edge of the top to provide an alternate fence position.

Make a guard ring to fit over the fence gap, which can also be used on an extension arm when nonstraight edges are being shaped. The loop, made from ⅛-in. rod, is soldered to a brass plate drilled for 6–32 mounting bolts. The extension arm, made from ¼-in. plywood, is stepped to bring it nearer the cutter and improve rigidity. Bolts holding the guard and extension arm should be in one half of the guide fence only so you can adjust the other half for depth of cut.

Because the router switch is not easily reached when the cabinet door is closed, you'll need an outside control. This consists of a single-pole switch and outlet (provided with ground connection) housed in a surface-mounting switch box screwed to the cabinet side. The router is plugged into the outlet.

A sizable assortment of cutters suitable for forming edge moldings, smoothing edges and other shaping chores is available. For use without a guide fence, as in cutting moldings along irregular edges, there are bits with pilots or shoulders to limit the cut. The setup illustrated had no tendency to "walk" because vibration is light. If desired, you can use C-clamps to anchor the cabinet on a table or bench.

Fingers should, of course, be kept away from cutters. Instead, various work hold-downs—such as springy steel strips—can be designed as needed, mounted on the fence and supplemented by push sticks to hold work against the cutter.

Your shaper cabinet can be finished conventionally. For the top, an easy finish is a sealer, such as thinned shellac, followed by two polish coats of floor wax. The rest of the cabinet can be varnished or painted.

TO SHAPE edges on straight work, a ring-type guard goes on the rear fence to protect fingers.

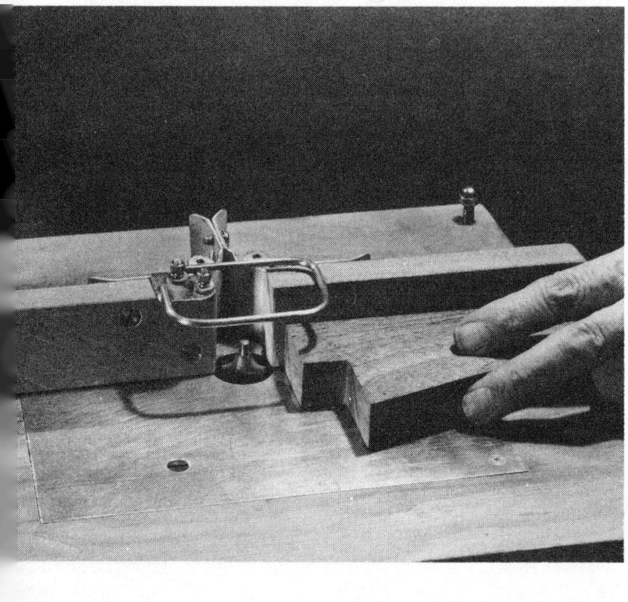

FOR CURVED work, guide fence is moved back. The ring guard is mounted on the extension.

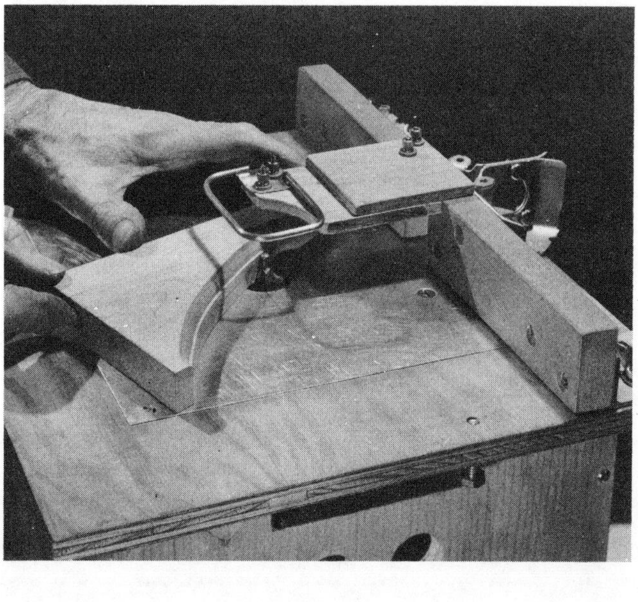

How to keep cutting edges sharp

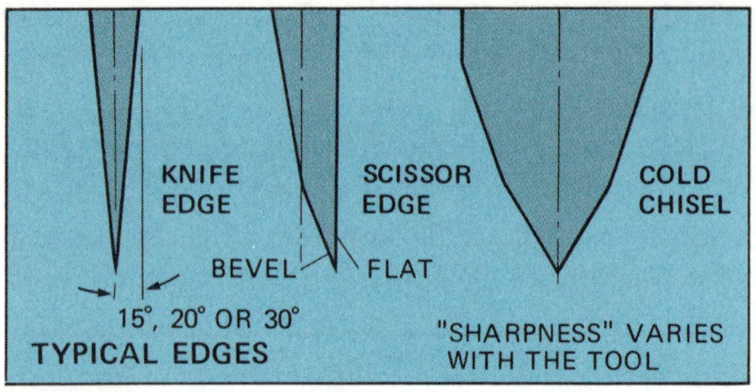

THE HOW AND WHY OF SHARPENING

It won't take you long to discover that you'll get twofold benefits from keeping all cutting edges of your various tools sharp. First, your skills with chisels, knives, gouges and the like will increase because you will have better control over the tool. Second, since a dull cutting tool is far more dangerous to work with than a sharp one, you'll minimize the chance of unfortunate accidents. (A dull chisel, for example, forces *you* to do the work that the tool should be doing, by applying extra pressure.)

Though most beginning workshoppers believe that efficient sharpening is beyond their skills, the opposite is true. Almost anyone can obtain, and keep, a sharp cutting edge rather than be forced to work with a ragged one—if he follows the basics listed on these pages.

Two sharpening rules of thumb you should always keep in mind:

☐ *Sharpen cutting tools regularly;* don't wait until they are dull and nicked because the cutting edge will then have to be reshaped on the grinding wheel.

☐ *Maintain the tool's original cutting-edge shape* (see examples above) *when sharpening.* Various tools call for specific degrees of bevel and shape: These shapes (degree of bevel) have proven to be the best for the particular job for which the tool is intended.

Any cutting tool that has been abused—lost its shape or nicked in its cutting edge—requires two steps for reconditioning: reshaping and sharpening. The reshaping may be done on a grinder, or with files if the tool is "soft" enough (of low carbon steel). To reshape, use coarse-grit grinding stones or files. The object of reshaping is to true a tool's edge, restore proper bevels and remove all nicks. Sharpness is *not* obtained with the coarser grits. Sharpening differs from reshaping in that only the edge requires work—removal of small particles of metal to achieve a razor edge.

GRINDING AND GRINDING WHEELS

There are two principal types of grinding wheels: natural and man-made. The first are of fine grit and are used in water at relatively low speeds for sharpening and fine honing. To reshape an edge, switch to one of the man-made stones (available in fine, medium-fine, medium-coarse and, occasionally, in coarse). Though several types are made, best for all-around use are long-wearing bonded and vitrified aluminum-oxide abrasive wheels. Grinding generates heat; stop frequently and water-cool the tool so its temper is not drawn. If tool becomes bluish, it's too hot and has lost its hardness. After frequent use, metal particles may fill (load) the stone's pores. To dress a stone, use a steel wheel dresser; to dress natural stones, use a stone or a chunk of concrete.

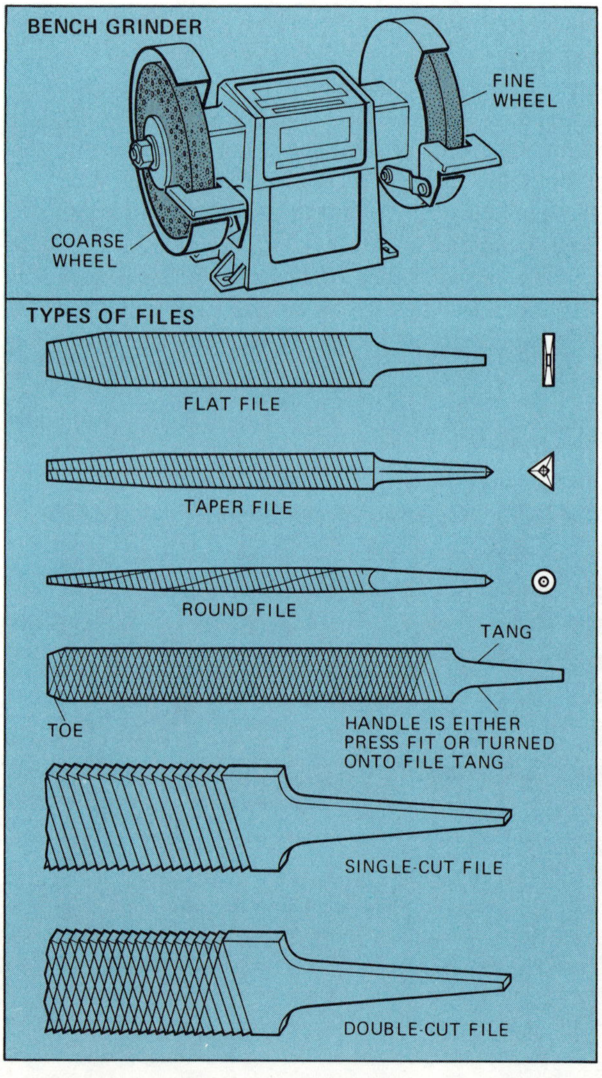

SEE ALSO

Bandsaws, sharpening . . . Knives, hunting . . . Scrapers . . . Shop tools . . . Toolboxes . . . Tools, hand . . . Twist drills

TYPES OF HONING STONES

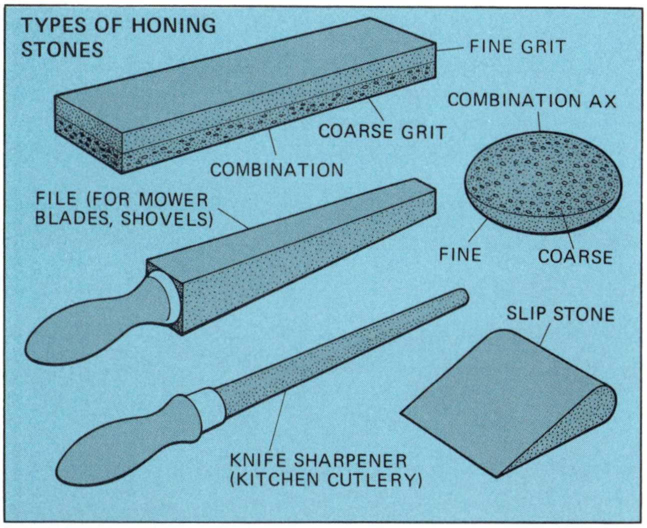

FIG. A

FIG. B

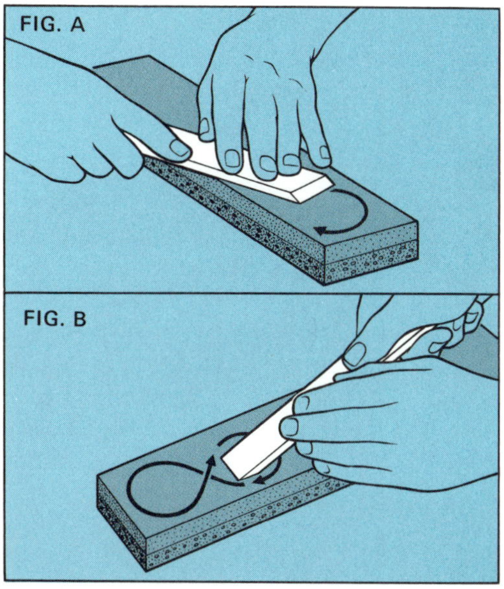

HOW-TOS OF HONING

Like grinding wheels (natural and man-made), stones must be lubricated during use, either with water or a couple of drops of fine-grade machine oil. The lubricating agent is a matter of personal preference, but most pros prefer to use oil. Oilstones are probably the most commonly used honing stone; these are flat and may be of one grit throughout, but the combination type (see drawing above) is more practical to own.

The idea of honing is to feather the cutting edge as fine as possible. To do it, alternately stroke each side with progressively lighter pressure and finer grit abrasive. It is important that every stroke be delivered in the right direction and at the right pressure. Once you have achieved a feather edge, stop. Additional honing can be, in fact, damaging because there is good chance that you will change the tool's edge shape. The tool will be sharpened properly if, when passed lightly across your thumbnail, its edge delicately removes a scant amount of nail.

Honing stones should also be redressed occasionally and stored in a covered box.

HONING A CHISEL

To stone an edge without rounding it, use one hand to control the angle and the other to apply uniform downward pressure. In Fig. A above, burrs are removed using a circular motion. To hone bevel edge (Fig. B), keep wrists rigid and move the blade in a *continuous* figure-8 pattern. To maintain an edge which is started right, it must be occasionally whetted. In A (below), the blade needs attention all around; bevel must be taken all the way down as in B and then feathered to a razor edge as shown in C.

USING FILES

Low-carbon cutting edges can be reshaped and sharpened with one of the files shown at left on facing page. The bottom edge of the cutter bar on a reel-type mower, for example, can be touched up using a flat metal-cutting file. (*Never* attempt to sharpen the reel blades unless you have the special equipment such sharpening requires.) When using files to sharpen a plane iron or chisel, support tool in vise so bevel edge is horizontal and cutting edge is facing away from you. File toward the edge. For straight-edge chisels, use mill files; for gouges, round files. Follow filing with a honing.

WHEN TO WHET THE BLADE BEVEL

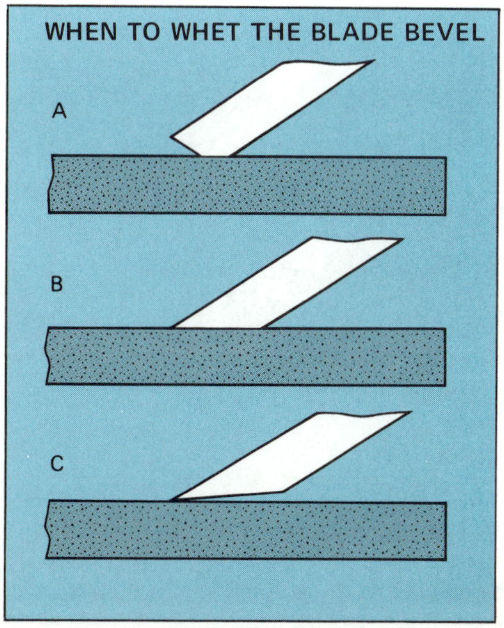

SHARPENING TOOLS is less of a chore with this unique self-oiling oilstone box. Apply steady pressure on the plunger and the pump is refilled in just a few seconds.

Make your oilstone self-lubricating

By KENNETH WELLS

■ THE OILSTONE HOLDER shown above looks like an ordinary box used to house and protect an oilstone. Inside, it's another story. The box houses a simple pump in the base that ejects just the right amount of oil onto the stone automatically. The dimensions given in the drawing (facing page) suit the most popular-size stone—1x2x8 in.

THE QUICKEST WAY to remove the stock from the waste portion is with a hefty bit in a drill press.

SEE ALSO

Knives, hunting . . . Scrapers . . . Shop tools . . . Toolboxes . . . Tools, hand . . . Twist drills

To make such a box, prepare a block of hardwood to the sizes given, then mark out the recesses in the base and lid to receive the stone and pump barrel. A drill press fitted with a router bit and equipped with a depth stop makes short work of removing the waste from the recesses although it can be done with a drill bit and chisel as shown at the right. Make the lid recess slightly larger than the base recess to provide an easy fit, and use a chisel to square up the corners of the recesses so that the stone will fit.

The base and lid of the box can be finished with two or three coats of polyurethane seal or shellac polish.

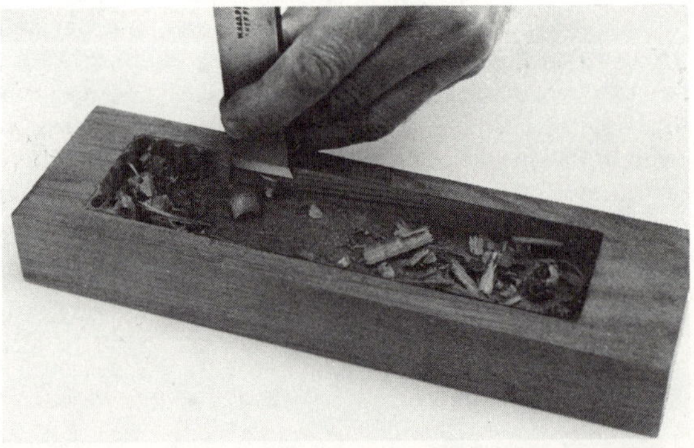

WITH MOST WASTE drilled out, a sharp chisel is used to cut a precise recess to suit your oilstone and pump.

THE BOX is rigidly clamped and the hole for the pump barrel is bored using a hand brace and bit. Be sure to keep the bit vertical.

THE PUMP BARREL is being fixed in place. Besides keeping the oil at hand, the box protects your stone from collecting dust and dirt when it's in storage.

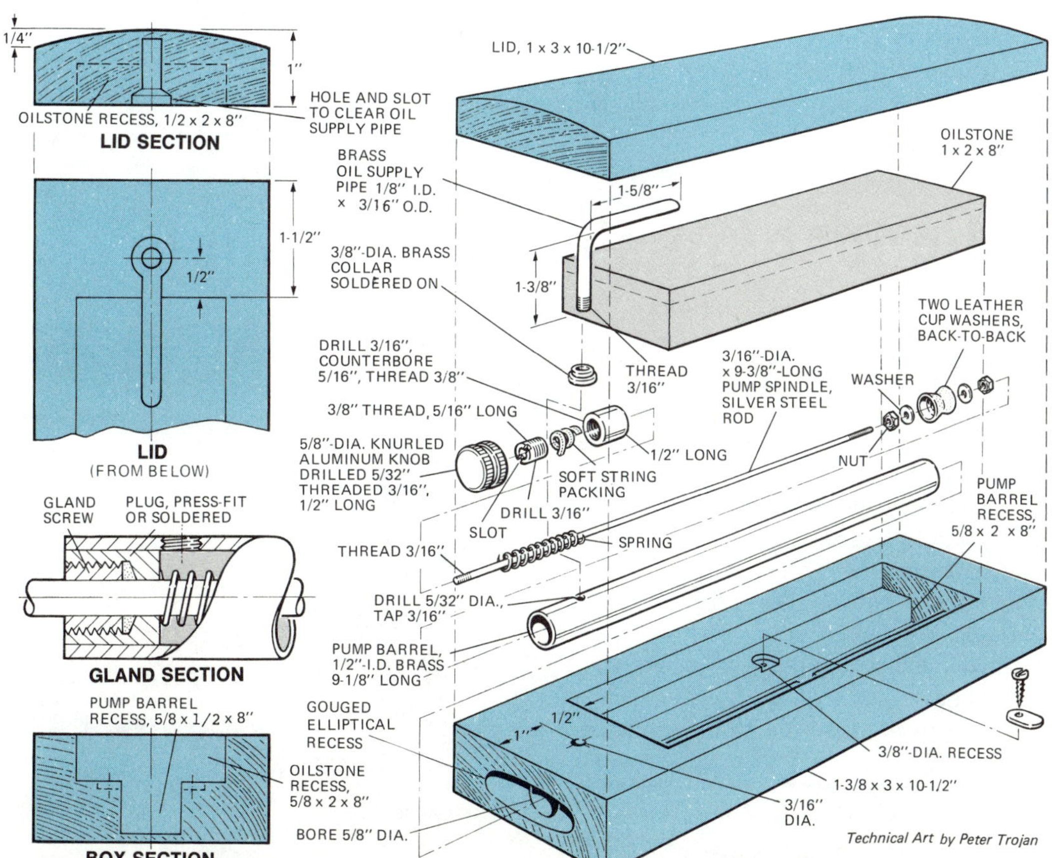

Technical Art by Peter Trojan

Escape from that crowded family medicine chest by building yourself one of these shaving cabinets. Both are equipped with mirror and shelf

Two handsome shaving cabinets

■ GOT THE FEELING you're being gradually squeezed out of the medicine cabinet by teen-age daughters and your better half? When there's hardly room left for your razor, it's time to move out and into one of these handsome shaving bars. Placed off limits to everyone else, they'll keep everything right at hand to give you that well-groomed look.

Both designs you see on these pages are wall mounted and have their own mirrors. Both feature counters, one a drop-front affair, the other

SEE ALSO
Bathrooms . . . Hinges . . . Towel racks

HANDY DROP-FRONT COUNTER reveals additional storage behind it. Magnetic catch holds counter shut.

an inside ledge. The former provides storage behind a lift-up mirror, the latter inside a swinging front. To top it off, both are smart looking and make handsome additions to any bathroom wall.

Styled by Gary Gerber, noted industrial designer, the bars combine select cabinet woods, with bright aluminum, glass and gleaming mosaic tile, and one of the handiest tools for putting all four together is a heat-type electric glue gun since it's made to order for bonding glass, tile and metal to wood. Using stick glue which bonds in 60 seconds, the gun eliminates the need for clamps.

The cabinet shown on this page is made of ½-in. solid walnut and fitted with a hardboard

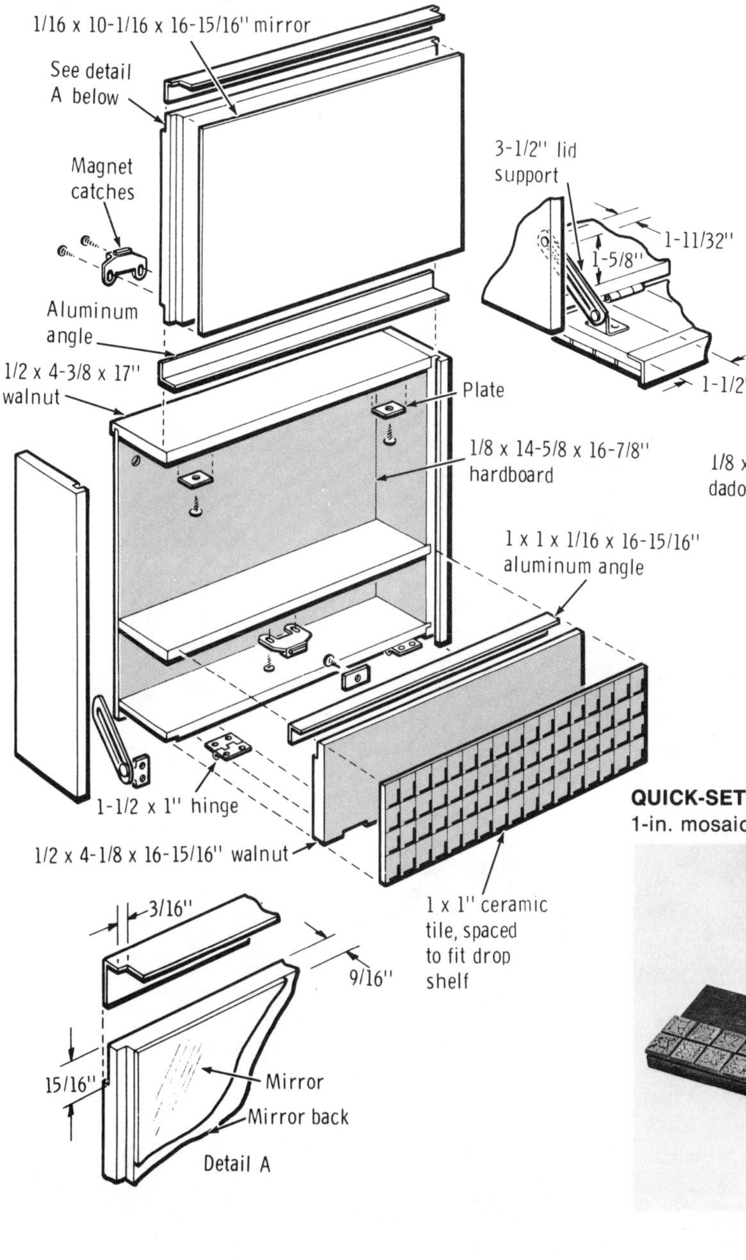

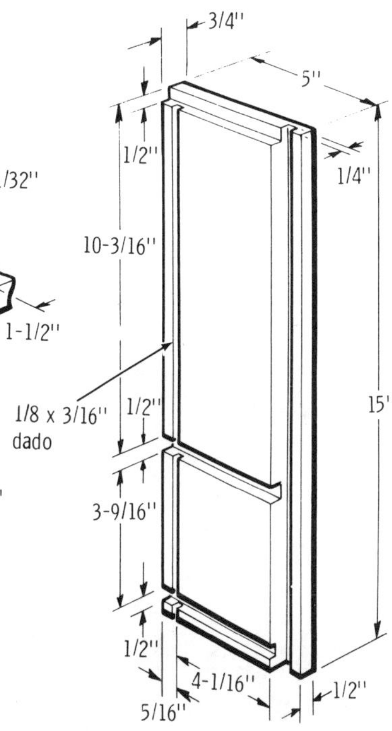

QUICK-SETTING GLUE makes a fast way of bedding the 1-in. mosaic tiles to the hinged walnut front.

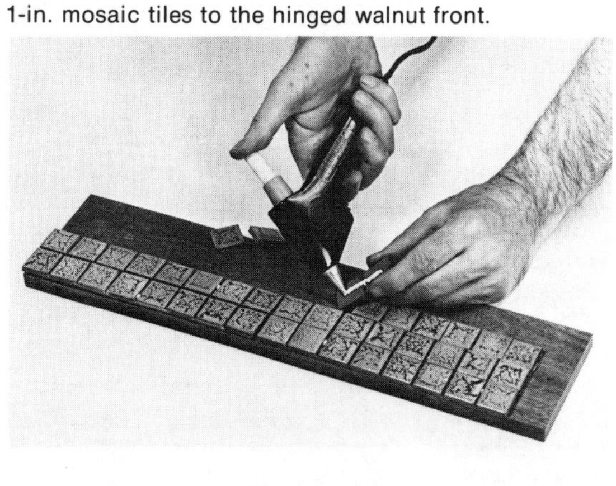

back. The ends are made right and left hand, and the closeup detail shows how they are grooved at the rear for the ⅛-in. back and at the front for the 9/16-in. sliding mirror. The latter is glued to a plywood backing which is rabbeted top and bottom for aluminum-angle handles, and along the sides to fit the grooved ends. The mirror is cemented to the plywood with the glue gun. Since magnetic catches are used to hold the mirror in the raised position and are screwed to the plywood from the back, the mirror assembly must be in place before the ends of the cabinet are finally glued. Because of the catches, you can't slide the mirror in place from the top.

An aluminum angle across the top provides a handle for the tile-faced drop front. When gluing this, as well as the two metal strips to the mirror, the aluminum should first be heated so it's warm

when you apply the stick glue. A magnetic catch holds the drop front shut, and a desk-lid support holds it level when open.

The swing-front cabinet detailed on these two pages consists of two separate assemblies, one nesting inside the other. The three-sided box holding the mirror is made of ½-in. solid walnut and has a hardboard back. Note how the parts are grooved and rabbeted to accept a post to which the swinging front is hinged. Since the weight of the latter is on this post, metal corner braces are added for extra support.

Pine and hardboard are used for the front unit, the pine for the ends. Aluminum angle cemented to the three shelves provides retaining edges. The swinging front is completely painted in a three-color pattern, whereas the walnut members are stained and varnished.

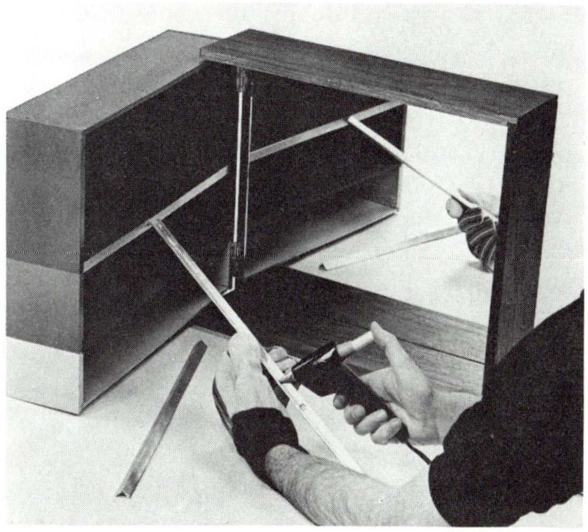

BETTER BOND is assured when cementing aluminum to the wood shelves if metal strip is first heated.

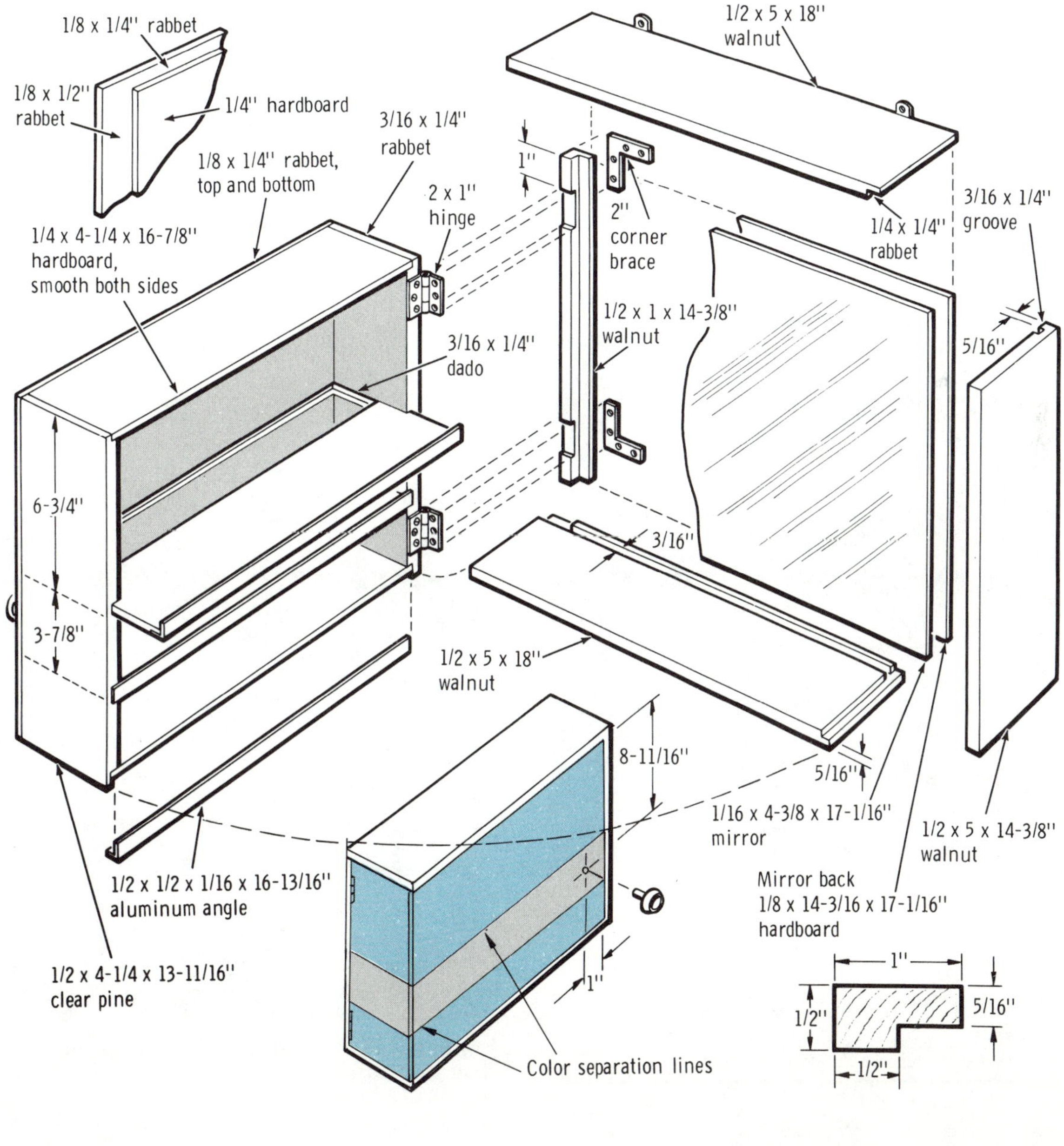

■ A CHARMING decorative piece for almost any room, this early American shaving console is also functional. You can use it to hold shaving gear or other items. A shelf above the mirror can display an old shaving mug, and the small drawer provides more than adequate storage for the usual assortment of shaving paraphernalia. Additionally, a comb and brush box is located at the base which is fitted with an American eagle hook that serves as a small towel holder.

Even if the console is not used for its original intended purpose, its colonial look fits in well in any room—including the kitchen where it can be hung next to the telephone to hold pads, pencils, calendars and other items.

The shaving console shown is built of cherry; if you prefer, it will still look good in walnut or knotty pine. If you wish, a side-view mirror salvaged from an old car can be used for the looking glass.

By DON SHINER

An early American shaving console

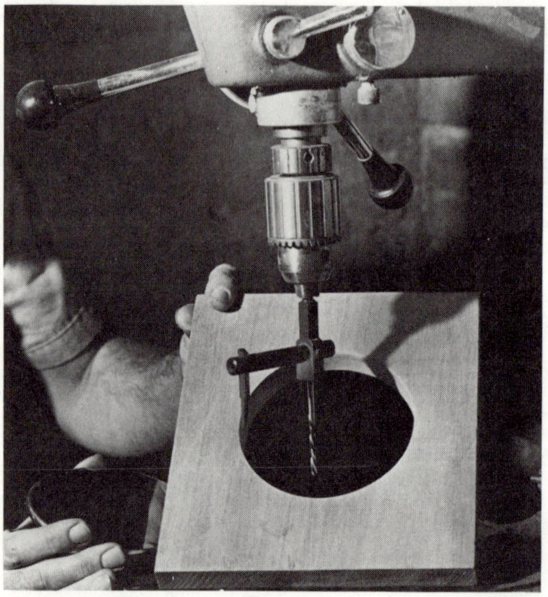

THE MIRROR CUTOUT in the rear panel is made with a circle cutter in a drill press or with a sabre saw.

BRACKETS for candle holders are glued and clamped to the side panels. Drawer is last step.

SEE ALSO

Bathrooms . . . Candle stands . . . Comb boxes . . . Dry sinks . . . Gossip benches . . . Kitchen accessories . . . Towel racks

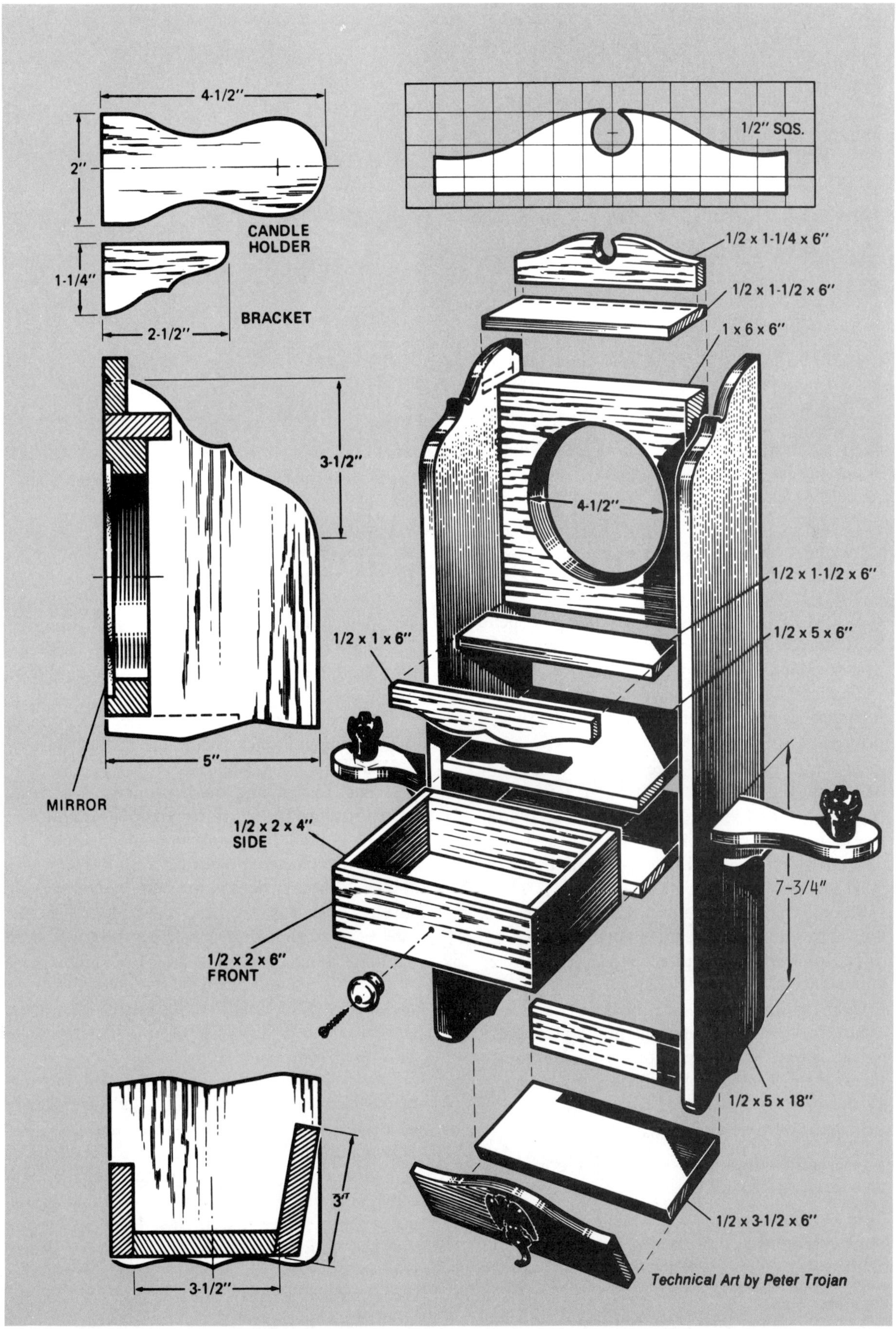

Technical Art by Peter Trojan

THESE FLOWER and thinning shears by Corona have straight blades that can easily reach into plant centers without pushing foliage and flowers aside. The 7¾-in.-long forged-steel tool has cushioned vinyl handles.

How to choose good gardenshears

■ WITH PROPER TOOLS, the time you spend outdoors caring for your lawn and garden can be as enjoyable as admiring the end results.

The list of common homeowner garden shears includes: flower/thinning shears, grass shears, pruners, hedge shears and loppers.

You can tell when you're holding a superior pair of shears. You can feel the balance and solid construction and see the finishing details. If your week's worth of gardening is lumped into a Sunday afternoon, the well-balanced handling of a good tool will cut down on fatigue.

Smooth action that helps produce clean cuts is built into well-made shears. Plants aren't frayed, ripped or heated and, therefore, have a fresher appearance and sprout sooner.

Over the long run, you can identify superior shears by their longevity and minimal maintenance needs. After years of use, when other shears are discarded, you can buy parts for quality shears.

uses, features of various types

One-hand shears are for light outdoor work. The flower shears also help with light thinning. There are two styles of grass shears: the scissors-type and the vertical-squeeze variety shown below.

There are also two basic types of pruning shears: bypass pruners, which cut by the action of a blade and hook (sometimes two blades) that pass each other, and anvil pruners, which cut with a straight blade against an anvil. Both types are widely used, but many professionals shun the anvil style because it tends to crush stems.

Hedge shears. Shears for shaping hedges and shrubs come in power and hand models. Some quality hand shears have a wingnut mounted at the pivot point for tension adjustment. One way of identifying a good hedge shear, according to a spokesperson for True Friends, is to quickly open and close it and "Listen to the whistle," which a good tool makes.

Electric hedge shears often feature two moving blades that reduce vibration. Teeth are sharpened on both sides to make clean cuts.

Lopping shears. The long handles on loppers give more cutting strength (greater leverage) and a longer reach than smaller shears. Loppers are available in bypass and anvil styles.

A last tip for identifying quality shears: When you shop, carry some paper with you. If the shears cut rather than bend it, you're probably holding a superior tool.

SEE ALSO

Benches, potting . . . Cold frames . . . Gardening . . . Grass . . . Hand mowers . . . Landscaping . . . Lawns . . . Mowers . . . Vegetable gardening

THERE ARE SEVERAL innovative details on these vertical-squeeze type grass shears by True Temper. The blades aren't connected by a common pivot pin. Instead, the top "floating blade" connects with a spring—the theory being that this assures even cutting along the length of the blades. When not in use, a gravity lock holds the shears in closed position. Work it by simply closing the blades and turning the shears upside down. Blades are hollow-ground, high-carbon steel.

TWO BASIC TYPES of pruning shears are the bypass pruners above and the anvil pruners below. The female blade on these by Wilkinson Sword has a groove to collect sap and keep blades clean.

WAVY BLADES of True Friends hand shears (top) are designed to maintain the proper cutting angle along their length. These have a shock absorber and hardwood handles. Blades on True Friends electric shear have opposed cutting action—both move simultaneously to reduce vibration. Blades are chrome-vanadium steel and have a ½-in.-dia. cutting capacity. The tool is double-insulated with a friction-safety clutch to prevent motor damage if the blades jam in use.

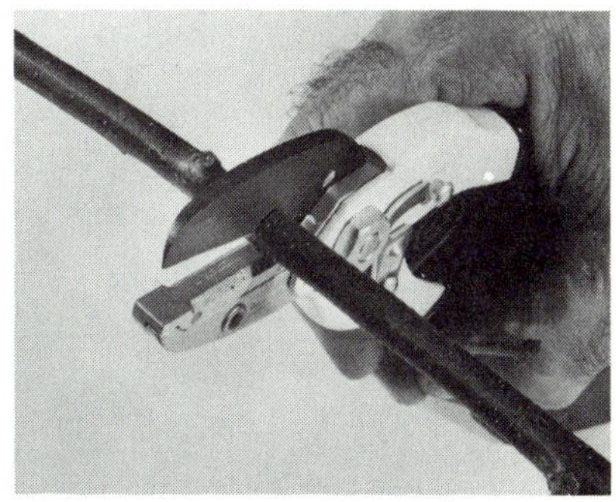

SHOWN ABOVE are Wilkinson's anvil pruners. These feature an aluminum anvil to minimize blunting of the cutting edge. One possible disadvantage of this type is that they are more likely to crush stems.

Sharpening tools

Blades on quality shears are often hollow-ground. A few light file strokes should be sufficient to resharpen them, unless the blades have become badly dulled or nicked.

1. Use a small (about 6 in.) smooth, single-cut mill file on shears with straight blades.

2. Try to maintain the factory angle on the cutting edge as shown above. If the blade is filed flat and thin with no bevel, it will either chip or roll.

3. Hold the blade in a vise and sharpen from the blade point toward the handle in one straight motion.

4. Avoid filing the flat side or inside of the blade. However, you *can* use the file on these surfaces to remove burrs that have been caused by filing.

5. Hooks on quality lopping and pruning shears rarely require sharpening. However, you can remove nicks with a round carborundum stone.

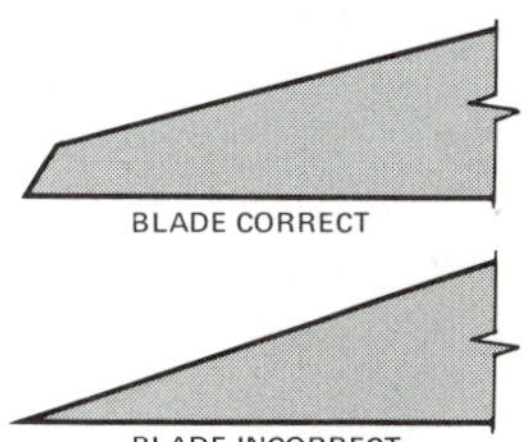

THESE ANVIL-TYPE loppers by Seymour Smith have a gear drive to develop extra cutting power—three times more than a conventional lopper of equal size. The tool cuts up to 1¼-in.-dia. limbs. Blade is replaceable and the bronze anvil is reversible for additional use. The anvil is also replaceable.

EXTERIOR plywood siding/sheathing, "Sturd-i-wall" is single-layer construction. Boards, battens dress it up.

All about sheathing

By RICHARD NUNN

It's a necessary building product to make your home comfortable, safe, and more economical to operate

SEE ALSO

Hardboard . . . House additions . . . Insulation . . . Lumber . . . Nails . . . Plywood . . . Siding

ABOUT 87 PERCENT of all homes built in the United States every year use some type of sidewall sheathing. Regardless of the type of siding on your home—new or existing—experts recommend that sheathing be used; without it, the house is not as structurally strong, safe and comfortable as one with properly applied sheathing. It forms a wall in itself, it strengthens the framework, and it has a significant insulating and sound-deadening value depending on the type of material used.

Wood sheathing consists of boards up to 8 in. wide with a shiplap or tongue-and-groove construction for added strength and weather resistance. When buying the material for new construction or making repairs, ask your lumber dealer for a quotation on "sheathing-grade" lumber. Through tests it has been determined that wood sheathing applied diagonally (and properly nailed) forms a wall four times as strong as one

INSULATION-BOARD sheathing goes up in big 4 x 8-ft. panels. It is rated for heat-resistance and also offers sound-deadening qualities.

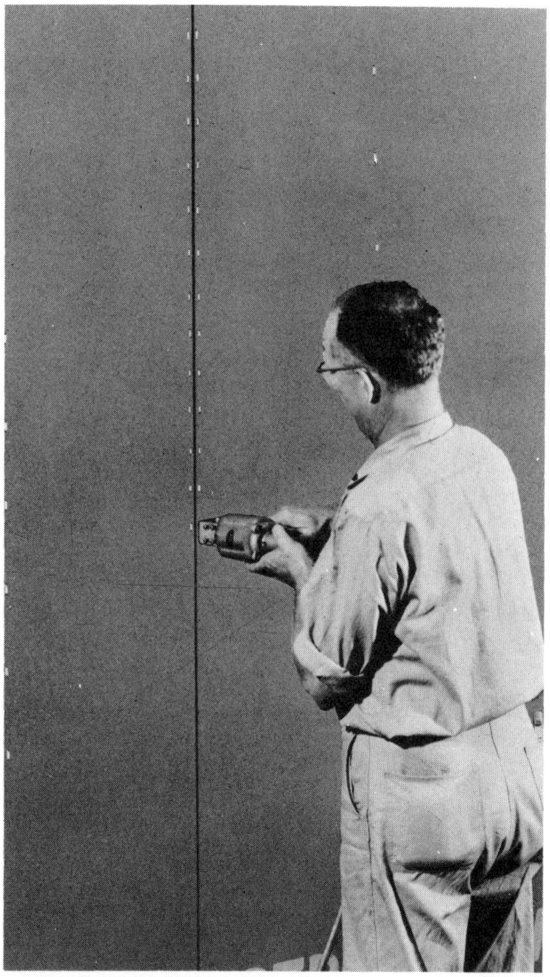

STAPLE GUN helps to install insulation-board sheathing as well as nails. Manufacturers imprint nailing schedule right on the material.

sheathed horizontally with exactly the same boards. Diagonal sheathing requires a little more material because of the trimming, but its added strength more than offsets the additional cost involved (see page 2622).

Plywood sheathing will add great strength and rigidity to any structure, and plywood also is ideal for shear walls engineered to resist lateral loads. Plywood sheathing produced by mills belonging to the American Plywood Association is marked "Standard INT-DFPA." The most common thicknesses are 5/16, 3/8, 1/2, 5/8, 3/4 and 7/8 in. The veneer grade is C face, D back and inner plies. When plywood sheathing is used, building paper and diagonal wall bracing can be eliminated. Common smooth 6d nails or annular, spiral-threaded galvanized box nails, or T-nails of the same diameter can be used. Staples can also be used, but at a reduced spacing. If siding such as shingles will be used over the plywood sheathing, you must apply the plywood to the studs with the face grain running across the studs.

Gypsum sheathing has a gypsum-rock core enveloped in a heavy, water-repellent paper. Because of the core, a conventional wall built up with a layer of gypsum sheathing has a fire-resistance rating, depending on the type of construction used. The sheathing is made in sheets 1/2 x 24 x 96 in., which are quick and easy to install. The tongue-and-groove horizontal edges fit snugly together to reduce wind penetration. The material costs less than wood sheathing. It does have one limitation, however: It can't serve as a nailing base. Wood siding, furring strips and wall ties must be nailed through the sheathing and into the framing members.

Insulation-board sheathing is probably the most common of all sheathing products used today. The material provides more insulation value than competitive sheathing products. Be-

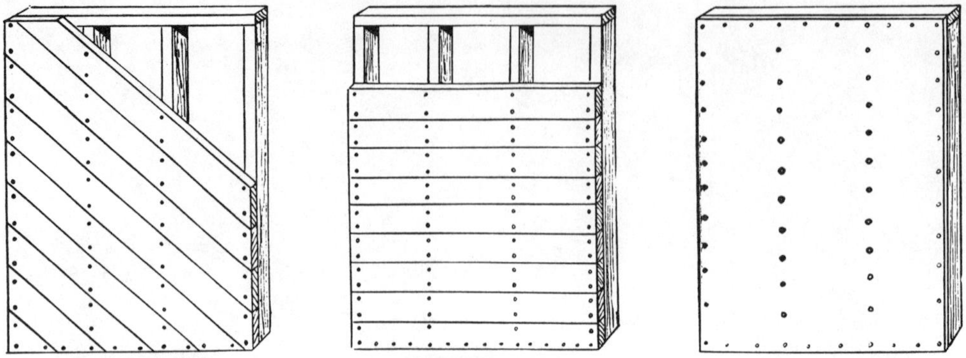

DIAGONAL WOOD
REQUIRES 1350* SQ. FT.
TO COVER 1000 SQ. FT

HORIZONTAL WOOD
REQUIRES 1150* SQ. FT.
TO COVER 1000 SQ. FT.

INSULATION BOARD
REQUIRES 1050** SQ. FT.
TO COVER 1000 SQ. FT.

*Includes Dimensional Loss and Estimated Cutting Waste
**No Dimensional Loss with Fiberboard

cause it is applied over the studs as well as across the spaces between the studs, the sheathing covers the entire wall area with a uniform layer of insulation. It is manufactured from scientifically processed wood or cane fiber. The fiber is reduced to a pulp and reassembled under heat and pressure to form the sheets.

Insulation-board sheathing is produced in two thicknesses: ½ and 25⁄32 in. Available board sizes are 2 x 8, 4 x 8 and 4 x 9 ft. Other sizes are made on a special-order basis. Two other products are also available: nail-base and intermediate fiberboard sheathing. Intermediate, manufactured in 4 x 8 and 4 x 9-ft. sheets and in ½-in. thickness, eliminates the need for corner bracing in frame construction when it is nailed according to recommendations.

Nail-base sheathing, available in the same sizes as intermediate sheathing, is a high-density product that also eliminates the need for corner bracing frame construction. With nail-base, you can apply wood and asbestos cement shingles directly to the sheathing with annular grooved nails. With regular fiberboard sheathing and ½-in. thick intermediate sheathing, wood furring strips must be used for wood or asbestos cement shingles. You can apply wood shingles to fiberboard shingle backer in combination with any fiberboard sheathing, using annular grooved nails. The wood furring strips can be omitted.

Other features of the material include easy handling, light weight, better workability and better bracing strength. Since the material is water repellent and forms a weathertight cover, no building paper is required, resulting in a savings of about $20 per average house.

The sheets of insulating-board sheathing are applied vertically to the walls. When the material is used without corner bracing, staples or nails should be applied to the intermediate studs first, and the fasteners must be spaced not more than 6-in. on center.

Where 2 x 8-ft. sheets of the material are used with tongue-and-groove or shiplap joints, apply it at right angles to the framing members. Supplementary corner bracing is required. The sheathing should be applied with a ⅛-in. space between the ends of the boards. Make sure the interlocking long edges of the boards fit snugly with the tongues up. Nail to the intermediate framing members first with the fasteners spaced 8 in. on center. Nail the vertical edges next, spacing the fasteners 4 in. on center and not less than ⅜ in. from the edge of the sheathing panel.

Cement-asbestos board is a special building panel manufactured by covering a core of cane-fiber insulation board with surfaces of cement-asbestos. The bonding adhesive is moistureproof, and the material somewhat resembles a sheet of precast concrete. This material can form a complete exterior wall in itself. The surface is durable, weather and fire-resistant, stone-gray in color and can serve as an exterior surface without any further finishing treatment. The material is also used for interior partition walls where fire-resistance is specified.

Shingle-backer board is an insulating material similar to insulating-board sheathing. It is used as a backing for shingles and some types of siding such as aluminum. The material eliminates the need for undercourse shingles, adds insulation value and strengthens and deepens the attractive "shadow line" of the shingles. Backer board is made in sheets measuring 4 ft. long and, depending on the manufacturer, something under 12, 16 or 18 in. wide to undercourse shingles of those sizes.

CUTTING SHEET-METAL stock calls for a saber saw or portable jigsaw as shown above; snips, several of which are shown in Fig. 25; or professional equipment such as the squaring shear shown in Fig. 2. Ordinary snips take care of metal as thick as 22 ga. handily. To follow a pattern accurately, it's important to score lines clearly on the surface of the metal, then to follow those lines carefully. When possible, use a straightedge to keep the scribe on the track.

Know-how of working sheet metal

By C. W. WOODSON

BASIC SHEET-METAL WORK requires only metal snips or shears and a squared hardwood block or two over which to make bends. Anvils, more tools and shaping devices, and bench stakes for seams and radius bends will let you go beyond simple projects. Beyond this point, you enter the professional area with its hand and powered machines and advanced ways to develop sheet-metal shapes.

Whatever your level may be, you'll find sheet-metal work is satisfying.

Three basic methods of developing a given shape are shown in representative form in Figs. 3 through 6. These by no means cover the field of development, but do indicate methods of procedure. The shortcut, rollation method in Fig. 3 is quite widely used in the development of the more simple forms. Figs. 12 and 14 through 16 show how it is carried out when making the top of a funnel or similar bell shape. The joint in the funnel top, or bell, can be seamed as in detail A, Fig. 11, and hammered flat as in Fig. 12, or can be sweat-soldered before soldering on the neck, Fig. 11, B. For procedure in laying down a conical shape (or what is to become a conical shape) note the right-hand detail in Fig. 3 and compare with Fig. 14. The cutout in Fig. 14 is then bent as in Fig. 15 and the edges chalked. The final step in the rollation method is pictured in Fig. 16. The other development methods such as parallel-line development, Fig. 4, radial-line development, Fig. 5 and development by triangulation, Fig. 6, are used in advanced work in the laying down of large and involved shapes.

Nearly all sheet metals, both ferrous and nonferrous, of 22 ga. or thinner can be cut easily with ordinary tinner's snips, Figs. 14 and 25. Heavier metal is best cut with compound-lever shears, or

SEE ALSO
**Cutoff machines . . . Cutters, sheet-metal . . .
Metal casting . . . Metalworking . . .
Power hacksaws . . . Racks, book . . .
Sabre saws . . . Torches**

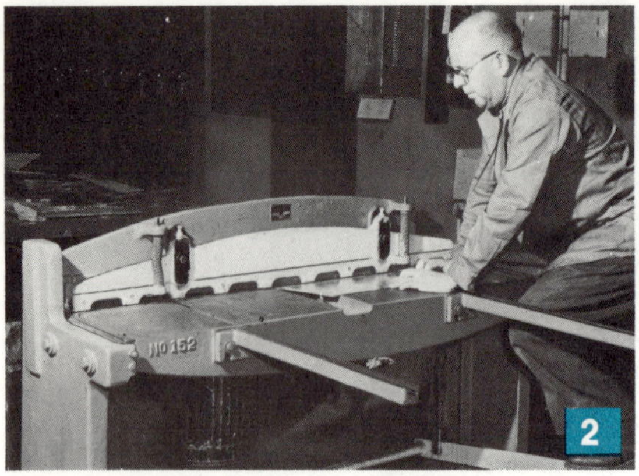

FOOT-OPERATED squaring shears like this are standard in professional or large school shops.

with a hacksaw with a blade having at least 24 teeth per inch. You also can use a portable jigsaw (or saber saw), Fig. 1, with a metal-cutting blade. Many sheet-metal shops and some school shops have a squaring shear, Fig. 2. Foot-operated units of this latter type usually handle mild steel to 16 ga. with a nominal cutting width of 30 in. or more.

Hand-wiring an edge, Fig. 8, is a good test of one's skill as a tinsmith. In shops this job usually is done on a machine, Fig. 17, but you can do a creditable job by hand as in Fig. 8, using a wood mallet and a pair of pliers, as in the accompanying photo, Fig. 7. Start with a right-angle bend in the sheet as in detail A. Turn it back on itself with the wire inside as in detail B, using the mallet and the pliers in conjunction to make a smooth bend. Wiring usually is done before the part is formed. You'll find wired edges on such commonplace items as pails, pans, funnels, garden carts—almost any open-top container made from sheet metal. A wired edge adds greatly to their strength, durability and appearance.

Another step in simple forming that you should be familiar with before tackling any type of corner joining is the method of notching and clipping at corners to produce neat, attractive work. The square notch, used on simple boxlike forms, permits corners to be fitted tightly, details C and D, Fig. 9. The V-notch can be cut as in detail B, producing an overlap for riveting or soldering, or can be cut as in detail A to form a neat corner without an overlap. It also is used for double seaming on work having inside flanges. Bend the flanges against a solid hardwood block as in detail E, using a wood mallet or a soft hammer to prevent denting or scoring the metal.

Progressive steps in making a dovetail seam of one type are shown in Fig. 13. This method is

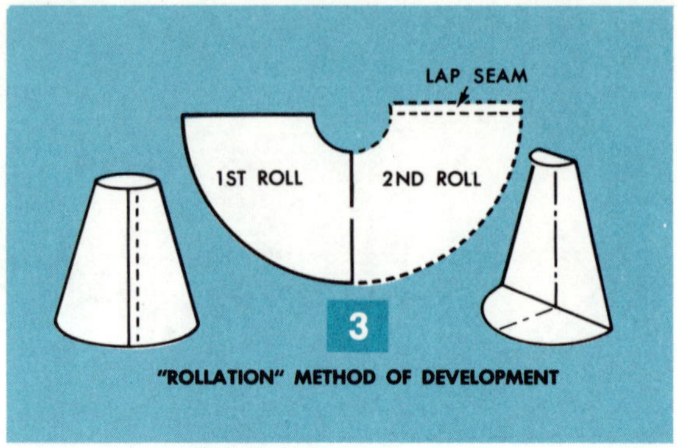

"ROLLATION" METHOD OF DEVELOPMENT

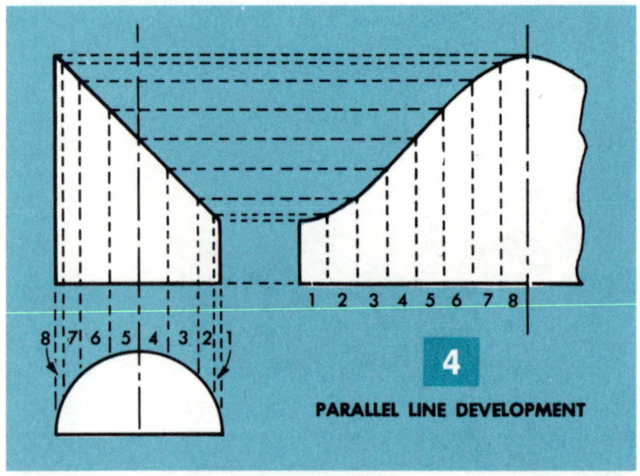

PARALLEL LINE DEVELOPMENT

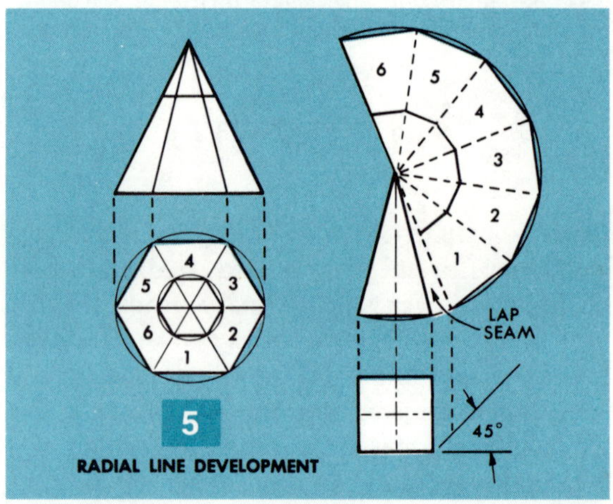

RADIAL LINE DEVELOPMENT

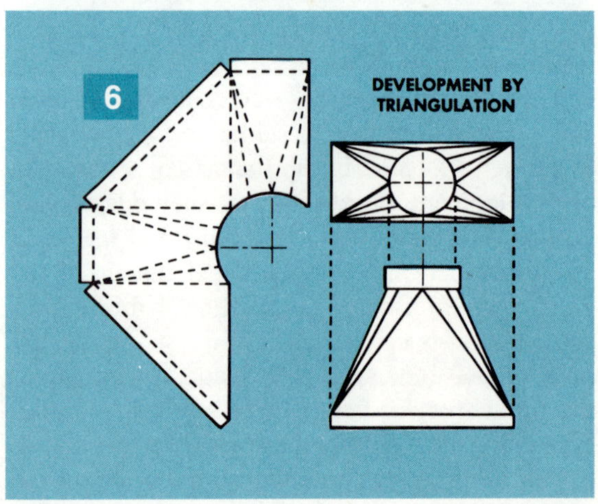

DEVELOPMENT BY TRIANGULATION

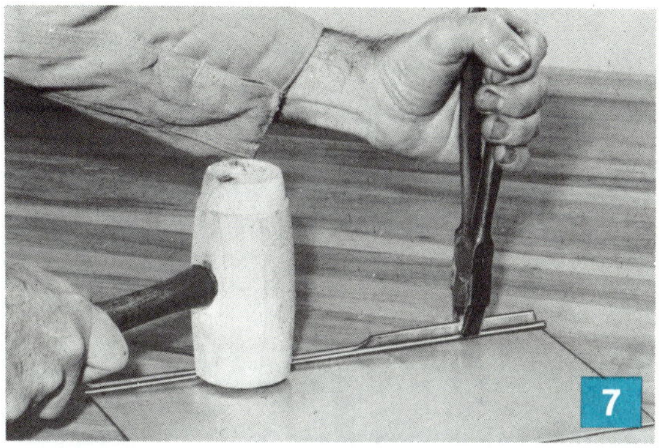

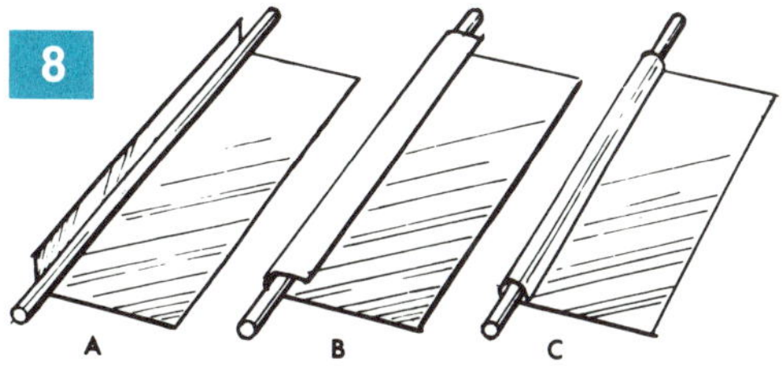

WIRING AN EDGE by hand tests tinsmith's skill. Photo at the left shows how mallet and pliers are used together to bend the edge. The detail drawings above show the three basic steps in the hand-wiring process.

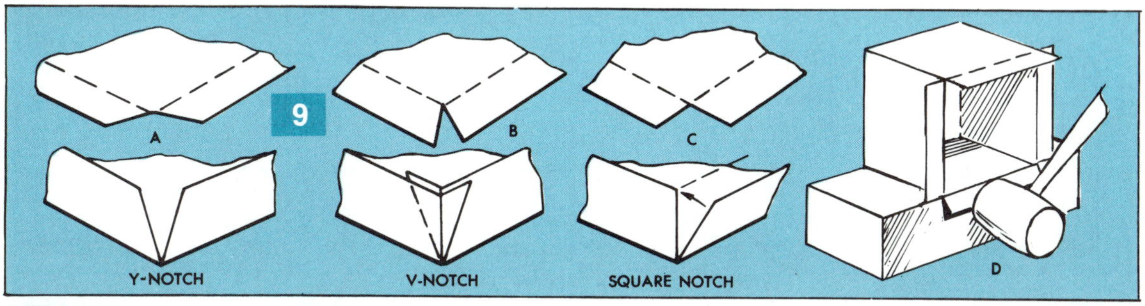

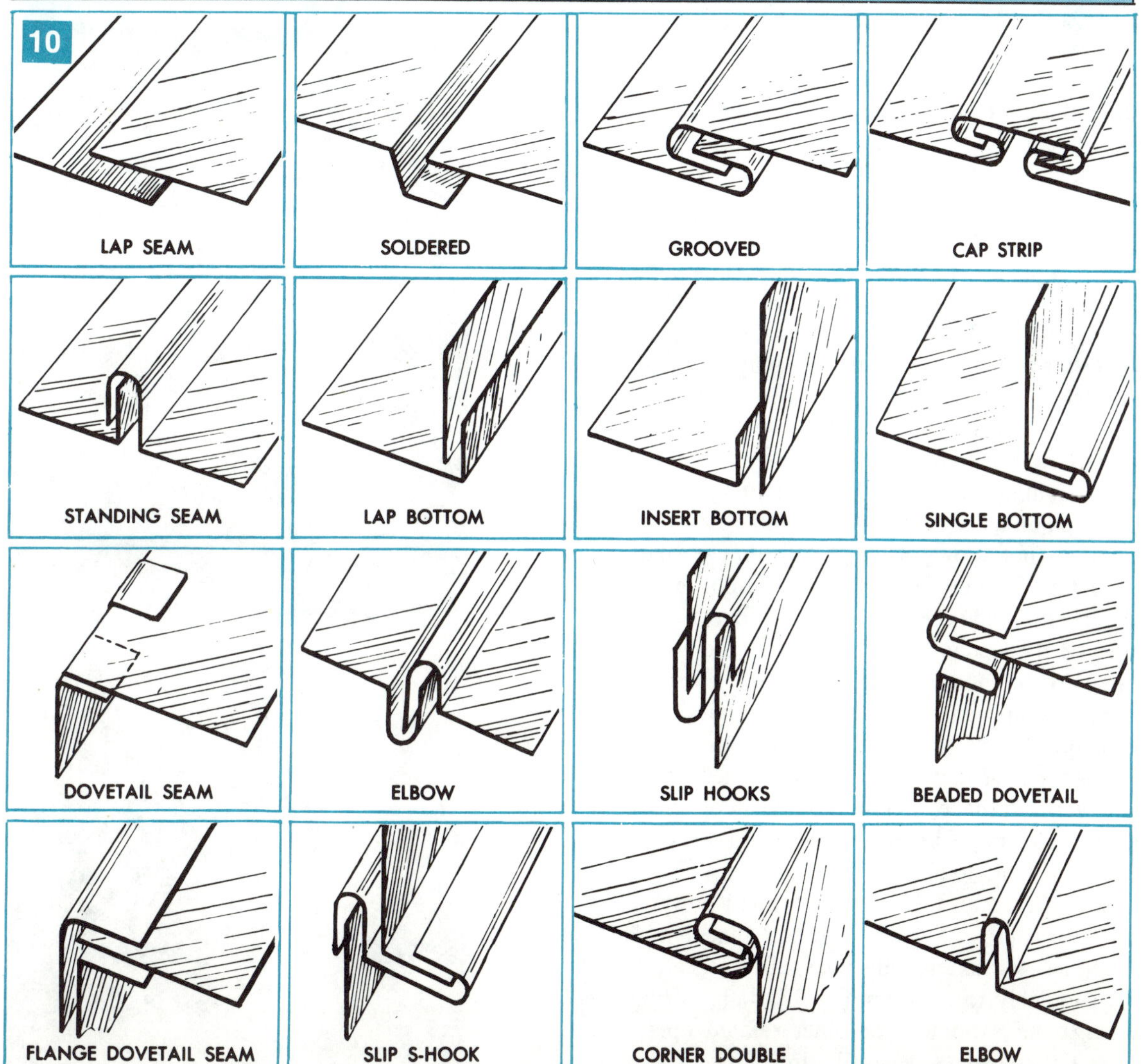

11

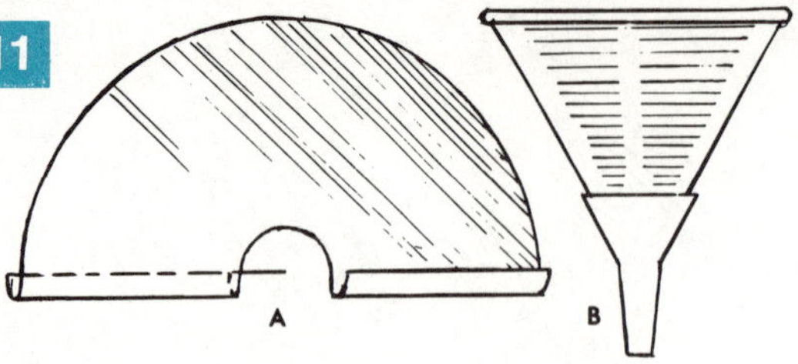

IN CUTTING a funnel top or bell, leave room for a lap joint at an end—or a grooved joint at both ends. Use of the rollation pattern is shown in Figs. 14 through 16.

12

working sheet metal, continued

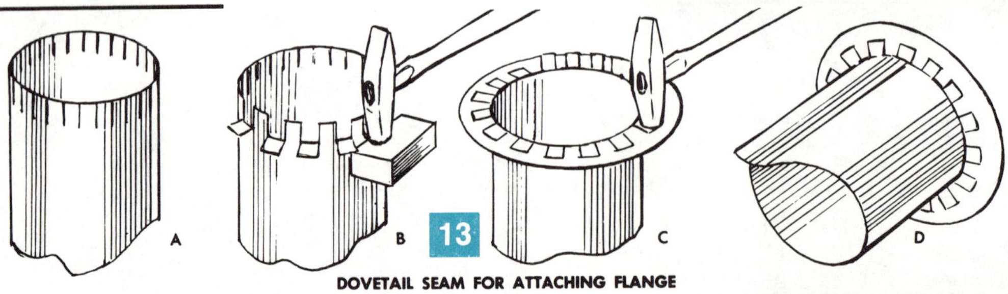

13

DOVETAIL SEAM FOR ATTACHING FLANGE

often used when joining a flange to a cylindrical shape. The latter is scribed near the end with a visible line and is then clipped at spaced intervals as in detail A, the cuts stopping at the scribed line. Next the alternate tabs are bent out and at right angles as in detail B. Now the flange is cut and slipped over the remaining vertical tabs, which are finally bent outward over the flange as in detail C. The finished job is shown in detail D. For added strength the tabs may be sweat-soldered.

Fig. 10 details various types of locking seams and typical soldered seams that are commonly used in joining sheet metals. Most of these can be formed on a bar folder, Fig. 21. Of course, the seams are not shown as they will appear when completed. They are shown open, or unlocked, to indicate the relationship of the folded edges. Some of the seams must be sweat-soldered, of course. While most of these bends are made by machine, some can be made easily by hand with the simplest tools. You will find these seams on various types of metal containers, in sheet-metal duct work, furnace plenums—anywhere sheet-metal parts are to be corner-joined or in some cases joined end to end.

Figs. 17, 18 and 20 picture a hand-powered unit known in tinshops as a rotary machine. It is supplied with interchangeable rolls and can be set up quickly to do crimping, beading, wiring, burring, and a number of other related operations. The machines generally are of two types,

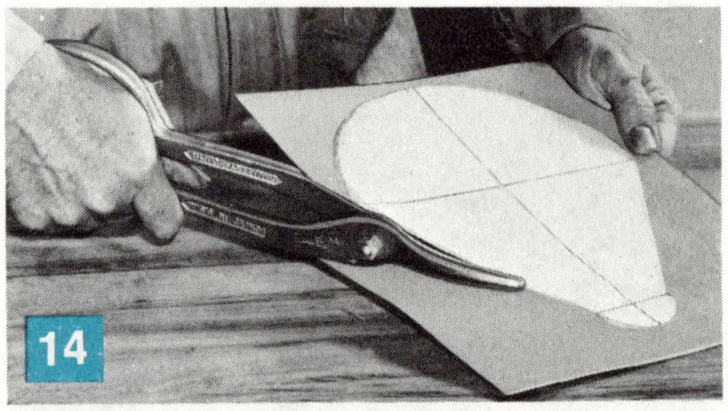

14

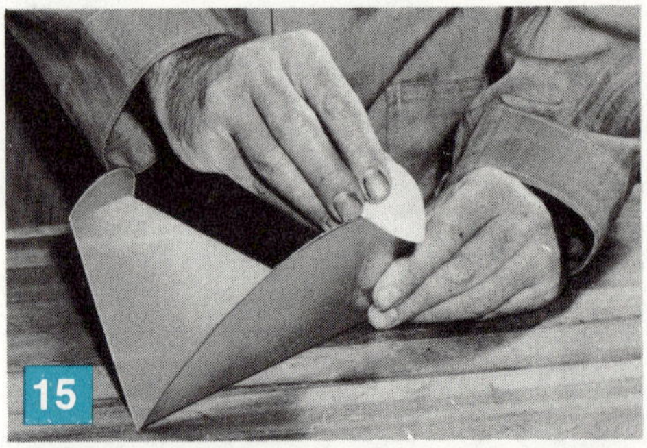

15

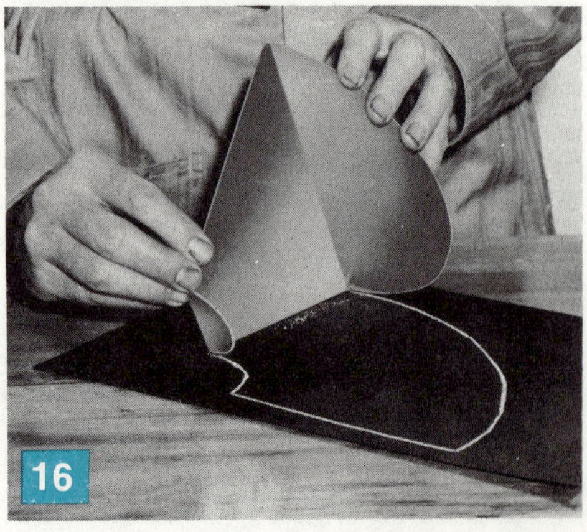

16

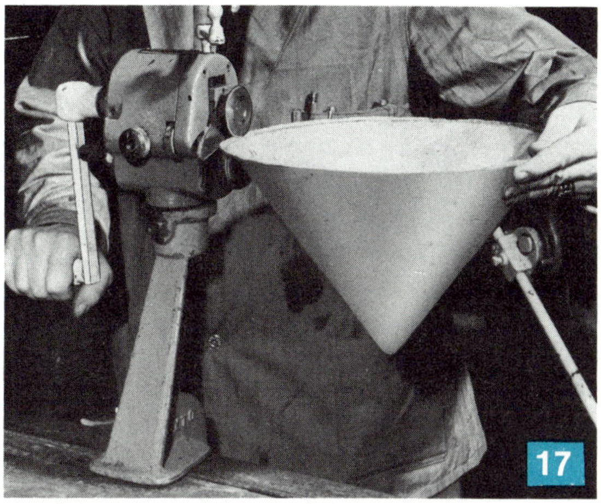

A STANDARD rotary machine is regular equipment in most sheet-metal shops. Here an edge is wired.

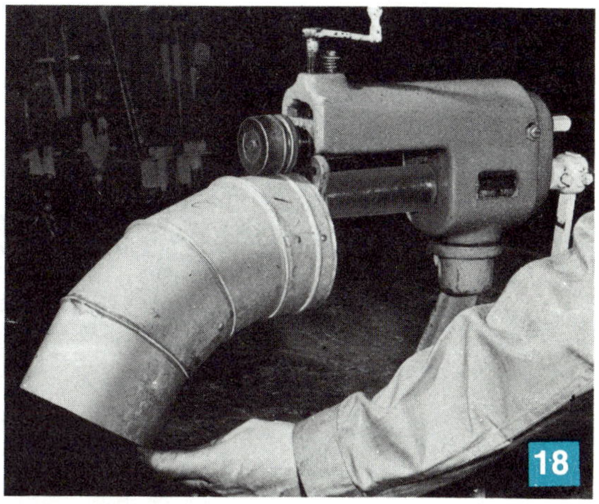

THIS ROTARY machine has a deep throat. Here a bead is being rolled on a smoke-pipe elbow.

the standard unit, Fig. 17 and the deep-throated unit, Figs. 18 and 20. A wiring operation is pictured in Fig. 17 and beading and crimping operations in Figs. 18 and 20.

In the well-equipped commercial shops and also in school shops you'll probably find an assortment of stakes and a bench plate. Fig. 19 illustrates only a few of the many types of stakes available for various types of sheet-metal work at the bench. One that is quite common, is the double stake, supplied with at least four heads, A, B, C, and D. Light sheet metals are worked on stakes and hollow mandrels.

Fig. 22 shows how the single hemmed edge is formed on a bar-type folding machine, Fig. 21. Fig. 23, details A, B and C, show the forming of a double-hemmed edge. In one method of making a grooved seam by hand, the locks on the two pieces of metal are folded and hooked together and the seam closed with a hand grooving tool, Fig. 24. The seam is then flattened with a wood mallet. The seaming tool, Fig. 25, enables one to do a better job of working a seam. It comes in widths up to 6 in. or more and facilitates making a sharp, clean bend. It is adjustable for depth, or reach, which determines the distance from the edge the bend is made.

Cylindrical forms can be made by working the metal over a hollow mandrel with a mallet, Fig. 19, or with a slip-roll former, Fig. 26. Straight cuts in the light sheet metals of 22 ga. and thinner are easily made with tin snips of the regular pattern, Fig. 25. For making short-radius circular cuts in from an edge you'll need the hawk's-bill snips. For intricate patterns involving curved cuts of medium radius you use what are known as pocket circular snips (not illustrated). Aviation snips, Fig. 25, come right and left and in combination and are designed for intricate work on light sheet metals.

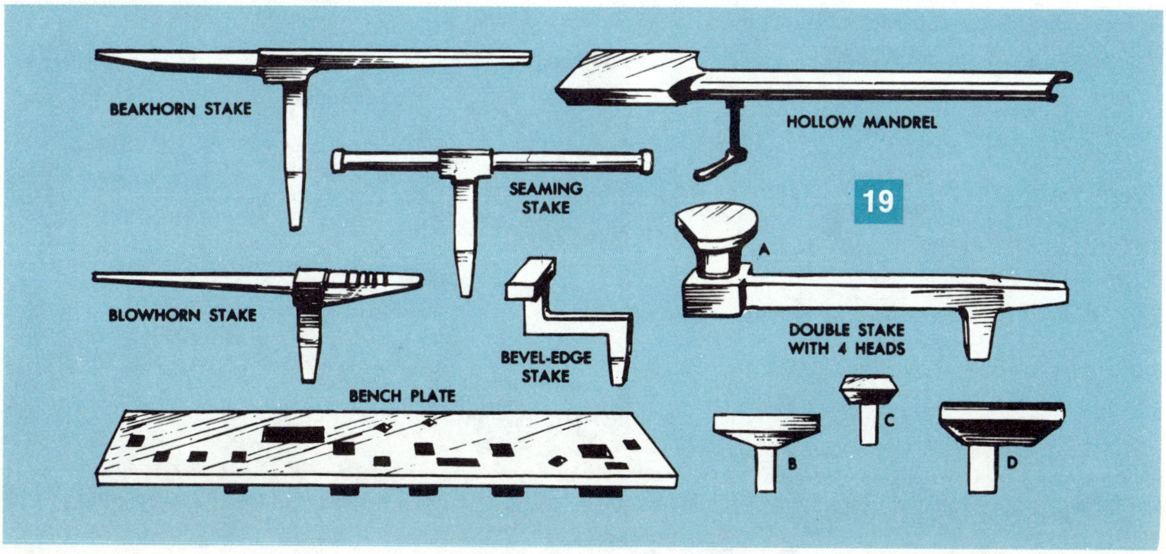

20

21

working sheet metal, continued

22

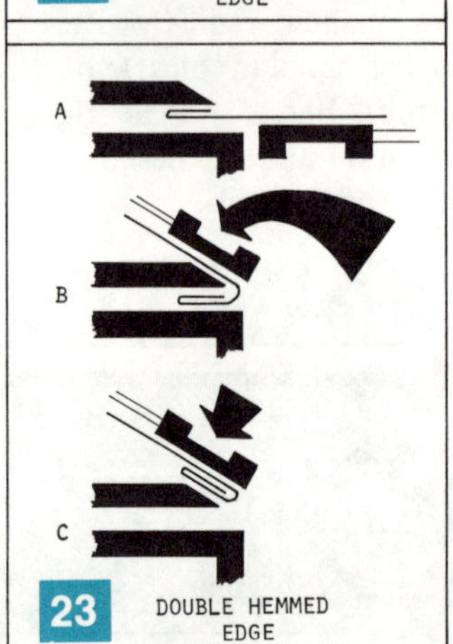

23

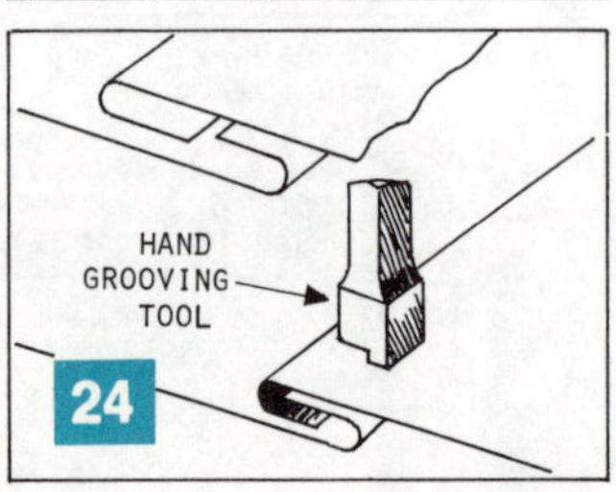

24

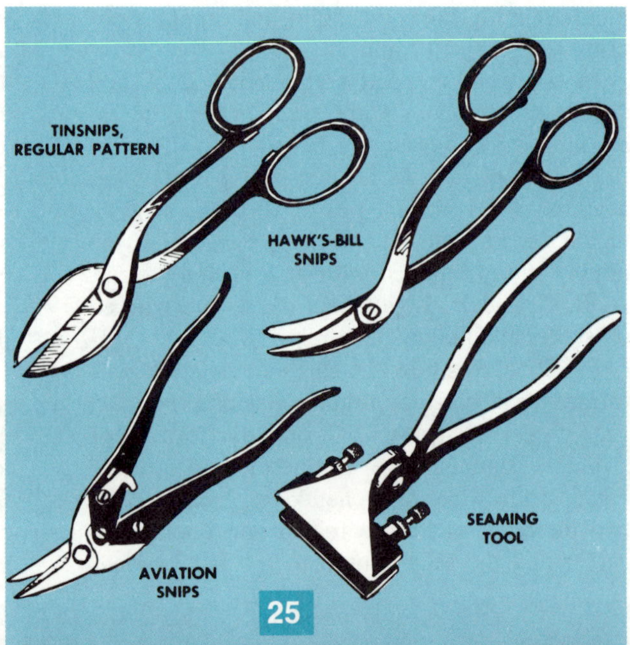

25

26

THE SHEET-METAL BRAKE, made of standard-size lumber, handles up to 26-gauge metal.

LONG PIECES OF METAL are as easy to bend as smaller ones with this homemade brake. You simply change the pressure foot.

NEAT right-angle bends and flat folds are easy to make with this simple, benchtop, sheet-metal brake. The metal is inserted under the pressure plate, the two handles are tightened and the hinged forming bar across the front is brought up to make the desired degree of bend. To flatfold an edge, you first bring the forming bar all the way up and against the beveled pressure plate; then the work is removed, flipped over and the bend is squeezed flat.

The brake is made mostly of wood of standard lumberyard sizes. Nuts, which are sweat-soldered in place, provide the tapped holes for each threaded handle, and the yokes are bent from strap iron to straddle the two hinged pressure arms. A compression spring under each arm raises the arms automatically when its handle is backed off.

To bend a metal box, the trick is to bend two opposite sides using the regular pressure plate. Then a special pressure plate is cut to fit the inside width of the box and only one pressure arm is used to hold the plate while making the bend. You can fashion boxes as small as 3x4 in.

SEE ALSO
Cutoff machines . . . Cutters, sheet-metal . . . Metal casting . . . Metalworking . . . Power hacksaws . . . Torches . . . Tubing, metal

Sheet-metal brake you make of wood

By RAY M. GATES

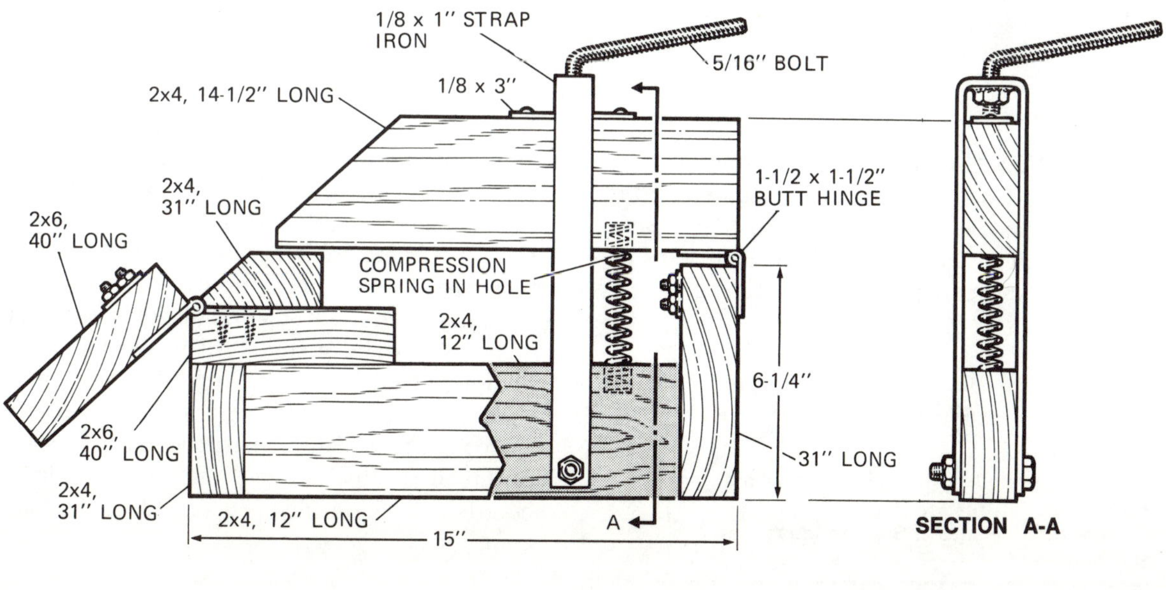

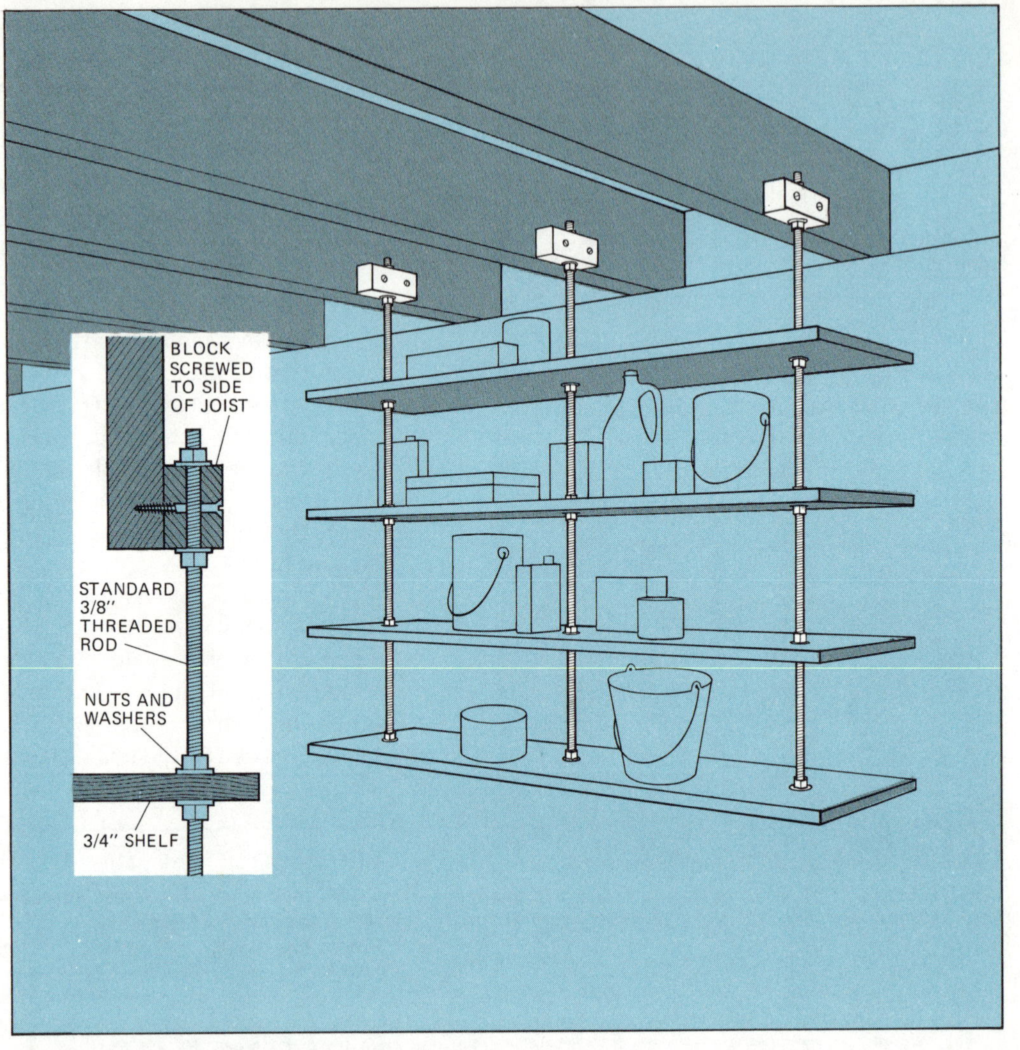

How to put up shelves that stay up

■ SHELVES CAN MEAN the difference between order and disorder in the basement, attic or garage, and they're something you can't have too many of for holding such things as cans of leftover paint, garden sprays and insecticides, balls, mitts and bats, clippers and shears, Christmas decorations, luggage, tools and boots.

There are about as many ways to support shelves as there are things to store. Shown on the facing page are six of the more common ways for installing them between end uprights or fastening them to walls or studs. All arrangements will hold a considerable load without giving way.

A novel way to hang shelves is shown above: Two or more boards are suspended from a series of threaded rods that pass through holes in the boards and wood blocks screwed to the basement joists.

SEE ALSO
**Basement remodeling . . . Book shelves . . .
Bookcases . . . Fasteners . . .
Garage remodeling . . . Storage ideas . . .
Storage walls**

DADO

CLEAT

ANGLE
BRACKET

DOWELS

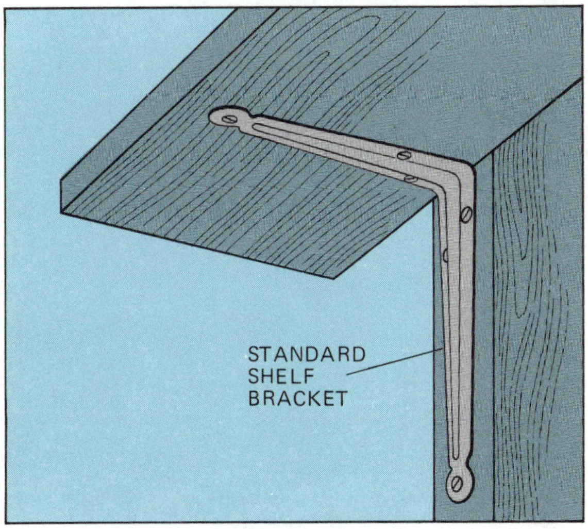
STANDARD
SHELF
BRACKET

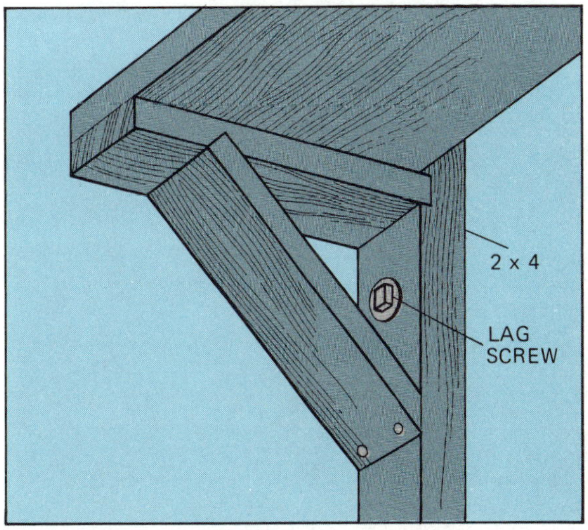
2 x 4
LAG
SCREW

How to build wall shelves

THE TROUBLE WITH shelves is that they collect things. You put up something originally intended for decorative glassware or a collection of beer mugs—no problem. Later, your needs change and you start loading on hefty books, hi-fi gear and that souvenir ship's anchor you found last summer. After a while, time and gravity take their toll. Suddenly your shelves fall off the wall.

Because most shelves, by their nature, will have to handle heavy loads—either now or later—it pays to get them up right the first time, especially wall-hung shelves that have no floor support. The job needn't be difficult. Commercial shelf hardware comes in types and styles to suit any need. Mounting fasteners are available for any wall surface you're likely to encounter. It's just a matter of choosing the right system.

SEE ALSO

Book shelves . . . Bookcases . . . Fasteners . . . Remodeling . . . Room dividers . . . Storage walls

THE ADVANTAGE of a homebuilt unit is that it can be tailor-made to provide exactly the storage you need. Such a unit is shown above. See the drawing at the right for construction details.

ADJUSTABLE WOOD SHELVING mounted on slotted wall standards is easy to put up anywhere and permits a wide variety of attractive arrangements. As your storage needs change you can change shelf spacing.

METAL UTILITY shelving now is available in decorator colors, and has moved into upstairs rooms.

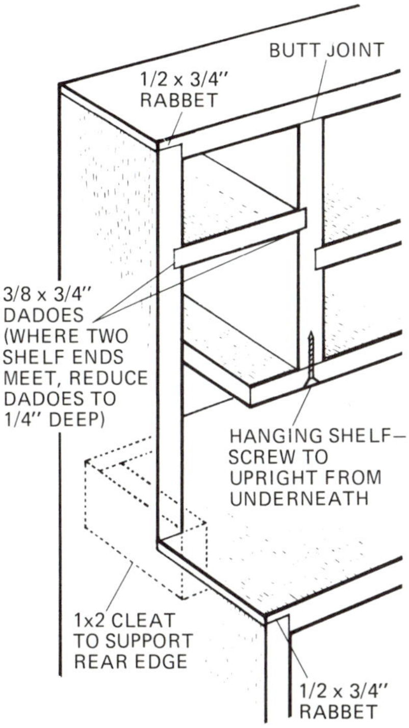

FREE-STANDING BOOKCASE
Handsome bookcase/storage wall (facing page) looks like a built-in, is actually free-standing unit that can be moved. Made of rich, warm-toned redwood, it suggests how similar units can be designed to suit individual needs. Open niches provide space for pictures and decorative objects. Deeper base cabinet houses TV set, also acts as foot to stabilize shelves. Basic joinery used in such self-supporting shelf units is shown in drawing above. Assemble joints with glue and finishing nails.

CLIP-TOGETHER ORGANIZERS
You can design your own bookcase or closet organizer with these versatile shelf connectors from Knape & Vogt. The metal, tack-on clips fit standard ¾-in.-thick, prefinished shelf boards and come in corner, tee and four-way-cross styles. By combining the connectors in various arrangements, you can create compartmented storage units to suit any space and need.

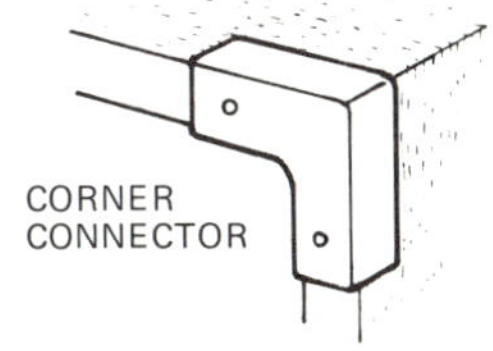

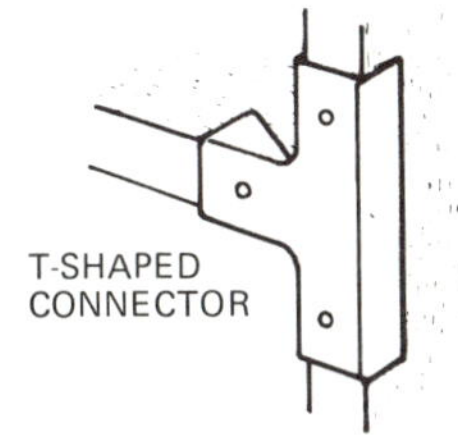

VERSATILE STORAGE WALL
Perforated hardboard provides flexible storage for changing needs, can support shelf brackets as well as many special fixtures that simply hook into prepunched holes spaced 1 in. apart. Mount panels on ⅜-in. spacers to give clearance in back for the fixture hooks (drawing below). You can also use plastic wall anchors that come with standoff collars, made especially for this purpose. Installation at right features attractive "shadow box" frame around it, with fluorescent fixtures recessed into cove at the top to give soft, indirect lighting.

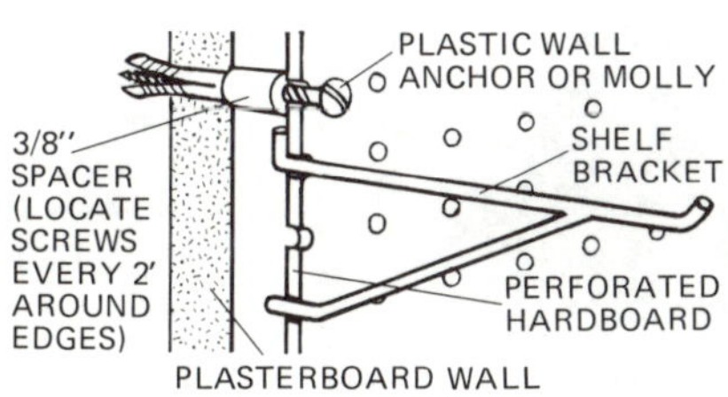

When you put up wall-hung shelves you face two basic considerations: proper wall attachment to support the total load, and proper bracket spacing to prevent the sagging of individual shelves.

For example, assuming that screws are driven into solid wood, a ¾-in. pine shelf on brackets spaced 12 in. apart will support a whopping 670 lbs. per sq. ft. But the same board on brackets 36 in. apart will hold only 38 lbs. per sq. ft.—and at 72 in., just 5 lbs.

In general, the maximum safe span for a heavily loaded ¾-in. wood shelf, with no support at the back edge, should not exceed 32 in. (Shelves in enclosed bookcases with back support can span up to 48 in.) Glass shelves of ¼-in. plate, such as typically used in medicine cabinets, should not exceed about 20 in. between the supports, though much heftier ⅜-in. plate can safely span up to 40 in.

Screws turned into thin wood paneling or plasterboard will soon pull loose. Wherever possible, it's best to screw shelf brackets into wall studs. This way, the studs—not the surface wall—support the load and no special anchors are needed.

Since studs are spaced on 16-in. centers, you can screw into every other one and maintain a sturdy 32-in. spacing. For lightly loaded shelves, or shelves of 5/4 or two-by stock, you can go to every third stud.

But studs are often hard to find or may not fall exactly where you want your shelf brackets. Here you need anchors made especially for hollow walls. Screws turned into simple plastic sleeves will support hundreds of pounds and stay put indefinitely. Other types of anchors are made for solid masonry walls.

Once relegated to the basement, steel utility shelving now comes in bright, attractive decorator colors, making it equally at home in a family room, den, pantry, home office, children's room and other upstairs areas.

Consisting of predrilled angle-iron legs and lipped metal shelves, these handy bolt-together units can be assembled in minutes with only a screwdriver. They provide quick, flexible storage wherever substantial shelving is required. The leg angles have rows of closely spaced bolt holes so the height of the shelves can be adjusted easily.

Most metal utility shelving is designed to be free-standing, making it readily movable. Some units, however, can be wall-hung with special clips. Stock sizes range from 47 in. high by 30 in. wide up to 71 in. high by 42 in. wide. Shelves come 9 to 24 in. deep. For storing preserve jars and other breakables, the shelves can be mounted lip side up to keep such items from sliding off.

homemade shelving

You can make your own utility shelving, using commercial brackets that take wood planks or big plywood sheets. Such hardware is especially handy for custom-tailoring large or odd-shaped shelves to fit a particular space, such as in attic eaves, under a stairway or over the hood of a car in a garage. Particleboard, available in sheets or in standard shelf widths, is cheap and ideal for utility use.

In a basement, where appearance is not a consideration, you can make your own hanging shelves by bolting pairs of 2x2 or 2x4 uprights, spaced several feet apart, to ceiling joists. With cross cleats nailed to the uprights at appropriate heights, you can suspend a tier of shelves from overhead. For extra-sturdy support, extend the uprights down to the floor.

perforated hardboard

Masonite's versatile Peg-Board, widely used for storing tools, sports equipment and other gear, can also serve as the basis for a flexible shelf system. Metal shelf brackets, made to hook into the prepunched holes in hardboard, are available in 4- to 8-in. lengths and can take prefinished or homemade shelving boards.

UTILITY SHELVES, RACKS

Open-work shelves and racks made of vinyl-covered welded rod have light, airy look, collect less dirt than solid surfaces and are handy for use in closets, kitchen, pantry, laundry room, workshop and garage. These from Closet Maid come in many shapes to hold typical household supplies and are easy to mount in special snap-in wall clips (below).

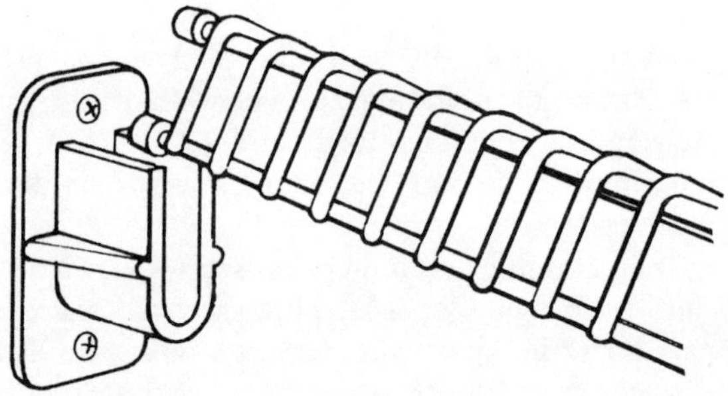

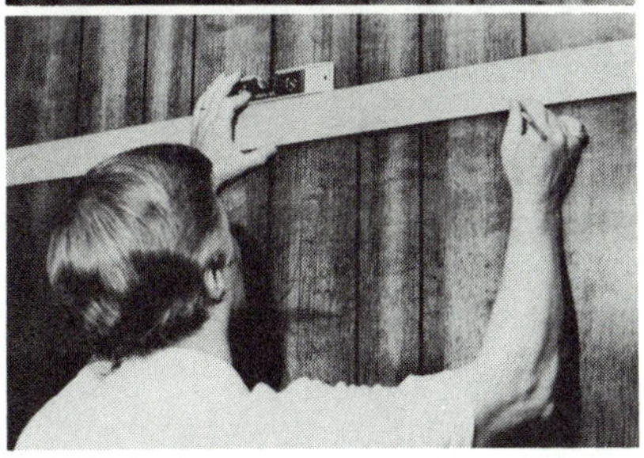

ADJUSTABLE SHELVES

When installing wall standards for adjustable shelves, care must be taken to mount all uprights at the same height so shelves will be level. Use this simple procedure: Locate first standard, mark for topmost screw and install wall anchor. Standard will hang vertically by gravity, but should also be checked for plumb with a spirit level. Mark for and install remaining anchors. Then, with first standard in place, rest a straight board and spirit level on top and mark location for top of second standard (lower left). Do the same for all succeeding standards. Check to make sure slots are at same elevation. Note in this case that standards are positioned over grooves in paneling. This avoids marring face of paneling if the shelves must be removed later.

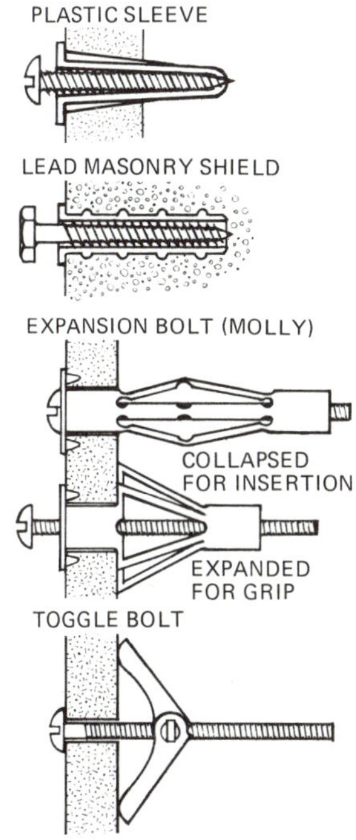

METAL UTILITY SHELVING

Metal, bolt-together shelf units are designed to be free-standing, but can also be wall-hung using special clips (right). Shelves have lipped edges that can be turned up or down. Turned up (below), the lips keep jars and other breakables from sliding off. Predrilled leg angles, available in lengths up to 6 ft., allow easy adjustment of shelves to any level.

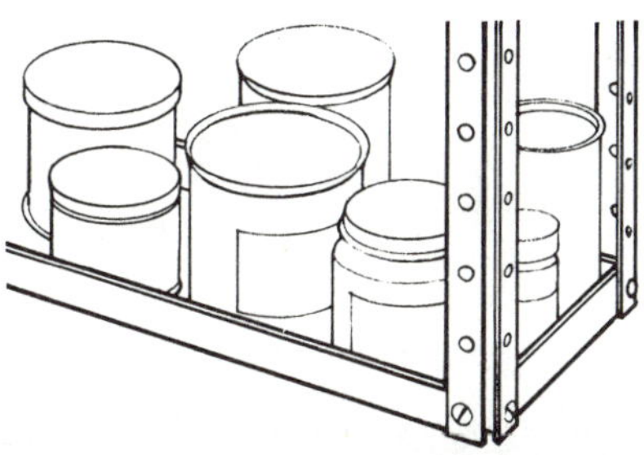

WHICH WALL ANCHOR?

Wall-hung shelves need sturdy support. Where you can't screw into wall studs, special anchors are required to keep screws from pulling loose. For hollow walls, there are three basic types: plastic sleeve, expansion bolt (Molly) and toggle bolt. Plastic sleeve is simplest, requires only small pilot hole, is good for light to moderate loads. Mollies and toggles both work by gripping back of wall and are a better choice for heavily loaded shelves, especially deep ones that put considerable outboard strain on brackets. On solid masonry walls, you should use lead shields. These expand as lagscrews are turned into them, locking them securely in place.

INSTALLING CLOSET AND CABINET SHELVES

Installing shelves in an enclosed space, such as a closet or alcove, is easy because side walls can support the ends of shelves. Cleats of 1x2 or chair-rail stock can usually be nail-fastened to studs. Put up back cleat first, using a spirit level to ensure that it's straight (lower left). Then install end cleats, leveling them as well (bottom center). Most closets have waste space above clothes, can usually take two shelves. Where you want adjustable shelves in a cabinet or bookcase, the drawings at right show two alternate mounting methods using slotted pilaster strips or L-shaped clips that fit into rows of ¼-in. holes. (A strip of perforated hardboard makes a handy guide for locating holes 1 in. apart.)

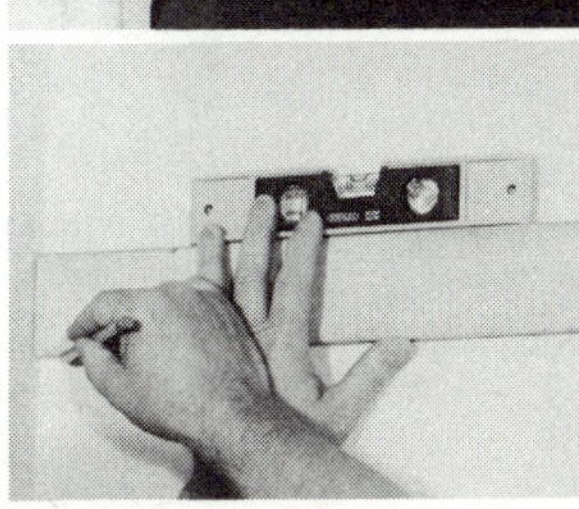

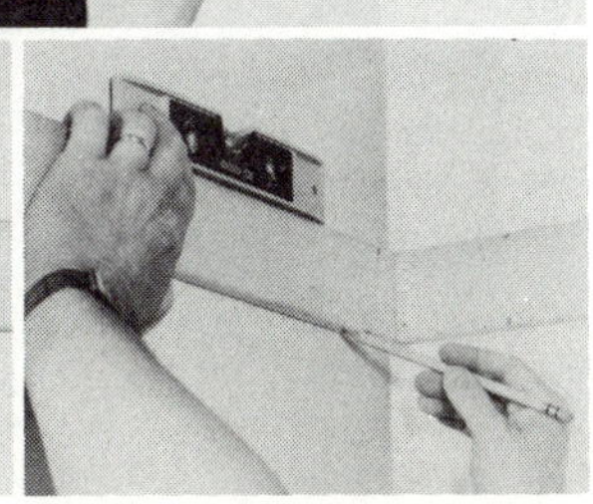

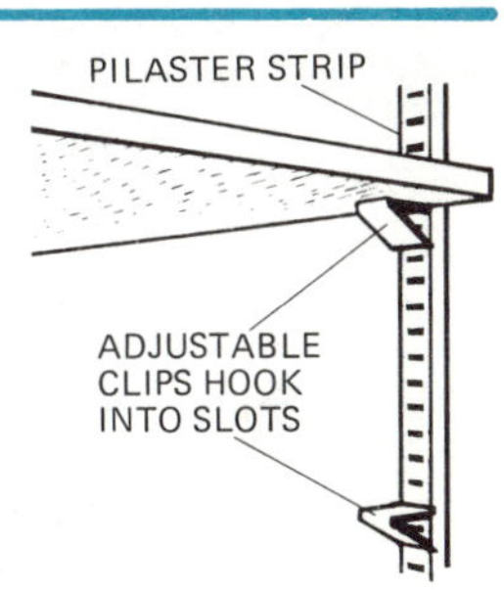

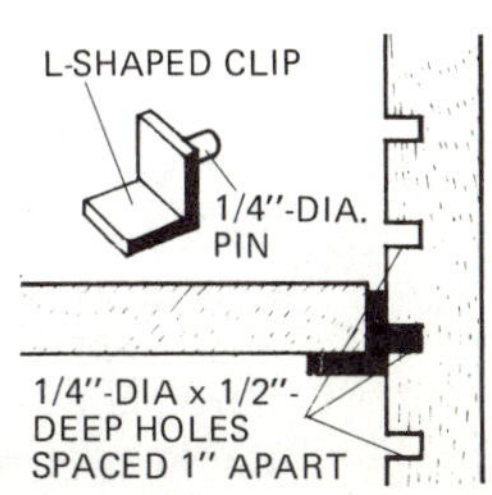

A handsome cover-up for utility shelving

By CRAIG WILSON

UTILITY SHELVING is functional but not very pretty. If you use your basement for recreation as well as storage, or if you'd just like a neater looking garage, you want those cluttered shelves out of sight. I covered mine up inexpensively with a few sheets of prefinished ⅛-in. plywood paneling.

Panel doors slide in double grooves in kiln-dried 2x4 rails; it's important that the lumber you buy for these rails is straight. Grooves are made with a router or cut on a table saw (or you can have this step done at the lumberyard.) Shelving must be securely fastened to the wall. Fasten the rails to shelf uprights and to ceiling joists, where possible, with wood screws. The rails must be level; if shelves were made inaccurately, shims may be necessary. Vertical 1x2 end strips are fastened with glue and finishing nails. Make the framework wider than the shelves, close the sides in with perforated hardboard, and you'll have extra space for hanging storage. Panels are cut ⅜ in. shorter than the distance between bottom of lower groove and top of upper groove; cut a test strip to be sure of this dimension. Cut wide enough to allow at least 1-in. overlap between panels; bowing will be less likely if grain is vertical.

After the framework has been sanded, primed and painted (with gloss enamel for easy cleaning), bottom grooves are rubbed with beeswax to help panels slide smoothly. To dress up panel edges, glue on ⅛-in. plastic report-cover spines. These are sold in a variety of colors by office-supply outlets. Spines that will fit ¼-in. paneling are also available.

SEE ALSO

Basement remodeling . . . Family rooms . . . Fasteners . . . Garage remodeling . . . Hardboard . . . Paneling, plywood . . . Routers . . . Storage ideas . . . Storage walls

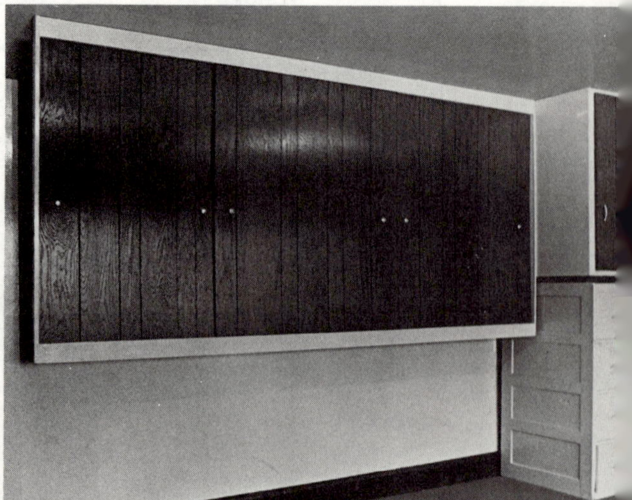

FRAMEWORK AND PANELING produce a handsome cabinet look. Recessed pulls are pressed into 1-in. holes in panels, should be above children's reach.

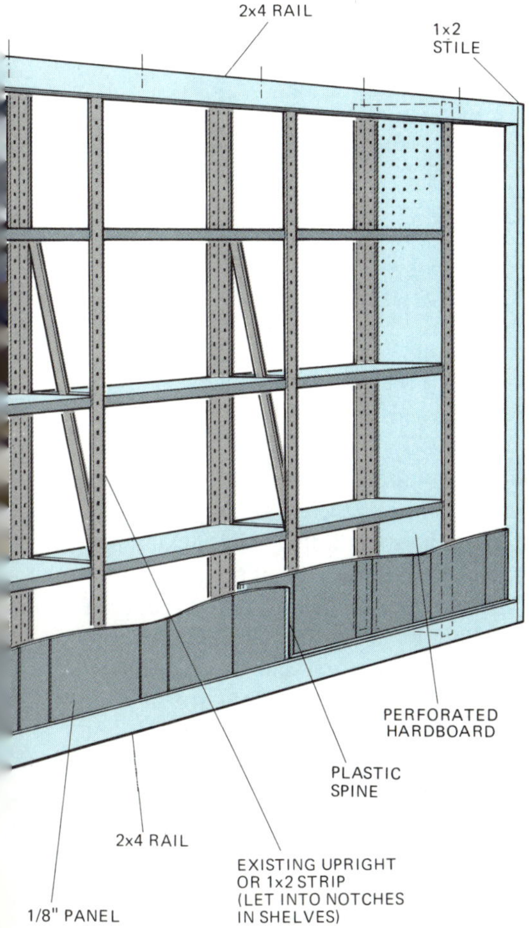

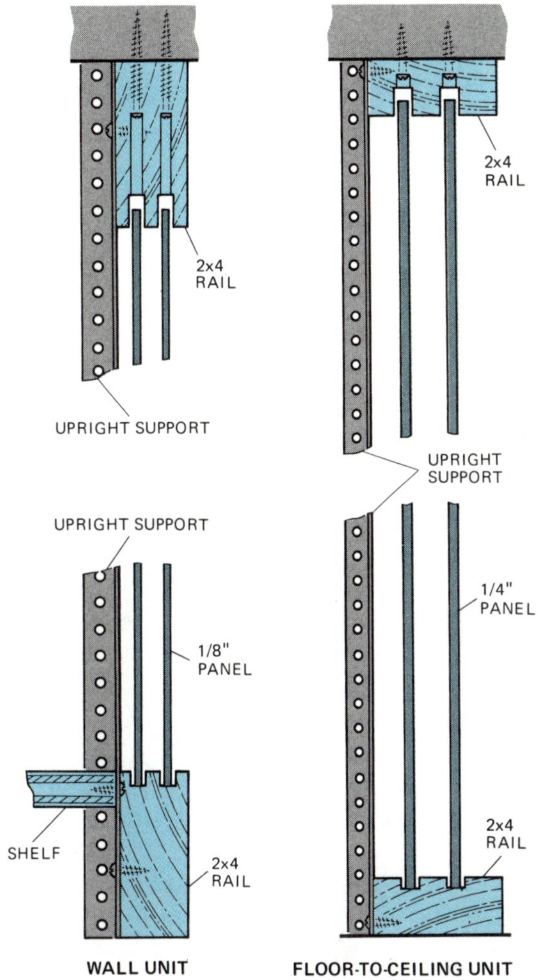

STORAGE SPACE inside is plentiful. Enclosure with a hinged door (paneling on ½-in. plywood) was made oversize for maximum space above the existing cabinet.

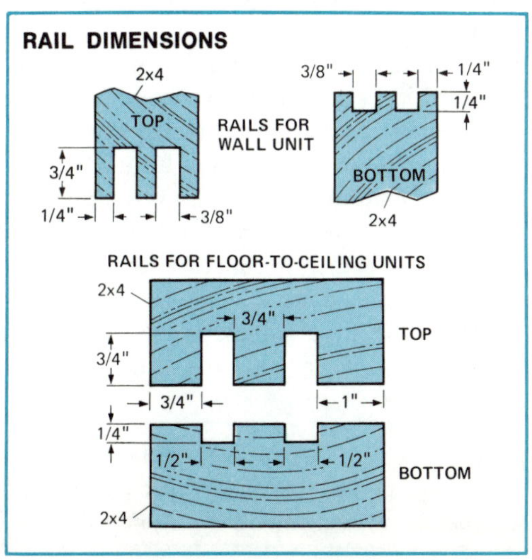

How to use shims

By MIKE McCLINTOCK

NOT MANY building materials come perfectly straight or perfectly even. Not many houses are perfectly level or plumb. This situation is referred to as "conditions in the field."

The total effect is that when you install a window, the sill may be out of level, or when you hang a door, the jamb may not be plumb. You may also run into the same trouble when you frame a new addition. To solve these and other field condition problems, use shims.

A shim is a small piece of material, usually wood, that will make up a small discrepancy in measurements. They are usually made out of the

SHIM FROM BOTH sides of the work. This will help to keep the board level and stable.

same material that they are supporting. Where great compression can be expected (like a girder resting on a masonry footing) a static material like slate is used. The most common shimming material is wooden shingle points.

The most common mistake in shimming is to drive a single shingle point in from one side. This frequently results in an uneven and unstable condition. The beauty of shingle shims is that use of a pair together produces automatic leveling. Here's how it's done:

First, split up a shingle to make 2 or 3-inch-wide pieces. Then start the thin edges toward

SEE ALSO

Additions, house . . . Doors . . . House additions . . . Lumber . . . Measurements . . . Shingles

DRIVE THE SHIMS across each other. This will effectively raise the board as much as you want.

each other from opposite sides of the board. Drive them in so they meet in the center under the board. Here, you might find that backing one up with a block and sharply tapping the other will help the thin points overlap. Now you can put your level on the board and check the bubble as you tap the shingles—first one, then the other. With gentle taps you can raise a board in very fine degrees until you get exactly the right amount of rise to a level condition. Don't worry about the excess shingle—it's easily trimmed. Firmly score the edge of the shingle flush to the board with a razor knife. A sharp blow from the opposite side will break it off cleanly. If most of the shingle has been driven through, and only a

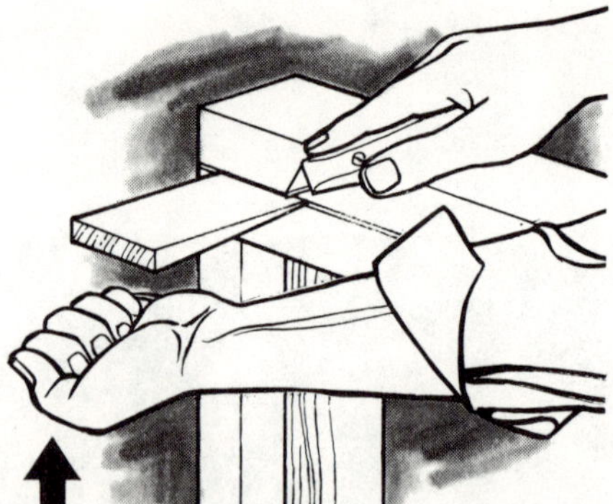

TRIM OFF excess by first scoring with knife. This will keep edge flush for sheetrock or siding.

few inches of the thickest part remain, you should trim it with a handsaw.

It's really a simple process worth doing carefully. Remember, you don't need shims to rectify a mistake, although they are great for that purpose if you really build yourself into a problem. Careful shimming on the frame will save you a lot of time and a lot of headaches when you start to put up sheetrock and trim.

WHEN YOU NEED an adjustable wrench but are unable to find one, try improvising with this trick. Just thread two square nuts on a long bolt, the longer the better. Turn down the nuts so they slip tightly over the nut to be removed or tightened; apply leverage as needed. For small nuts you likely can make do with hex nuts on the bolt instead of square nuts (as shown).

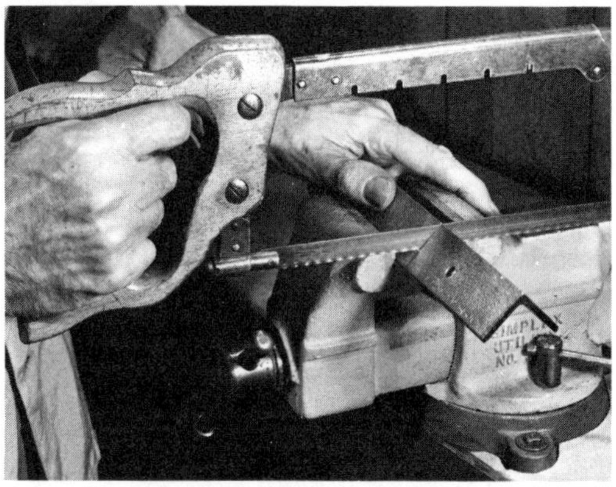

SAVE TIME by starting a hacksaw at the corner of a piece of angle iron instead of sawing down one leg and across the other. Obviously, fewer strokes of the saw are required to completely cut through the angle, thus saving time and labor. Another advantage, although not as obvious, is that the saw will cut more smoothly because more of the teeth will be engaged in cutting through both legs of the angle at the same time. Be sure, however, that the angle is firmly secured in a vise.

TO KEEP from producing undesired bends while twisting a piece of flat iron, slip it in a piece of pipe with a diameter slightly larger than the width of the strip of flat iron. Secure one end of the strip in a bench vise and grip the other end with a large monkey wrench. Twist slowly to spiral, but not kink, the strip. If the strip wedges inside the pipe, gently tap it out with a hammer. Alternatively, you could leave one end secured in the vise and tap off the pipe, instead of forcing the strip.

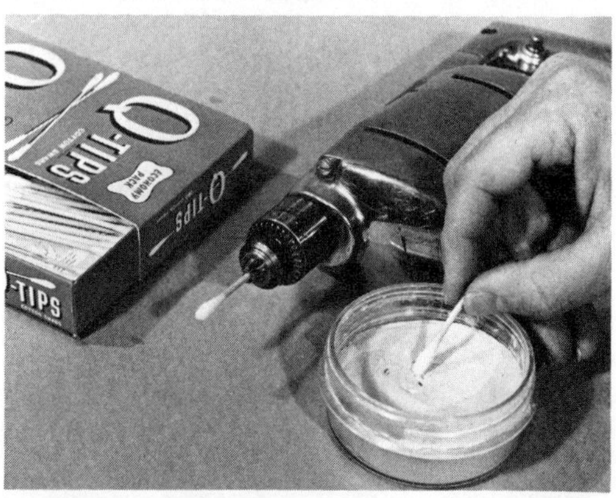

FOR DELICATE POLISHING tasks, especially those involving a small, intricately shaped area, try using this highly effective shortcut. Dip a cotton swab into polish, then chuck the swab in an electric drill or hand grinder. With very light pressure, feed the spinning swab against the work until all tiny recesses have been covered. Then clean off the excess polish, chuck a clean swab into the drill and buff the work, again using only light pressure to avoid breakage of the wood shaft.

How to repair a damaged roof

■ HIGH WINDS and heavy rains are never welcomed by homeowners. When such storms strike, most of us consider ourselves lucky if damage to the house and property is minor. Unfortunately, very often the damage is up on the roof. Shingles that have been exposed to weather for 10 years or more are particularly susceptible to being blown off. (However, the self-seal, tab-type shingles, which have been around a while, have reduced the incidence of this type of damage considerably.) Of far greater concern is what to do when your roof—not just the shingles—has been damaged by a toppled tree or fallen limb.

If you are afraid of height and working from a ladder, don't fight the feeling: Call in a pro. But if you do the repair work yourself, be advised it is a must to thoroughly cut out all the damaged area and replace with sound material. New sheathing must be of the same thickness as the existing, and all joints must be properly covered with 15-lb. felt. Weaving-in of shingles is a must or the patched-in area will leak.

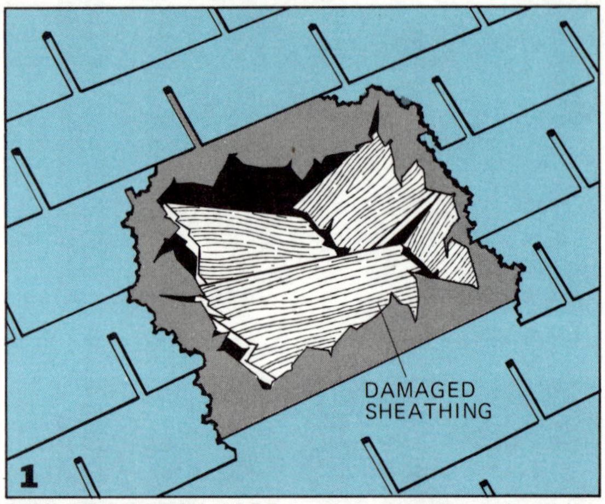

SEVERE ROOF DAMAGE, such as shattered sheathing shown here, can be caused by falling limbs. Sheathing problems can also result from leakage, which rots sheathing. Rot damage is often not apparent. If you spot a bulge under the shingles, chances are the sheathing needs replacing. Inspect the area from inside where possible.

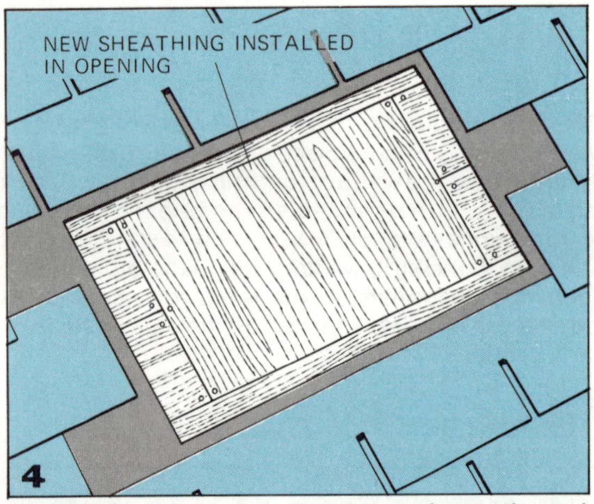

USE EITHER 1x6 tongue-and-groove roofers or plywood as shown, but it must be same thickness as existing sheathing. Plywood goes faster because it requires cutting just one piece (for a small hole). Next, cut 8-in.-wide felt strips and cover joints. Do bottom horizontal first, then the verticals and top horizontal; use overlaps.

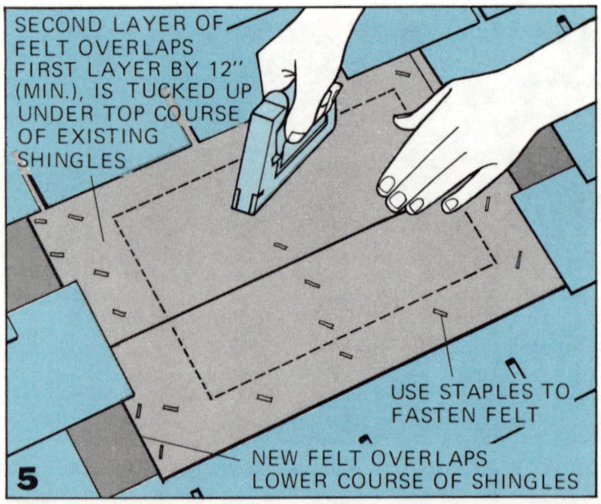

APPLY 15-pound felt so it overlaps existing shingles on downside and is tucked under row at top. Completely cover joints discussed in Step 4 and slip felt beneath shingles to right and left. Apply felt with 12-in. overlap, making sure it's flat or shingles will bulge. Use ample number of ¼-in. staples to secure felt.

SEE ALSO
Gutters and downspouts . . . House additions . . . Ladders . . . Scaffolding . . . Sheathing . . . Siding

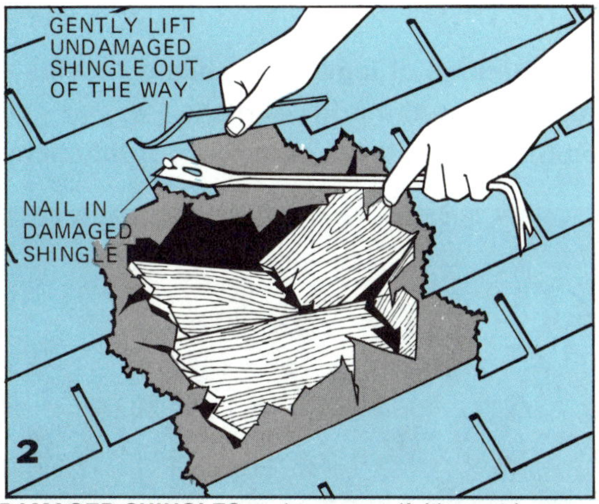

DAMAGED SHINGLES and tarpaper (felt) must be entirely—and cleanly—removed. Completely remove any partially damaged shingle so you can weave in a replacement shingle. Start with top course and work down. Use a ripping bar or large screwdriver to pry up nails from damaged shingle, or tear out shingle and drive nails home.

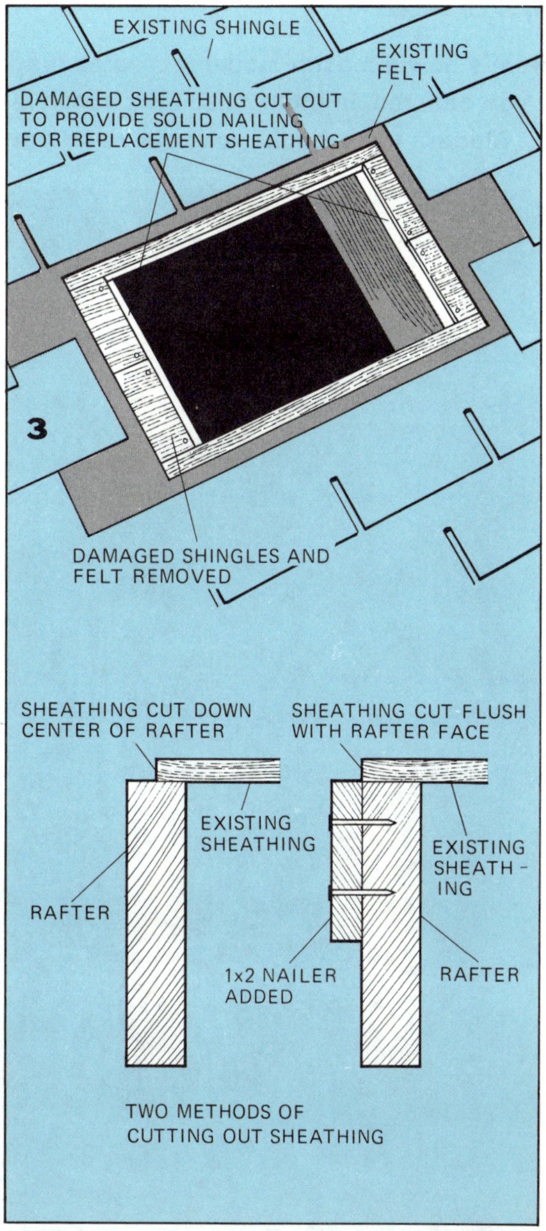

NEXT, remove all damaged, split and cracked sheathing to obtain a squared, easy-to-fit opening. You need solid nailing to attach new sheathing; use either method above to cut out old. Either cut down center or a rafter or cut alongside and add a 1x2 nailer for the new sheathing to be fastened to. The latter method is easier.

WEAVE NEW SHINGLES into existing ones so alternate rows overlap. *Never have an unbroken vertical line (shingle joint).* Here, for clarity, new shingles are shown slightly lighter than the existing. On repair jobs, take a piece of old shingle when you buy the new. Try to match so your repair job will be virtually invisible.

The challenge of modeling fine ships

By JAKE GRUBB

Here's how a master modeler creates magnificent miniatures of legendary sailing vessels—and how you can, too. In many cases it's possible to obtain and use the original plans. Modern tools, books, materials and parts speed the work without sacrificing authenticity

■ MAKING AN AUTHENTIC REPLICA of a mighty square rigger used to be considered beyond the skills of the average do-it-yourselfer, requiring expert know-how, specialized tools and massive amounts of time and patience. Time and patience are still requisites, but beyond these the task is not necessarily as awesome as it might seem. Authentic construction plans are available from a variety of sources. Books, tools, materials and even many ready-made parts can be obtained at hobby shops. Modern power tools make the job easier than ever, speeding once laborious, time-consuming hand operations.

Recreating in miniature the majesty of an ancient sailing ship is a rewarding challenge—filled with fun and excitement—that any hobbyist can master, says veteran modelmaker Ed Sims of Laguna Beach, CA, a man who for 27 years has made his living duplicating legendary vessels in precise scaled-down detail. The first thing to do, he says, is obtain plans for the ship of your choice, often easier than you may imagine. This is done by contacting the proper historical institution. If the ship is American, Sims writes directly to the Smithsonian Institution in Washington, DC. "Specify the ship you are looking for," he advises, "and the Institution will likely have the original plans or duplicates on file. They will send you copies for a nominal fee—one or two dollars. If they can't supply the plans you want, they will often refer you to a source that can."

good sources: museums

Other sources for plans are hobby shops and maritime museums. Most hobby shops stock or can order plans for well-known historical vessels. If the ship you want is of foreign origin or an obscure design, your best bet may be a maritime museum. "There are 82 national maritime museums throughout the world," says Sims. "You start by finding out where the ship you want was originally built, then you write the national maritime museum of that country. They will either have the plans or suggest other sources." Sims recommends the museums of Great Britain, Paris, Rotterdam and Barcelona as being most helpful.

Plans will probably be in 1/8 or 3/16-inch scale. Beware of a larger scale or you may find yourself with a model the size of your living room on your hands, Sims warns.

Tools required for ship modeling are basically simple, says Sims: a pair of needle-nosed pliers,

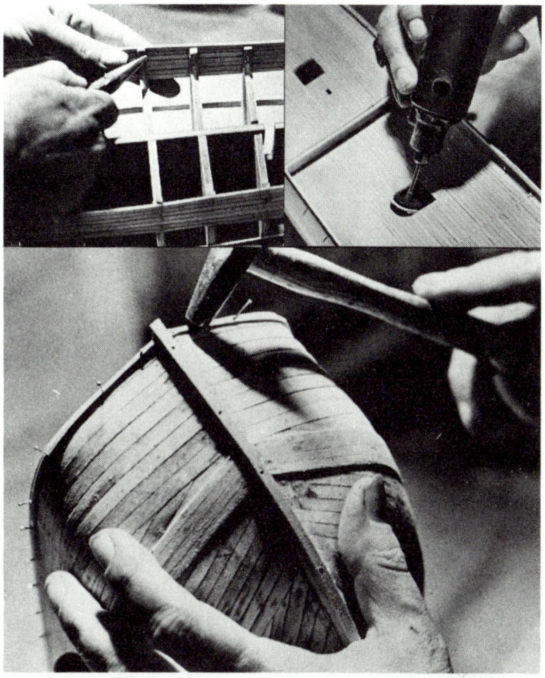

MIGHTY THREE-MASTED SQUARE RIGGER, shown in all her ornate glory on facing page, begins to take shape above. First step is planking hull. Thin wood strips, watersoaked to make them pliable, are glued and tacked on with brass pins as temporary fasteners. After glue sets, pins are removed with long-nosed pliers (top left) and holes "pegged." At top right, square holes for masts are formed in deck with tiny disc sander.

cuticle scissors for fine cutting, an X-Acto knife with No. 1 blade, X-Acto modeler's chisels, tweezers, a 1/32-inch-scale ruler, fine sandpaper and a miniature electric hand drill or hand grinder of the Dremel type. Sims uses a hobbyist's jigsaw for cutting out ribs, keels and other parts demanding precise accuracy. He also uses a small bench sander for shaping and finishing. If necessary, a coping saw can be substituted for the powered jigsaw and hand sanding for the bench sander.

Working from original plans is relatively easy if you take them a step at a time and don't allow yourself to become confused by the mass of intricate detail. Take your time and study each part before attempting to reproduce it. Wherever possible, obtain pictures of the ship you're modeling as these will serve as an additional aid in deciphering the plans.

SEE ALSO

Airplane models . . . Cannon models . . . Hobby centers . . . Jeweler's saws . . . Metal casting . . . Modelmaking

First step in the building process is to make precise tracings of the ribs and keel. These are then cut into templates, laid on ⅛-inch-thick plywood and traced again to produce the actual parts. The ribs and keel are cut out with a jigsaw or coping saw and matched against the original plan for accuracy.

Gluing begins when the keel and all ribs are cut. The ribs are slotted and glued along the keel at intervals specified by the plans. The next step is to add planking. The planks are usually ¼ by 1/16-inch spruce or bass wood, purchased from a hobby shop. These fine strips are attractive in color and grain and, because of their flexibility, are easy to apply to the curving contours of a wooden ship hull. The planks are treated in two stages. First the edges are painted black so that when the strips are butted together they're separated by thin black lines that simulate the caulking between teak planks in traditional sailing ships. A quick way to do this is to bunch the strips together in a stack and spray all the edges at one time with black lacquer.

Stage two is to separate the planks, let the paint dry, then soak them in a tub of water for two or three days. Soaking makes the wood pliable and easy to work. You begin planking by first laying a strip of wood in a straight line down one side of the hull, positioning it halfway between topside and keel. This gives you a straight starting point for laying up the remaining planks. You glue the plank at each point where it meets a rib, using a water-soluble cement. At the same time, you tack the plank in place with tiny ½-inch brass pins. These hold the plank until the glue dries. After the first strip has been applied, others are added alternately on each side until the entire half of the hull is covered. At the bow and stern, the ends of the strips are carefully trimmed. Then the opposite side of the hull is planked in the same way. When all planks are applied, the small brass pins are removed with needle-nosed pliers, leaving holes which are then drilled out and filled with tiny doweling "pegs" to simulate the pegged planking used in real sailing ships.

AUTHENTIC PLANS of early sailing ships provide accurate data for superdetailed modeling. Copies of such originals are available at nominal cost from maritime museums and from historical institutions like the Smithsonian.

MASTER MODELMAKER ED SIMS (above) checks "ratlins" for proper tautness of rigging before putting finishing touches on a 17th-century British warship. Photos at left show fantastic detail and workmanship in masts, rigging and deck fittings that are typical of an authentic replica made from original ship's plans. Shown below is Sim's unique method of mounting his models. Instead of being held in a conventional cradle, the vessel sits on rows of wood blocks simulating heavy timbers, giving it the appearance of resting on ways ready for launching. Bolts that run through the keel hold it in place.

Careful hand sanding with very fine paper smooths and tapers the hull, removing minor flaws in the planking and adding the graceful, sweeping contour lines typical of traditional square riggers. Planking the deck comes next and is done in much the same way as the sides of the hull except that the job is simpler and faster because there are no intricate contours involved.

The hull is finished in several steps, depending on the effect and appearance desired. Sims starts with an overall coat of all-purpose sanding sealer, then usually follows this with an oil-base wood stain rubbed on with a soft cloth. In some cases, wood trim is highlighted with paint, depending on historical accuracy or builder preference. Finally, the hull is given a second application of sanding sealer; this time it serves as a varnish to produce a softly gleaming satin finish.

With the hull complete, the ship is now ready for a stand. In fashioning his stands, Sims uses an unusual method. Instead of the conventional cradle or flat base, he mounts his hulls between rows of small wood blocks fastened in turn to a plank. The blocks create the effect of a ship perched on ways ready to be launched.

Hull detail begins with deck components such as hatches, winches, cabins, windlasses, capstans and transom. Here is where the use of pictures becomes an important supplement to the plans. While the plans will give the physical dimensions of such deck details, they will not show how they really looked. Many of these are highly distinctive and decorative in design, and only pictures can give you a true feeling of their appearance. The miniature woodwork is all made by hand. Tiny cabin windows are cut out with X-Acto chisels, hatch covers are shaped from thin spruce, lifeboats are carved from solid pine and winches are built up from a number of tiny individual pieces.

The transom, often the most ornate part of the ship, is usually a highly intricate arrangement of windows and scrollwork. Here's where a few special tricks, developed over years of experience, can be a valuable aid to the beginning modeler. Sims has a unique way of making window panes, for example. In each small carved opening for a window, he merely dabs a tiny spot of transparent glue and lets it dry, forming a mottled pane of simulated glass. The result is amazingly realistic. For scrollwork and other textured effects, Sims uses liquid gesso, a surface-preparation material employed by artists for oil paintings. When the fast-drying gesso is applied in repeated coats with a fine brush, it builds up a thick, irregular base that, when stained, takes on the appearance of intricately carved wood.

The technique can be used on figureheads, scrolls, flowers and other ornamental details. In fact, Sims often simply rough-cuts his designs, then works them over with gesso to achieve the final results—like modeling with clay, but in miniature.

Masts, yardarms, booms and bowsprits are all made from standard wood dowel stock. Sims selects dowel diameters to match the fattest portions shown on the plans, then tapers down the ends by eye. He does rough tapering on a bench sander and finishes up with hand sanding. Square holes for stepping masts are made by first drilling small round holes in the deck, then enlarging these into square openings with a disc sander chucked in a hand grinder.

"Rigging is a subject in itself," Sims explains. Before trying it, a beginning ship modeler should study the technique thoroughly from readily available published sources. For this, Sims recommends Harold Calahan's books on rigging for sailing ships, especially his volume entitled *Masts and Rigging*. This can be obtained at most libraries and bookstores.

"You begin with the running rigging—the white lines that control the sails—and work upward," advises Sims. "Once you get past the lower shrouds, the task is 75 percent complete." Sims uses white Irish linen thread in varying weights depending on the ship's size. The ratlins, or ladder-type side rigging, are also of Irish linen thread and are rubbed generously with beeswax to stiffen them. Sims warns against using synthetic nylon or rayon threads because they tend to stretch in time.

Miniature metal fittings such as cannons, pulleys, chains and anchors are available ready-made for nearly every purpose on a ship. These can be obtained at, or ordered through, most hobby shops. While such items *can* be handmade—and a perfectionist would insist that they be—Sims is willing to concede that they offer a handy way to avoid a lot of tedious work and are especially convenient for the beginner. In other words, it's no sin to add a few commercially made details if they'll improve the appearance of your handiwork. The important thing is the end result—and the thrill and satisfaction you'll get from turning out a masterpiece that's your very own from keel to crow's nest. And it's not all that hard, if you really want to do it.

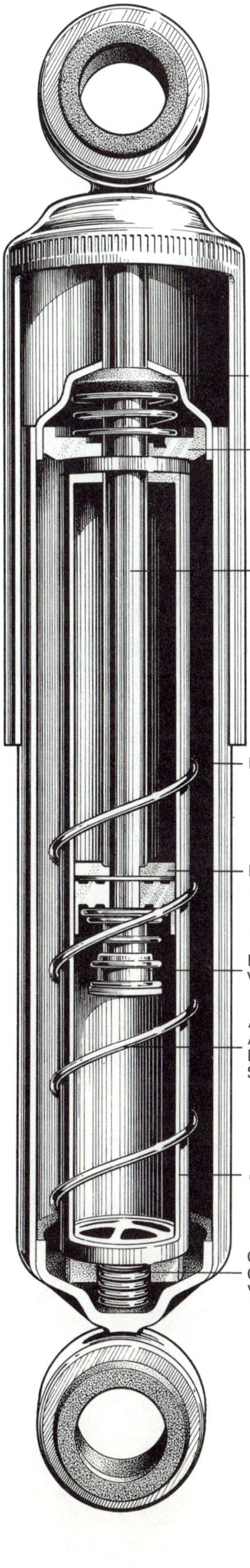

All about shock absorbers

By MORT SCHULTZ

■ SHOCK ABSORBERS are often taken for granted. Yet these relatively simple little devices are vital to your safety and comfort. Poor shocks cause a rough ride and sloppy road handling. Bad shocks can be downright dangerous. Fortunately, failing shocks are comparatively easy to detect and replace.

Oddly enough, shock absorbers do not themselves absorb shock—they control the action of your car's springs, which in turn absorb road shock. Without shocks, your springs would not function properly.

Technically, shocks are direct-acting, velocity-sensitive dampening devices—direct-acting because they're mounted directly between a car's frame and axle; velocity-sensitive because the faster they move, the more resistance they offer. As the speed of a typical shock is increased on a shock-absorber dynamometer from 30 to 85 to 170 cycles per minute, control on rebound (extension) increases from 165 to 285 to 430 pounds, respectively. Control on compression (jounce) increases

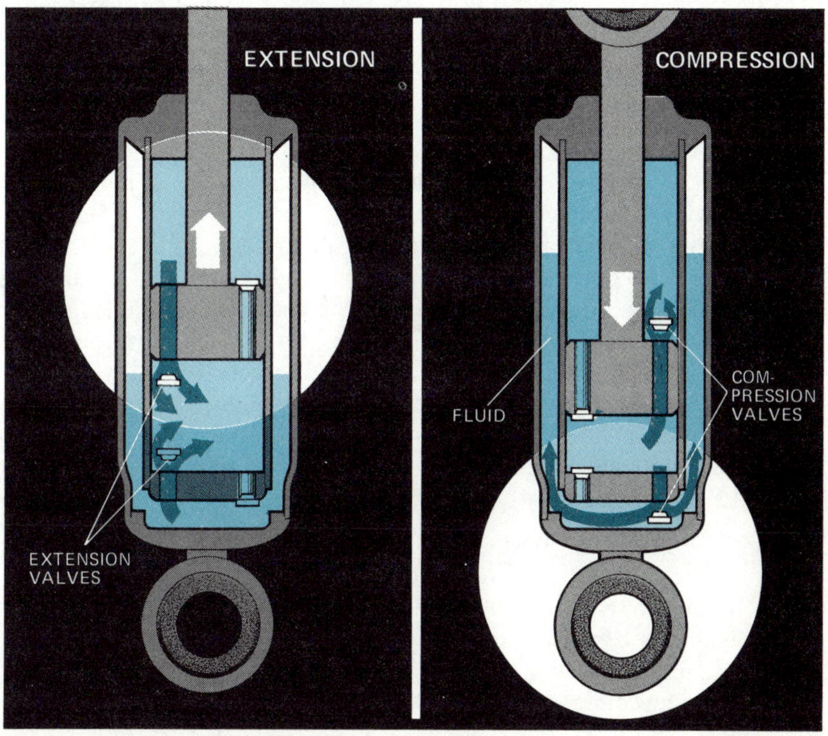

TYPICAL SHOCK ABSORBER (left) contains hydraulic fluid that quickly dampens the continuous up-and-down motion of a car on its springs. System of valves (above) controls flow of the fluid through compression and extension cycles.

SEE ALSO

Autos, maintenance . . . Autos, ramps . . .
Gaskets, auto . . . Ramps, auto repair . . .
Steering and suspension, auto . . . Tune-up, auto

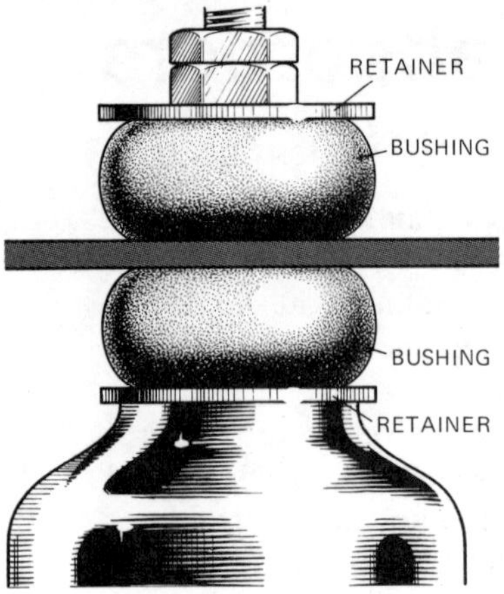

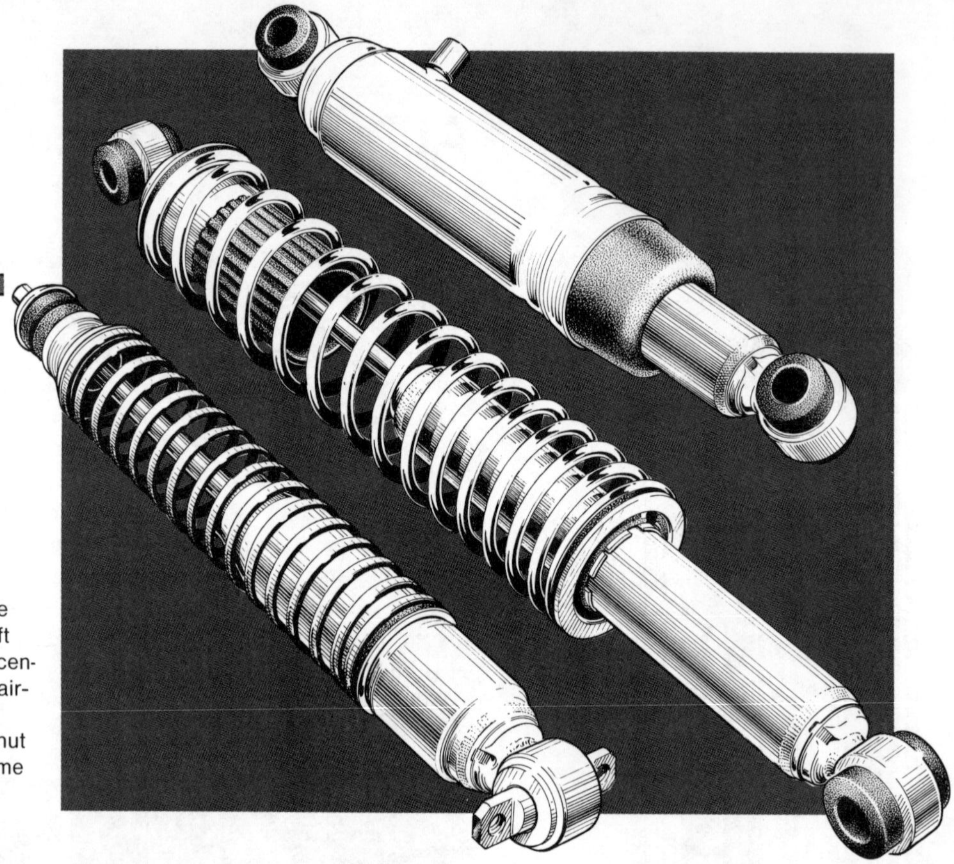

LOAD-CARRYING SHOCKS combine springs with shock absorber. The left shock (right) is a front-load carrier, center is a rear-load carrier, right is an air-adjustable shock. Drawing (above) shows stud-type mounting. Tighten nut only until bushing spreads to the same diameter as retainer.

from 60 to 185 to 275 pounds, respectively. Greater extension control is needed to compensate for the more powerful springing action that takes place during rebound.

The term "dampening" refers to the fact that shocks dampen, or restrict, the action of a vehicle's springs. If there were no shock absorbers, springs would bounce and rebound freely, making steering difficult, causing wheels to lift off the road, reducing braking efficiency and shaking up the car's passengers.

convert motion to heat

Shock absorbers convert mechanical energy of up and down motion into a heat energy that is dissipated through the shock. The principles of fluid displacement are employed.

During compression, the piston rod and piston move down in the working cylinder, which causes a pressure drop in the upper part of the cylinder. The volume of the lower part is reduced.

path of least resistance

To correct the pressure imbalance, hydraulic fluid follows the path of least resistance. This route is up through the upper compression valve, which is unseated by the force of the fluid. Thus the upper part of the cylinder is filled.

However, all the fluid which was originally in the lower part of the working cylinder cannot fit into the upper part because the piston rod has filled some of the void. This fluid is forced down through the lower compression valve into the reservoir area.

The amount of compression (jounce) control is dictated by the amount of force needed to transfer hydraulic fluid from the working cylinder into the reservoir.

do you need new shocks?

Shock absorbers deteriorate gradually, especially shocks originally installed by the automobile's manufacturer and replacement units that are warranted for a specific period rather than "life." Deterioration is deceptive. It doesn't happen suddenly. Drivers become accustomed to the gradual changes in driving "feel" that take place. You never really know how much you need shocks until after you've replaced them. Suddenly your car will be riding like it was new again.

However, being aware of trouble signs will allow you to spot worn shocks before they cause too many problems. Problems include loss of stability, driver control and braking efficiency; decreased tire life; premature damage to springs, suspension and steering-linkage components; and a decrease in your riding comfort.

trouble signs

The following are signs which indicate that your car may need new shocks:

■ Shocks that have seen 20,000 to 25,000 miles if they are original equipment, or replacement units that have exceeded the mileage warranty set by the manufacturer.

■ Oil on a shock's barrel, which signifies seal deterioration.

■ Worn bushings. Test by trying to shake the shock. A shock that shakes is one that either has loose mountings or bushings that are worn.

■ Physical damage. A broken rod that you can see by lifting the car, so shocks are extended, is physical damage. Also, large dents in the case.

■ Scuffed or badly spot-worn tires.

■ The car bottoms out when negotiating harsh bumps or when coming to a sudden stop.

■ The car is hard to handle, swaying on turns, bouncing on smooth roads, and/or lacking control on curves.

■ Shocks that fail the push-and-bounce test. Push down hard at each corner of the car two or three times. Let go on the end of a downstroke. If the corner bounces more than 1½ cycles, the shock should be replaced.

two important tips

1. **If one shock needs to be replaced, the other shock on the same axle should be replaced.** The other two can be left in service if they aren't damaged or worn.

2. **Replacing shock absorbers won't cure riding and driving problems caused by other conditions.** According to Gabriel, a maker of shocks for J.C. Penney and K Mart, "Excessive bottoming due to weak or sagging springs can't be helped by new shock absorbers. Nor can they (shocks) correct shimmy caused by unbalanced tires, bad front-wheel bearings or worn front-end parts."

picking a shock

Shock absorbers come in three general types: replacement, load-carrying or special purpose.

Replacement shocks look like original-equipment shocks. Some *are* comparable. Others have larger cylinder bores and pistons, greater-diameter piston rods and heavier valving. These heavier-duty units compensate for wear to the car's suspension system, withstand more rigorous driving conditions, and/or support heavier loads.

Replacement shocks may be classified as OEM-comparable (original equipment), heavy-duty, extra-heavy-duty, adjustable or MacPherson. Here, in general, is the purpose of each:

■ OEM-comparable shocks are similar to the vehicle's original equipment. They are designed for normal driving and light loads. Being the least expensive units available, they usually carry a specified rather than "lifetime" warranty.

■ Heavy-duty shocks can provide longer life than OEM-comparable units. They normally have a "lifetime" warranty and cost more. They should be used on a car with suspension parts that have "set." Heavy-duty shocks allow the car to handle heavier loads and more high-speed driving.

■ Extra-heavy-duty replacement shocks are designed for light trucks, recreational vehicles, station wagons and cars that pull lightweight trailers of the boat and camper types.

■ Adjustable shock absorbers are offered by a few manufacturers. They allow you to set the shocks for various conditions, permitting regular, firm or extra-firm support.

■ MacPherson replacement cartridges allow you to replace original equipment cartridges without discarding strut housings. MacPherson units are used on most imported cars, including Arrow, Audi, Capri, Colt, Datsun, Honda, Mazda, Porsche 914, Toyota, Volkswagen and Volvo 240 and 260.

load-carrying shocks

Load-carrying shocks are front and rear units that have the shocks combined with coil springs. Air-adjustable shocks also fall into this classification. Front and rear load-carrying units help you maintain maximum vehicle control and prevent damage to the suspension when hauling house trailers.

air-adjustable shocks

Air-adjustable shocks provide the *occasional* trailer-towing driver with flexibility. When towing your trailer, adding air to the shock provides maximum support. When the trailer isn't being towed, air should be bled from the shocks.

An air-adjustable unit is the same as a regular replacement shock absorber with the exception of the added air chamber. Owners of vans, recreational and off-road vehicles who vary the weight of the load they carry from one time to another will also find air-adjustable shocks useful.

REPLACEMENT cartridges for MacPherson-strut, front-suspension shocks make do-it-yourself work easy.

Special-purpose shock absorbers include those for racing cars, medium and heavy trucks, and buses.

replacing shocks

Don't buy shocks unless they are accompanied by instructions. In addition to the manufacturer's suggestions, here is a list of "dos" and "don'ts" you should keep in mind when replacing shocks.

■ Just before you begin work, lay out all parts from the packages. Make sure the mounting components of each shock are present. Take each shock in hand, hold it vertically, and pump it up and down to work air out of the chambers.

■ Make sure the car is firmly supported. You don't want it dropping on your head. If you are replacing rear shock absorbers of a car equipped with rear coil springs, don't let the rear wheels hang. The rear axle must be supported by a jack stand close to the shocks to keep springs in place when old shocks are removed, because shock absorber tension holds springs in position. Springs may also be supported by placing wedges between the suspension and axle.

Caution: If shocks are removed without the axle being supported, the axle can drop suddenly and may injure you and damage vehicle components.

■ Don't twist studs off old shocks. You can damage the threads of the mounting seat, which is a part of the car. If nuts are rusted, give them a liberal dose of penetrating oil a day or two before you are going to do the job. Before applying oil, use a wire brush to remove rust and dirt from the mount threads.

■ As you remove the mounting hardware, notice the order of position. Be sure to reassemble new mounting hardware in this order.

■ Normally, to remove front shocks, hold the upper stem so it doesn't turn as you remove upper hardware. Then remove hardware holding the lower mounting and pull the shock out from the bottom.

Note: Lower hardware of front shocks is accessible from below. Upper hardware may not be. If not, get to it through the engine compartment. Hardware is either atop the fender housing or is reached by removing a rubber splash shield over the housing.

■ Normally, to remove the rear shocks, disconnect upper, then lower hardware. If upper hardware is not visible, get to it via the trunk.

■ In some cases of front shock installation, you may have to enlarge the hole in the lower suspension arm slightly to permit insertion of the shock's stem. Do this by tapping the inside edge of the hole, or by filing or grinding. Enlarge the hole just enough to accept the stem. You must never file or grind the shock as a perfectly smooth finish is required if the shock is to perform its function.

■ When installing rear shocks, see that brake and fuel lines and exhaust pipes clear the units. Clearance should be checked with the car's body extended up and then pushed down after shocks have been installed—that is, with the wheels hanging and then by pressing down on the corners of the car. If necessary, move lines and pipes to obtain clearance.

■ Never grip the piston rod of a new shock with any tool. Just a small nick or scratch in the rod can cut the seal. This will allow fluid to leak out and the shock will be useless.

■ When installing shocks having stud-type mountings, don't overtighten the nut. The rubber bushing should be squeezed only enough to give it the same diameter as the retaining washers. Keep your touch delicate.

■ Replacing air-adjustable shocks is similar to replacing standard shocks. However, there are additional steps to observe. For one, you have to disconnect air connections. Make sure you know these steps. They are listed in the instructions that come with the shocks.

A roll-out shoe drawer

■ HOW MANY TIMES have you stumbled over your wife's shoes sticking out from under the bed, or opened a closet door to be greeted by an avalanche of dusty footwear? That's why I built this closet roll-out shoe drawer.

The drawer is designed to accommodate two common metal shoe racks. It rolls smoothly on a metal drawer track and seven nylon rollers. I cut off about 4 in. from the shoe-rack legs, leaving 1¼ in. for attaching with half-round clamps. At the front the racks are clamped directly to the back of the front uprights; at the rear the uprights have to be notched slightly in four places. Cover the sides, top and the drawer front with ⅛-in. perforated hardboard to provide ventilation.

SEE ALSO
Closets . . . Drawers . . . Joinery . . . Storage ideas . . . Storage walls

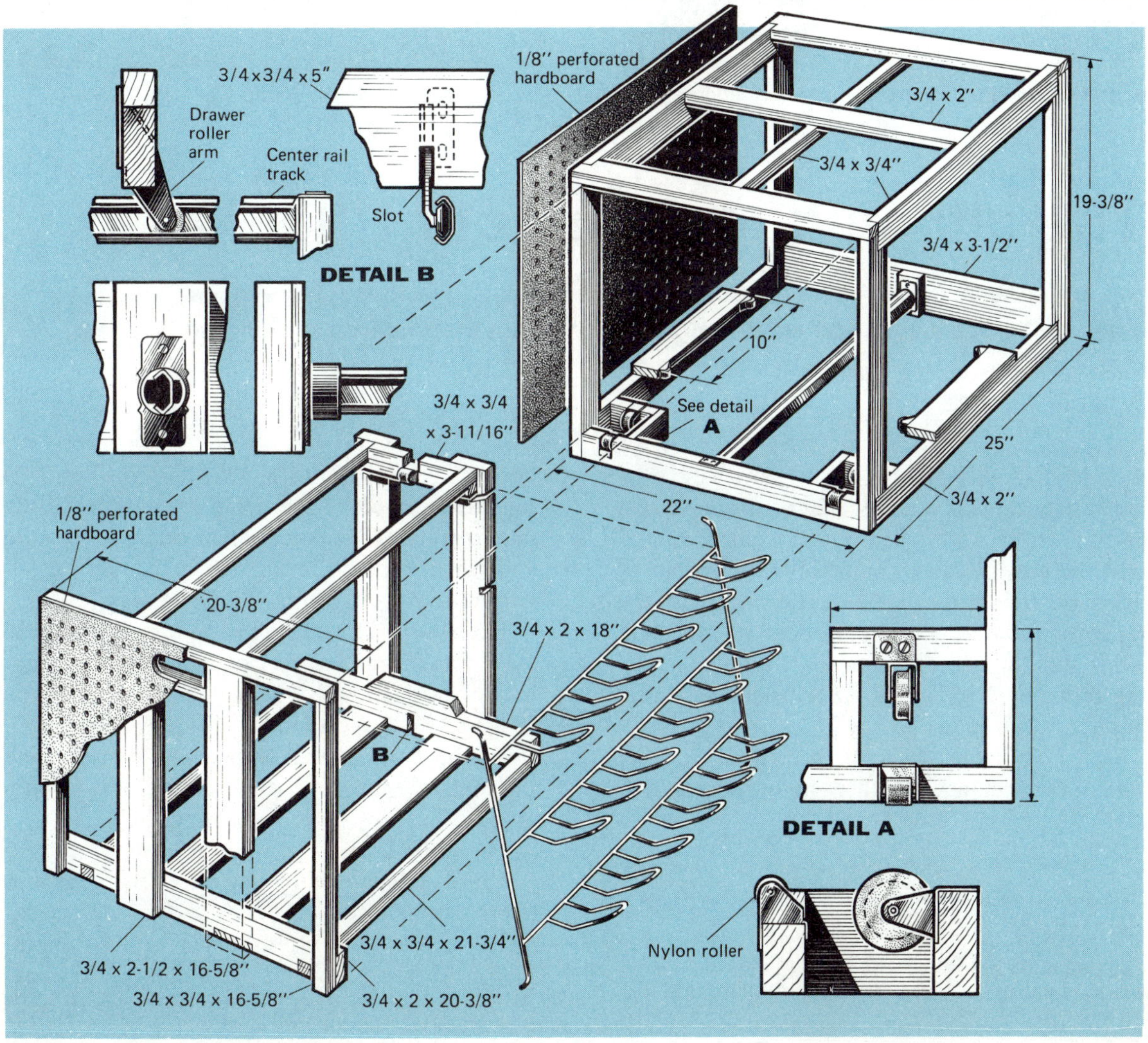

FOR BENCH-REST competition, massive concrete benches of special design provide support for weighty rifles.

The ultimate test for your rifle

Bench-rest is the name of the game for determining accuracy. Use these techniques to get all the bull's-eyes you want in practice and then be prepared for hunting success

By GEORGE NONTE

MANY A SHOOTER takes his trusty rifle, fires a few shots at a gallon can or similar target and figures he knows just how his gun is zeroed in. If he hits the can a couple of times in four or five shots at 50 yards, he figures he's ready for the range or the deer season. He does his shooting while standing, or leaning against a tree, or resting across the hood of his car or from some other haphazard position.

But shooting that way does not give a true picture of the accuracy of either gun or shooter, and doesn't really indicate whether the gun is sighted-in properly. More important, it can give a false picture of the potential accuracy of the gun, and might jeopardize an important and expensive hunt as well. There is a better way.

The absolute tops in rifle accuracy is produced by a rather small group of enthusiasts belonging to the National Bench Rest Shooters Assn. (NBRSA), 607 West Line St., Minerva, OH 44657. Even the most casual shooter can benefit from the methods they use to shoot five and 10-shot groups that are often indistinguishable from a single bullet hole.

These bench-resters measure their groups (from center to center of the most widely separated holes) with sophisticated optical instruments. Groups shot at 100 yards have been recorded with measurements that are less than 1/10

SEE ALSO
Gun cabinets . . . Gun racks . . . Hunting . . .
Marksmanship . . . Muzzleloading . . . Shotguns

inch between centers of the widest shots. That beats legendary tack-driving by a considerable margin.

This degree of accuracy is obtained with specially built guns, very precisely hand-loaded ammunition, unusual shooting techniques, and a rigid shooting table, called a bench rest, with sandbag or mechanical supports on it.

accuracy for the rest of us

The special guns aren't suitable for the hunter, but bench-resters do shoot a category of "sporter" rifles that are quite suitable for hunting. The specially loaded ammunition is usually out, too, because the average hunter normally shoots only factory cartridges. He can, however, borrow bench-rest techniques to better prepare himself and his rifle for that important big-game hunt.

First comes the shooting bench, or *bench rest.* Many ranges have benches of one sort or another, but they usually aren't the massive, reinforced-concrete or timber structures of the pure bench-rest range. As long as they are solid, they'll do, and if there aren't any available you can make up a simple portable bench as shown in our drawing. It won't cost much and will last a lifetime, improving your shooting every time it's used. The splayed legs give it a firm foundation, and it is further stabilized by the weight of your torso, the rifle and sandbags. This combined weight will give your rifle a firm, solid surface.

those bags

With any bench, you'll need sandbags. They can be bought in cheap or expensive models, of course, but it's also simple to make your own. Any close-woven strong cloth will serve.

Two or three rectangular bags 12 to 16 inches long and about six inches wide will serve up front. A couple of smaller bags will do back at the butt; often one is sufficient. Bags should be loosely filled so they can easily be squeezed to shape. Filled tightly, they won't work as well. Clean sand is the common filler, but lead shot is preferred by some shooters, in spite of its cost.

The large bags are stacked up near the front edge of the bench to support the fore-end of the rifle. The fore-end is bedded down into the top bag for the lateral as well as vertical support. Place the smaller bag(s) under the toe of the rifle butt, bedding the stock into it.

With malleable sandbags under the gun at both ends, the rifle's vertical angle can be changed easily to align the sights on target. Major changes are made in the front bags; minor ones by squeezing the rear bag with the left hand to raise or lower the butt slightly. In this manner, the sights are brought to bear on the target and all vertical support comes from the sandbags, eliminating the trembling and weaving present when the support comes only from your body. Lateral changes are made by moving the front bags or the rifle on them; minor shifts again by squeezing or moving the rear bag.

HEAVY WEIGHT and small caliber of bench-rest rifle dampen recoil and make unnecessary shooter's shoulder support.

COMBINING SANDBAGS and a mechanical support to bench-rest his hunting rifle, author Nonte test-fires his gun to check its sights and accuracy before the fall deer season.

HEAVY STEEL channel serves as stock for this unlimited-class specialty rifle. Shooter, like many bench-resters, brings along reloading equipment.

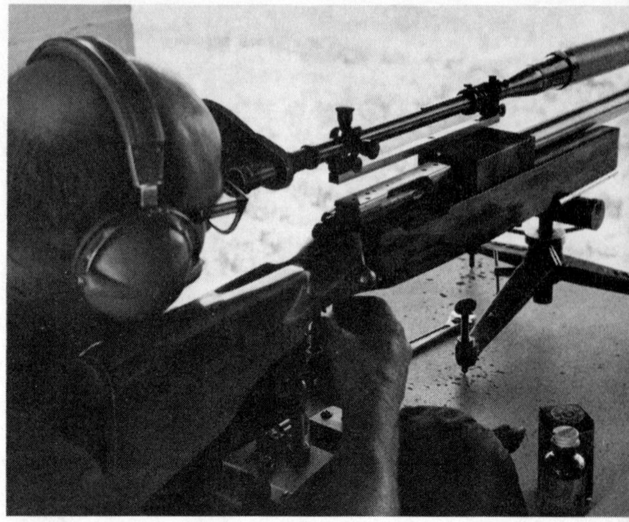

MASSIVE BENCH-REST model can be held by sandbags, mechanical supports as shown, or elaborate return-to-battery mounts that return to aim-point.

Hunting rifles generally recoil more forcefully than heavy bench-rest guns so the hunter must support the butt solidly with his shoulder. Alternately, a 25-pound bag of lead shot can be placed between gun butt and shoulder. This reduces recoil movement of the gun and eases the blow on your shoulder. It also damps out shoulder movement.

With this understood, here's how the shooting goes. First, as always, make certain the rifle is *unloaded.* Seat yourself at the bench, adjusting seat height so that your left forearm and right elbow (if you shoot right-handed) can rest comfortably on the bench top. Then adjust the sandbags so the rifle points at the target when solidly bedded and you can see clearly through the sights

PORTABLE BENCH can be easily made to help you test your gun and improve your shooting. It has splayed legs to give it a firm foundation that is further stabilized by your weight and sandbags. It can be quickly taken apart and then reassembled in the field for an accuracy check.

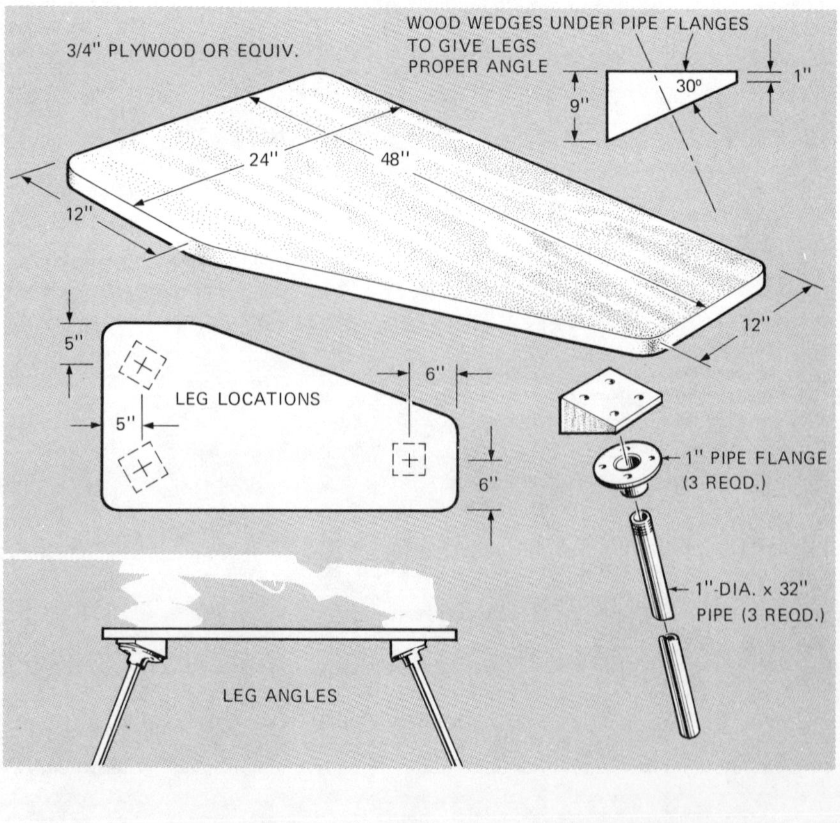

without muscular strain. Grasp the rear sandbag with the left hand and make minor adjustments by squeezing and shifting it to bring the sights dead-on. Don't try to shift the gun by nudging it around with your shoulder. The left hand shouldn't touch the gun, just the sandbag.

With sight alignment correct, support the butt solidly with your shoulder, but don't disrupt the rifle's seat in the sandbags. Grasp the trigger grip of the stock firmly but gently with your right hand. Squeeze the trigger carefully to fire, without disturbing that solid sandbag support. At first, do this dry-fire without loading the gun. The hammer or striker should fall without any disturbance of sight/target alignment. Practice this a bit before stepping up to live shooting.

So long as you've bedded the rifle well on the sandbags and don't disturb it with your shoulder or when pulling the trigger, the human error present in other forms of shooting is very nearly eliminated. Thus you'll be able to shoot accurately, and what shows up on your target represents the mechanical accuracy of only your rifle and ammunition.

Of course you must still control your breathing and keep your body as still as possible. By being firmly seated and resting your arms and torso solidly on the bench, such control becomes easy. *Any* movement of your arms, hands or upper body will be transmitted to the gun. If you note a very slight but regular twitch of the gun as you concentrate on the sights and target, it is most likely the effect of your pulse. This can come from the carotid artery in your neck and can be eliminated by carefully shifting your head and neck.

fire!

When sights and target stay in rock-steady alignment while the trigger is squeezed, you're ready for live ammunition. Load with one cartridge, get everything in position, align the sights and squeeze off a shot. Jack out the empty, relax, and then repeat the process for at least three to five shots at one to two-minute intervals. This keeps the barrel from heating rapidly, which can cause it to bend slightly, affecting the bullet's strike zone. Since the first shot is the most important to the hunter, the barrel should be kept relatively cool, simulating first-shot field conditions. Take care to position both rifle and yourself back *exactly* the same for each shot. Recoil will move the gun to the rear, and it must be repositioned on the sandbags before firing again. "Exactly" means just that. Deviations in position, bedding in the bags, grip on the stock or snugness of your shoulder to the butt will reduce accuracy.

study the grouping

Once you have fired a group of three to five shots from the bench you'll see clearly how well your gun is targeted, as well as just how accurately it can shoot. You may be surprised to find the sights weren't zeroed as closely as you thought. If the group isn't on point of aim, now is the time to shift the sights and then shoot another group to check them. In fact, you may need to shoot several groups to get the sights set exactly, and in doing so you'll learn more about just how much accuracy your gun can deliver.

Half a dozen groups will show what normally can be expected from your gun and ammunition alone. Average group size will indicate the smallest target that can be hit consistently without usual human error. Make allowance for your error and instability under hunting conditions and you'll realize that an offhand shot at a deer 300 yards away is a waste of time unless you and the gun are both exceptionally good.

bonus benefits

The use of a bench rest and related shooting methods are equally helpful regardless of the type or calibre rifle (or even handgun) that you shoot and the type of sights it carries. The light, open-sighted .22 rimfire squirrel or rabbit rifle is, in fact, less likely to be properly zeroed than a big-game rifle. Further, the usual targets of such a rifle are smaller so that one needs first-class hunt preparation.

Bench-rest enthusiasts shoot with high-magnification scope sights and use very small square black aiming points. They either quarter the square with the scope cross hairs or set the square in an angle formed by the intersecting cross hairs. Hunting scopes are usually of only 2½X to 6X power so a larger aiming point like a two-inch or four-inch square is much easier to use. With iron sights, open or peep, you may require an even larger aiming point, and a circular shape is better than a square.

varying the range

While the bench experts shoot only at fixed ranges of 100, 200 and 300 yards, your bench-rest work may be done at any range that suits the space available or approximates the range you normally shoot. And bench-resting before the hunting season or any other time is bound to increase your accuracy and enjoyment of the sport.

Modelmaker's shop in a cabinet

By RUDY KOUHOUPT

■ IF YOU NEED a good place to work on miniature engines, models or other small projects, this neat little cabinet will fill the bill nicely. It's an efficient and inexpensive cabinet workshop that takes up just 3½ sq. ft. of floor space and provides a place for everything. And your metal lathe, vise and large tools can be stored in the roomy bottom compartment between work sessions. Fourteen shallow drawers place all hand tools, lathe accessories and measuring devices at your fingertips. You will have more than enough bench space when you raise the hinged drop leaf to obtain the full 17 x 44-in. work surface.

All members of the cabinet are cut from ½-in. plywood and are fastened together with glue and brads. Start with the sides which are 16¾ x 26½-in. Dado the sides 7 in. from the bottom so the shelf will be well supported. Scribe and cut the sides to clear your baseboard when the cabinet is against the wall. Fasten the 16 x 29¼-in. shelf in the dadoes in the sides and use a length of dowel in front to give center support to the shelf.

The center divider is attached to the top of the shelf. Cut a piece 17 x 32 in. for the top. Put it in place nailing into the sides and center divider. Use a 4-in. triangle of ½-in. plywood at each corner in the rear to reinforce the shelf, sides, top and center divider.

Cover the exposed edges of the plywood with ½-in. half-round molding for appearance. Rip

SEE ALSO
Airplane models . . . Apartment workshops . . .
Cannon models . . . Drawers . . . Hobby centers . . .
Ship models . . . Tools, hand . . . Workbenches . . .
Workshops

IF FINISHED NEATLY, your cabinet workbench will look well in just about any room where you keep it.

SMALL TOOLS and lathe accessories are at hand in shallow drawers. Use thin wood for drawer partitions.

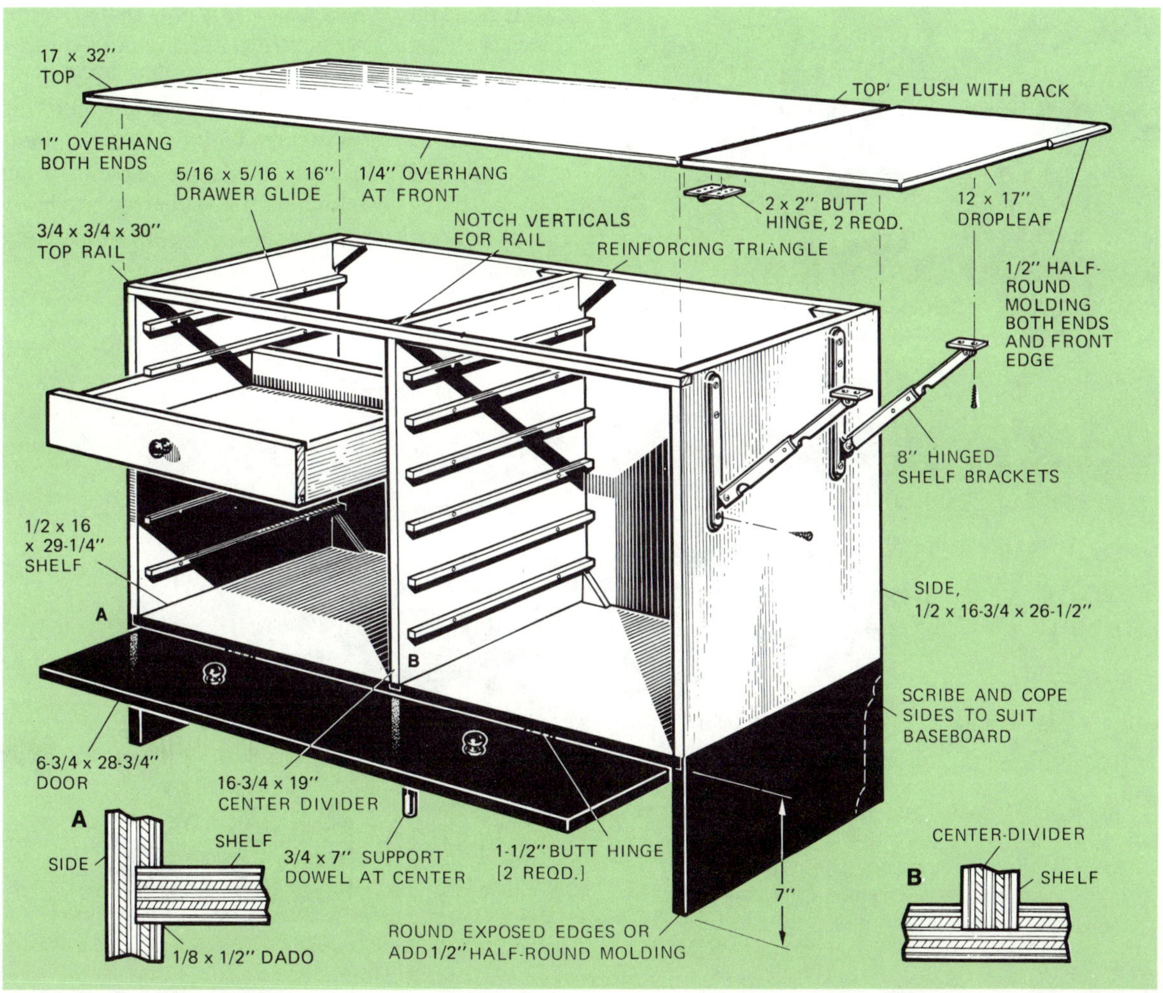

SMALL PERRIS LATHE (18½ in. long) is quickly and easily stored out of view behind the hinged door on bottom.

DRAWER CONSTRUCTION is simple as shown in the drawing below. Partitions (above) suit the owner's tools.

⁵/₁₆-in.-sq. strips to use as drawer slides on the sides and center divider. Fasten the strips with glue and brads.

The drawer sides, fronts and backs are also cut from ½-in. plywood with a ⅛ x ⅛-in. groove dadoed in ⅛ in. from the lower edge to receive the bottoms. Take drawer dimensions from the cabinet. Assemble the drawers and drill the fronts for the knobs. Add partitions and dividers to the drawers to suit your lathe accessories and tools.

Use butt hinges to attach the door to the bottom shelf so it swings down to close the large bottom compartment. Use 8-in. folding shelf brackets and another pair of butts as shown to attach the drop leaf. Put ½-in. half-round molding around the top and drop leaf. If you have the space, a drop leaf could be fitted to the other end also. Cover the top and drop leaf with plastic laminate. The cabinet receives a coat of enamel undercoater followed by a durable semigloss enamel.

Modelmakers who build engines and similar projects will require the use of a small metal-cutting lathe. The one shown is a British lathe built by Perris Engineering Ltd. and imported by Caldwell Industries, Box 170, Luling, TX 78648. A full range of accessories is available for this back-geared, screw-cutting lathe which measures just 18½-in. long. It is capable of handling a workpiece 9-in. long between centers and has a 4¾-in. swing in the gap and a 3½-in. swing over the bed.

	A	B
TOP DRAWER	1-7/16"	1-1/16"
SECOND DRAWER	2-7/16"	2-1/16"
LOWER DRAWERS	2-13/16"	2-7/16"

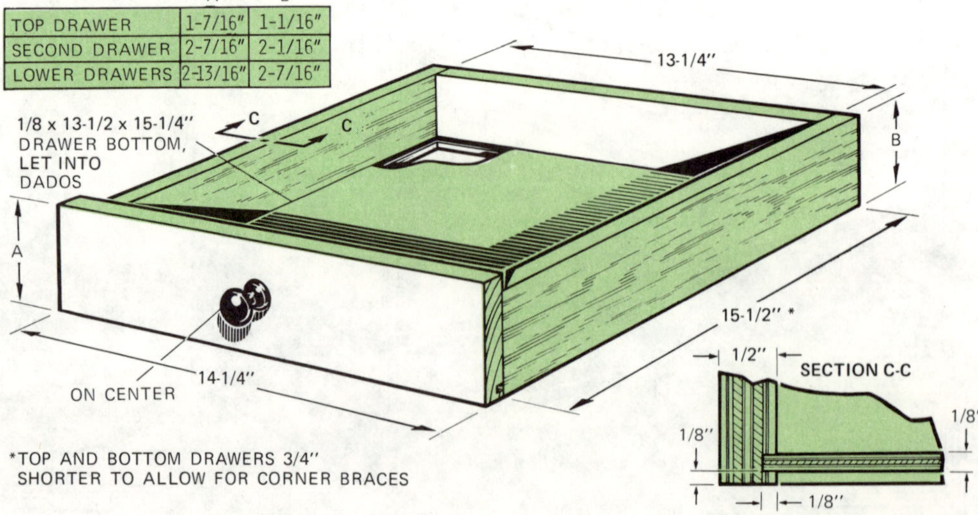

*TOP AND BOTTOM DRAWERS 3/4" SHORTER TO ALLOW FOR CORNER BRACES

A shop organizer

By M. R. KIRSTEIN

THIS SHOP organizer is not as tedious to make as it looks—you just need to know a couple of shortcuts. For the "drawers," you can use plastic boxes, sardine cans, tuna cans, jar lids—whatever you can collect in quantity and at low cost. Use ⅛-in. hardboard for a light-duty organizer, ¼-in. for heavy duty.

Determine strip lengths and widths according to the size and number of drawers you desire. To cut slots, clamp, drill and fasten about eight strips together with two fh bolts, washers and nuts. Countersink the bolt head if you intend to cut the slots on a stationary power saw. Lay out the slots on the top strip. You can cut the slots with a handsaw, bandsaw, jigsaw or table saw. (The latter allows you to cut more plies per pass, but don't cut more than six plies per pass.) Use one of finished strips as a template for laying out top strip on next stack.

Test-assemble the dividers without glue, front side down on a flat surface. Remove one vertical strip at a time and coat all contact surfaces with yellow carpenter's glue. Once all strips have been glued, square up unit and allow to dry. Finally, glue on sides.

I have made seven of these units for various drawer sizes and all turned out well. The first organizer I made is still in use after 25 years.

(Editor's note: *Sides can also be made of 1-in. pine for greater rigidity. To fasten sides to dividers, glue and clamp. Organizers can be used in kitchen, shop, child's room, studio.*)

SEE ALSO

Hardboards . . . Small-parts storage . . . Storage ideas . . . Workshops

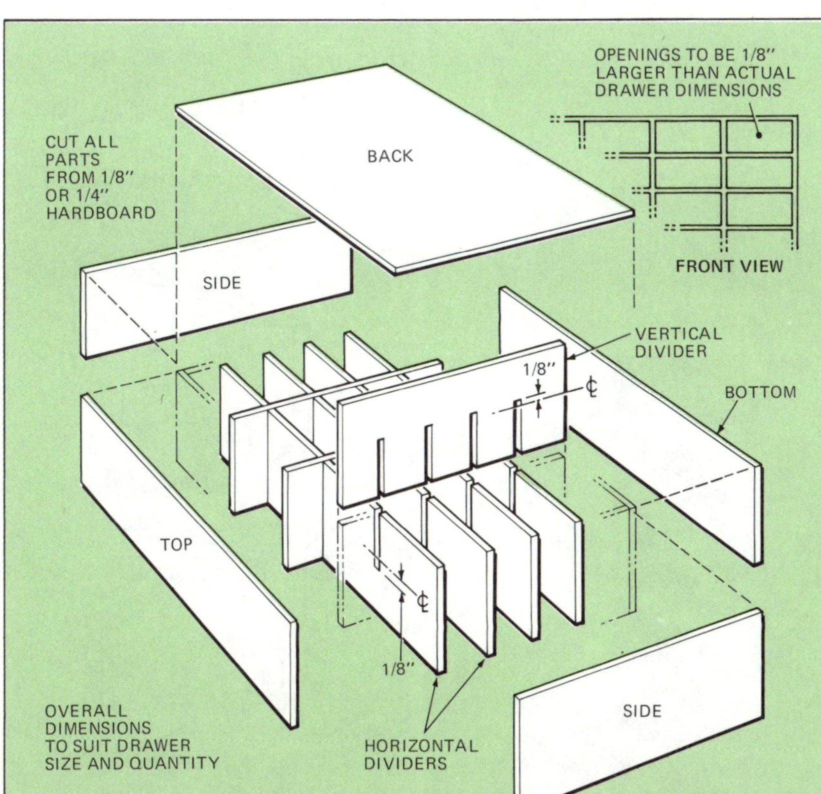

CHECK WIDTH of divider slots with scrap of hardboard prior to assembly.

APPLY GLUE to dividers and joints and assemble on a flat work surface.

Ten clever shop tips

1 With a spacing jig attached to the miter gauge, it's a simple trick to cut a perfect-fitting box or finger joint on your own table saw. The jig is little more than a wood fence screw-fastened to the gauge and fitted with a small projecting block which uniformly spaces a series of notches across the width of the work. The notches are made with a dado cutter, and their width and depth are generally equal to or slightly less than the thickness of the stock. With ½-in.-thick stock, the notches would be ½ in. wide, ½ in. deep and ½ in. apart.

To make the joint, stand the two pieces to be joined against the fence so the edge of one piece is even with line A and the edge of the other is even with B. Push the work across the cutter, then shift it so the notch just cut sits over the spacing block, and make a second notch. Place the second notch over the block and make a third notch and so on. Repeat the step until notches are made the full width of the work.

It is important that the two pieces of stock are held in the same position throughout the notching. This is assured when the spacer block projects far enough to catch both pieces. If desired, the two pieces can be clamped together with a small C-clamp. Adjustments can be made by moving either the spacer block or the fence itself to give you the perfect fit on your joint.

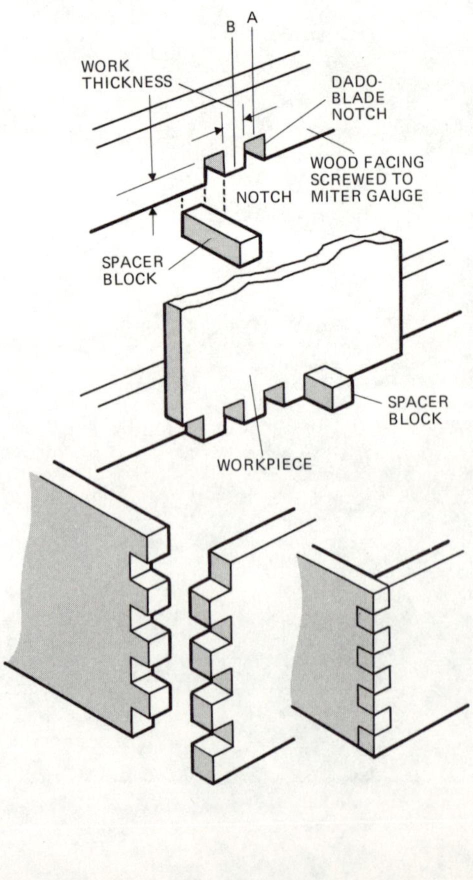

2 If you want to dish a disc, but don't have a lathe, there's another way to form a saucer-like cavity—with your table saw. All you need is a V-notched board clamped to the saw and positioned so it centers the blank directly over the vertical axis of the blade. With blade running below the table and the disc face down in the V-notch, crank up the blade ⅛ in. into the work and slowly rotate the disc 360°. You should begin to feel the blade cutting into the wood. Raise the blade another ⅛ in. and repeat the same procedure.

By taking a number of light cuts and slowly rotating the work each time, you'll produce a perfectly concave dish requiring very little sanding. If you want a cut which has a smaller diameter, try using a smaller blade. Remember, the sharper the blade, the better cut you will get.

SAUCER-LIKE CUT in the underside of a wood disc is made by rotating the work over a saw blade: V-notched board is clamped to the table so it positions directly over the blade.

3 If you must cut a lot of wedges, you can mass-cut them in jig time by using a notched board. The board is notched as shown to suit the desired taper, and the saw fence is set so the blade just clears the jig as it's passed along the fence. Sawing is done with the grain after the stock is first crosscut from wide material.

As each wedge is cut, the stock is flopped in the notch. Like slicing cheese, the jig is pushed forward, then withdrawn with the wedge in the notch. Select stock free of knots and with straight grain. If you use a hollow-ground combination blade, there will be no need to sand the wedges. Width of the stock from which the wedges are cut must equal the length of the notch so the wedges will have chisel points. If blunt points are wanted, make the notch in the board deeper.

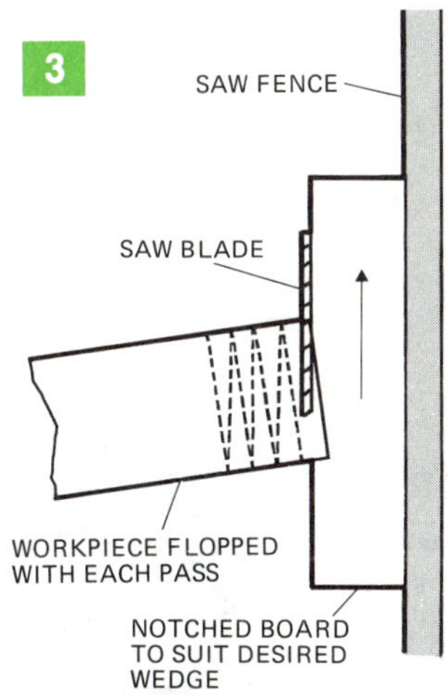

NOTCHED JIG pushed along a fence provides a fast way to mass-produce wedges on a bench saw. The work is held at an angle in the jig and is flopped over after each cut.

4 How do you bore a hole completely through a board edgewise that's 2 in. or so wider than the bit is long? You bore from opposite edges. In doing so, there's a trick to keeping the two holes aligned and here's how:

Clamp a scrap board to the drill-press table and bore a hole in it ½-in. deep. Then lower the table and bore a hole 3 in. deep in the edge of the work. Replace the bit with a long dowel of the same size. Align the dowel with the hole in the wood table by lowering the chuck, then lock the table. Put the original bit back in the chuck, insert a short dowel pin in the hole in the wood table, place the work over the pin and bore down from the top edge to meet the first hole. If you have carefully followed the correct procedure, both holes will be on target and align perfectly.

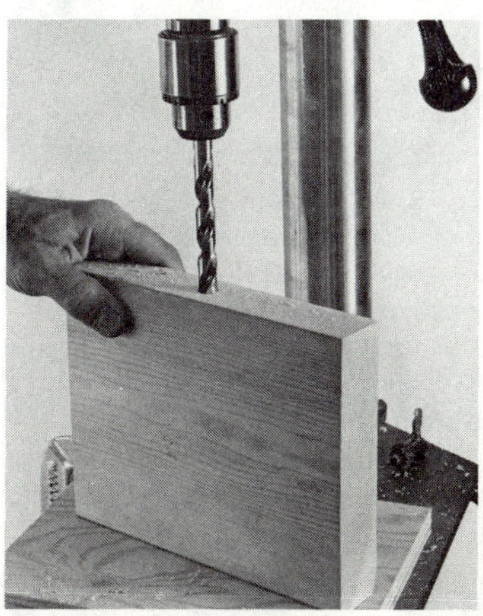

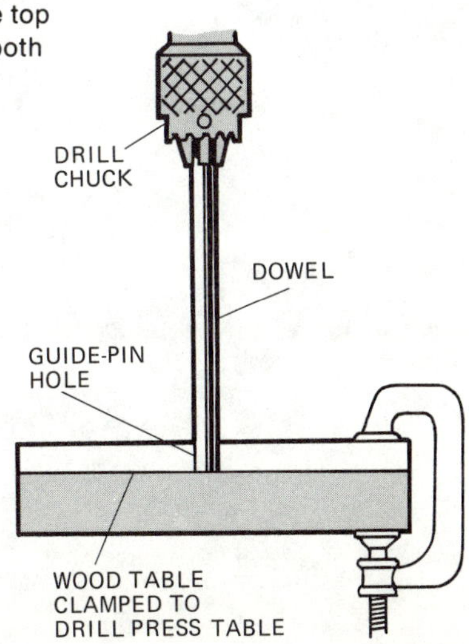

5 You can buy a tenoner that slides in the groove of your saw table and has a special clamping fixture to hold the work, or you can make one that rides the fence and uses a common C-clamp as shown here. Both are used to make the cheek cuts on a tenon after the shoulder cuts have already been completed.

When a single blade is used, the work can simply be turned edge for edge to make a second cheek cut. If you use two blades with a spacer between, one pass is all that is necessary and you're done. If your saw's fence is a simple box channel like the one shown in the photo on the right, the tenoner is made to fit it like a saddle with scant clearance to ride without binding and without play. Waxing the inside will help it slide easier. In following the dimensions, note that the tunnel is dimensioned for a 1-in.-thick fence and will vary in size with the particular fence you have. Note too that the vertical stop against which the work is placed, then clamped, must be at a right angle to the base to give you a properly cut tenon to fit your project.

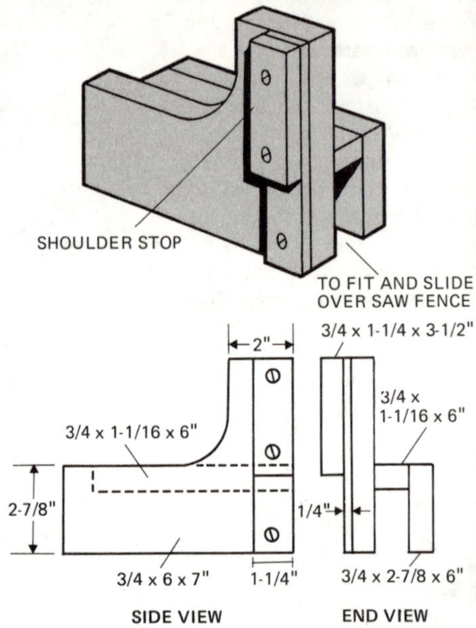

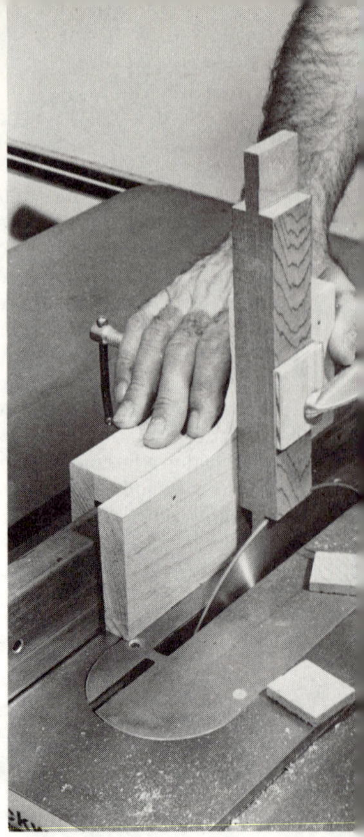

6 While you can set blade height by the saw's built-in scale, it's often quicker to do it with a stepped gauge block comprising a number of ⅛-in. thick plywood strips glued together in a stack. Each strip is ½ or ¾-in. shorter than the next. To use the block, you place it over the blade and crank the blade down (or up) until the block rests flat on the table. For example, if you want to set the blade ¾ in. high, you pick the sixth step.

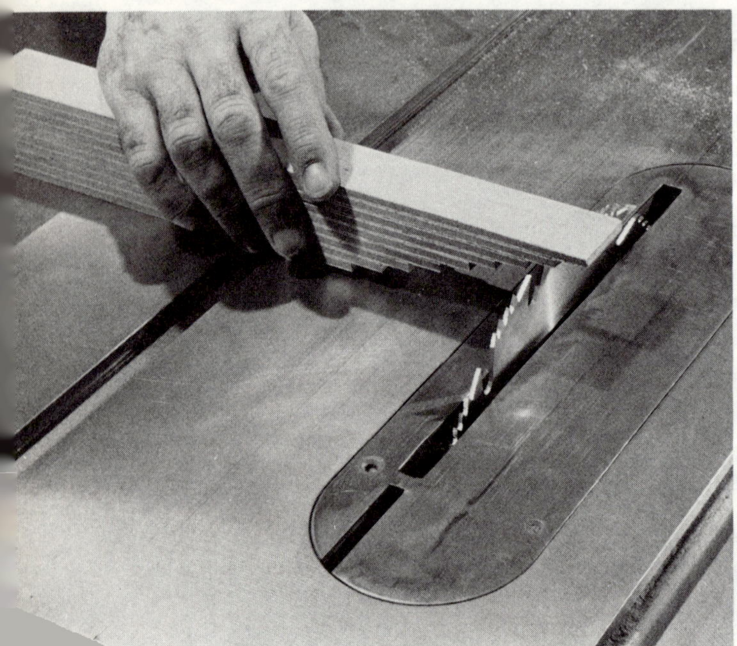

7 The best-holding glue dowels are dowels which have a spiral kerf. Not only does the kerf help line the hole with glue from top to bottom, but it affords an escape for glue trapped in the bottom of the hole when clamps are applied. To kerf a glue dowel on a bandsaw, tilt table 15°, clamp the miter gauge to it and slowly rotate the dowel as the blade cuts a 1/16-in.-deep kerf. Don't attempt this with a short length of dowel.

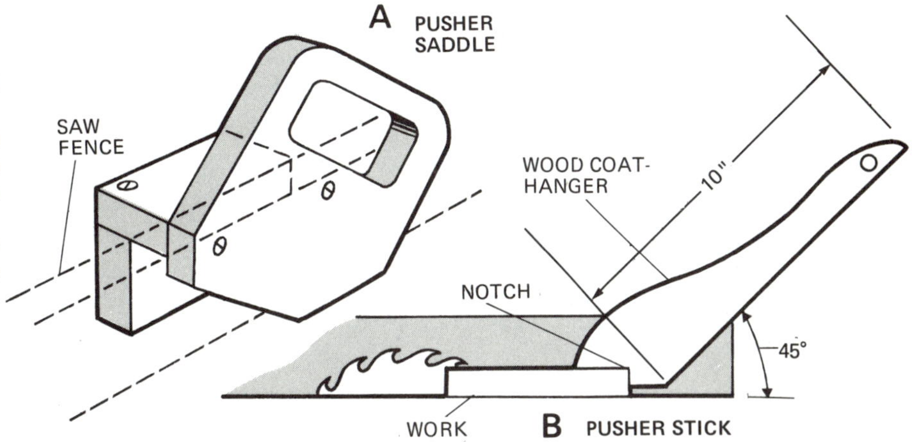

8 The first thing to make after you buy your first table saw is a push stick to have handy when you're ripping work narrower than 4 in. It is both for convenience and for safety. A wooden coat hanger will provide you with two ready-made push sticks which require only notching, although it's simple enough to make a push stick from scratch with scrap wood. The fence-straddling pusher is another type for use when the shape of the rip fence permits. Its D-grip handle keeps the hand securely in place and safe from the blade. Make it to ride the fence freely and not bind anywhere.

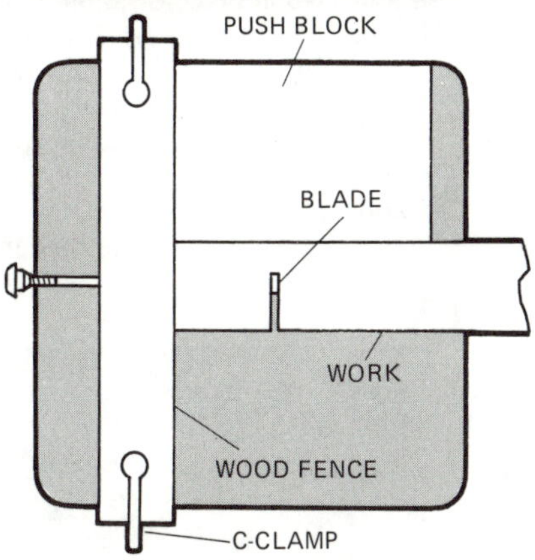

9 While a bandsaw is primarily for cutting irregular shapes, it still has other potential. Here it is being used for quantity cutoff work even though it has no fence or a groove for a miter gauge. As shown in the setup above, a scrap of wood is clamped to the table to serve as a fence and a wood block pinch-hits for a miter gauge. In use, narrow stock is guided squarely through the blade by the backup block used as a pusher. To maintain a high level of accuracy it is suggested that you make the block as perfectly square as is possible.

10 When work must be held in close contact with the fence for the entire length of a cut, the spring action of a spring board can often prove to be much better than the hand. It's simply made by sawing a 60° angle at the end of a hardwood scrap. Then rip several closely spaced "fingers" one-third its length. To use it, clamp it to the saw table. As you feed the wood through the saw the fingers will hold the piece to be cut in contact with the fence by bearing lightly against the wood.

An expert's best woodworking tips

By WAYNE C. LECKEY

You can bore a hole from one side of a board and wind up with a splintered mess, or you can bore from both sides and leave a hole as clean as a whistle. This is just one of the little tricks that is the mark of a good craftsman. One note of caution: Be sure to follow all safety procedures including using the blade guard on the table saw. To clearly illustrate some of the tips, we left it off in these photos

Angle in on screw pockets
Screw pockets for fastening tabletops are neatly formed in the table's aprons with a beveled 2x4 block clamped to the drill-press table. With the depth gauge set for the right depth, the work is clamped against the face of the slanting block. By cutting tangent to the surface, the bit forms a neat shouldered pocket for the screw. Using a much smaller drill, another hole is made in the bottom of the pocket for the screw

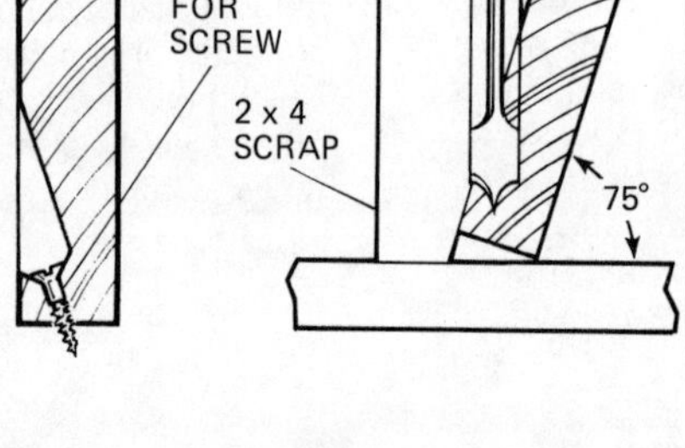

Rabbet wood discs on table saw
Rabbeting a disc is normally a job for a shaper, but when you don't own one, you can do it with a semicircular jig attached to the rip fence of your table saw. To start, gently lower the disc into the spinning blade, then rotate it slowly with your right hand while pressing inward with the left

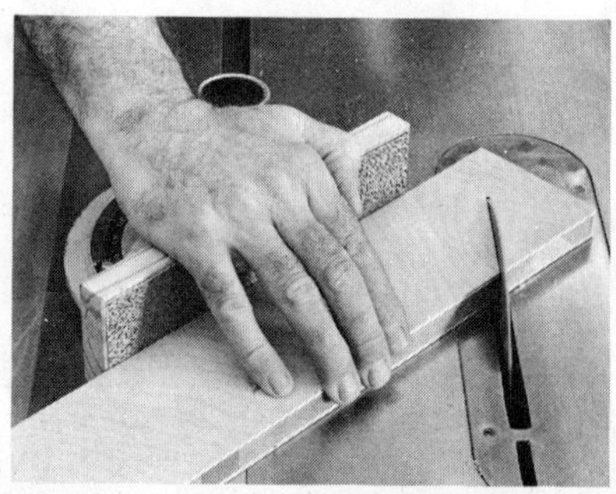

Prevent creeping with sandpaper
Workpiece creeping is difficult to prevent when you make angle cuts greater than 45°. The expert will cement a sandpaper strip to the face of his miter gauge to add a nonslip surface

Guide your saw for a bevel

It takes a steady hand and a good eye to saw a uniform bevel the length of a board with a handsaw. However, there's nothing to it if you clamp a 2x4 scrap to the top of the work against which the saw blade can bear at an angle as you guide it along the pencil line. The 2x4 must be positioned to suit the angle that you are cutting; the greater the angle the farther the 2x4 must be from the line

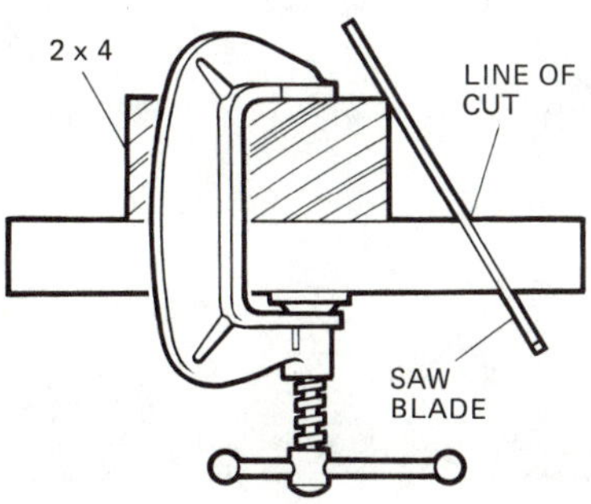

Two ways to rip tapers

Taper ripping requires a jig to hold the work at the required angle as it goes through the saw. Details below show two jigs; one a two-leg hinged affair, the other a stepped block. The hinged jig is set by measuring across the legs at a point 12 in. from the end. By opening the legs 1 in. you set the angle for a 1-in.-per-ft. taper. The nonadjustable stepped jig is good for work tapered on four sides, such as table legs. The work rests in the first notch for the first pass, then in the second notch

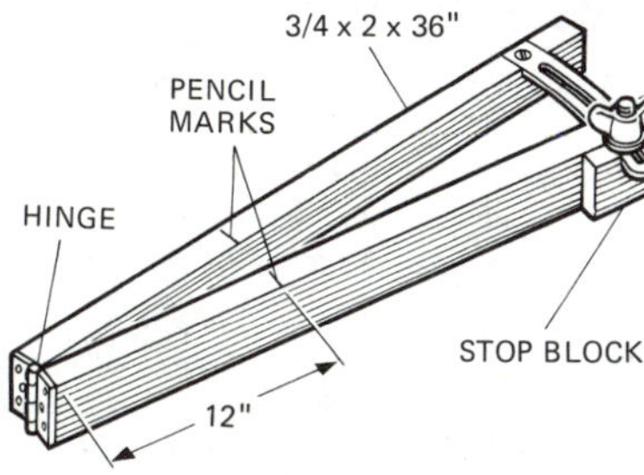

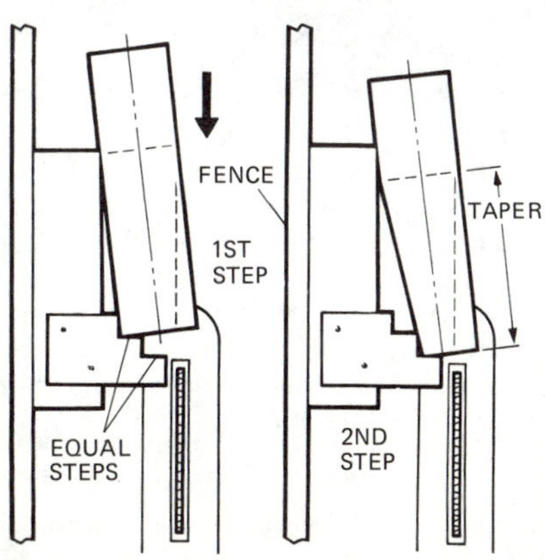

Board for squaring odd pieces

A squaring board comes in handy for cutting a straight edge along irregularly shaped plywood leftovers from your jigsaw and bandsaw. It's nothing more than a sliding platform fitted with a runner that rides in the table groove. The squaring board is used to support and guide the work as it passes through the blade. The rip fence should never be used to make such cuts. A squaring board is especially good for small pieces. When you want to square-up the edge of a large piece, a strip is clamped to the underside and then it is guided along the edge of the saw table itself. Placement of the strip is dictated by the size of your saw table, plus what is required to true up the ragged edge. If your saw is small in size it may be difficult to guide the work along the table edge without a helper

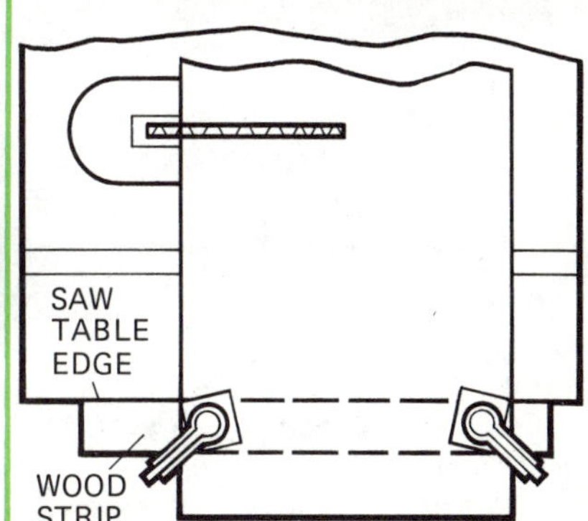

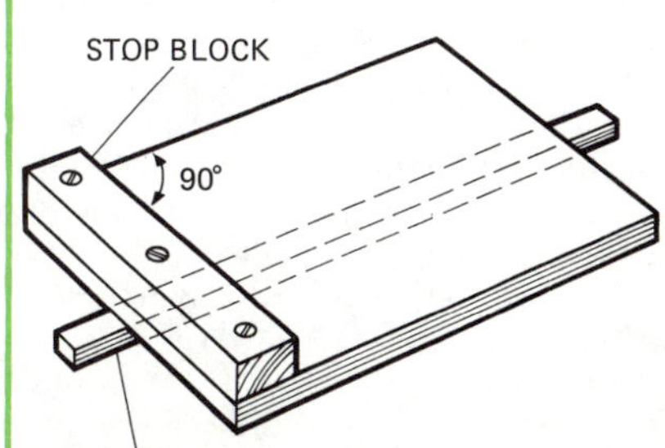

woodworking tips, continued

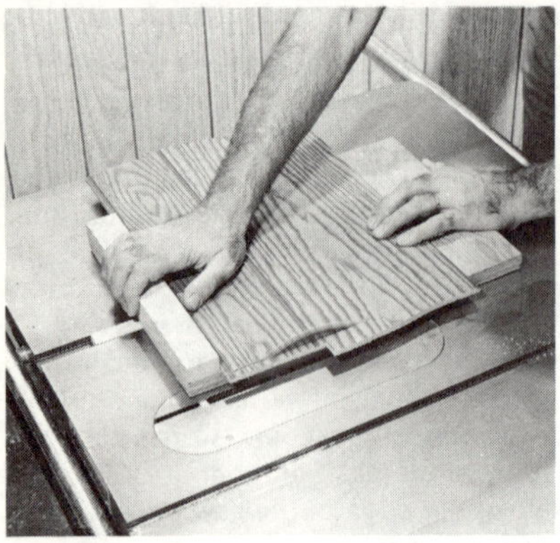

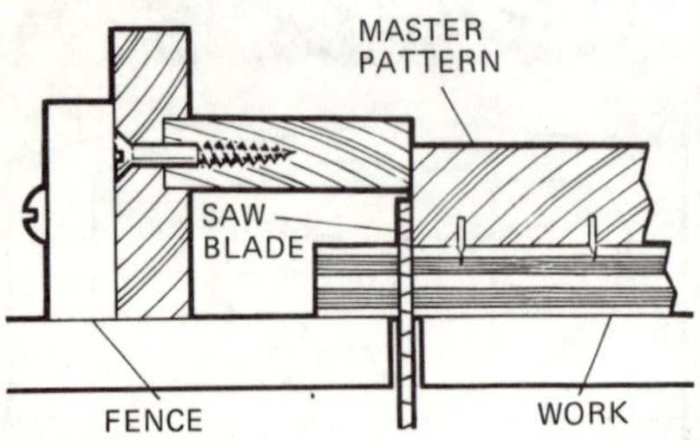

Mass-produce identical work
Pattern sawing is a fast way of duplicating straight-sided work. The setup requires an overhanging wood fence which is clamped or screwed to the saw's fence, and a master pattern of the part to be duplicated. The points of two brads in the master pattern embed in the wood. The wood fence is aligned flush with the outer face of the blade and the blade is raised just high enough to handle the thickness of the work. Clearance under the overhanging fence must suit the thickness of the work, and the pattern must be thick enough to ride the edge of the fence. The work must be cut up beforehand to the approximate (and slightly larger) size and shape

Miter molding faster with a jig
A miter jig is faster and more accurate than your saw's miter gauge for cutting right and left-hand miters. Runners are added to the underside of a plywood platform and the saw is used to make its own kerf. A plywood fence is positioned and screwed to the platform so it forms a perfect 90° angle at an exact 45° angle to the kerf. A strip of sandpaper glued to the face of each fence of the jig will help keep molding from shifting as it's being cut

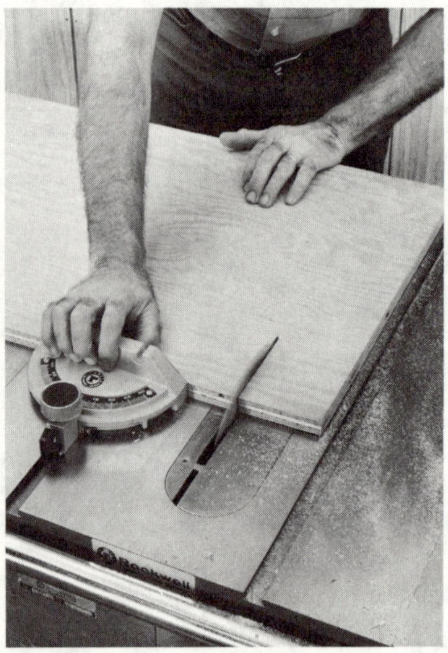

Crosscut wide boards
Place the miter gauge backwards in the table groove when crosscutting a wide board on a small saw. This utilizes all of the table in front of the blade and provides maximum support to the work. After you are halfway through turn off the saw and reverse the gauge in the groove to complete the cut

Cut duplicates safely with block
Never use the fence itself as a stop when crosscutting duplicate pieces. The work will wedge between the fence and the blade and be thrown with force. Always butt the work against a stop block clamped to the table. This way there is no chance of the pieces getting caught and thrown by the saw

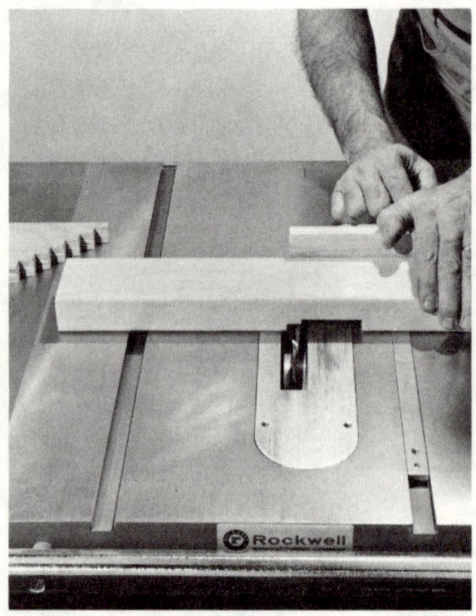

Duplicate identical dadoes
Extra-wide dadoes in duplicate work come out exactly the same length each time if you clamp a stepped block to the left corner of the saw table. Precut to suit the width of the dado blade and the length of the dado, the block determines each successive pass by resting work in the steps. The last step automatically sets the width. You can't miss since the block does the measuring

Forming cove molding

Making cove molding on your saw is possible by passing the workpiece repeatedly across the blade at an angle. The auxiliary fence is positioned to form the cove down the middle of the work, then clamped to the saw table. Stock is cut away by successive passes over the blade, cutting no more than 1/16 in. each pass. A combination blade works best and produces a smooth cut. Width of the cove establishes fence angle and is found with an adjustable parallel gauge as shown in the lower photo. Work is finally ripped down the center to produce two strips of cove molding

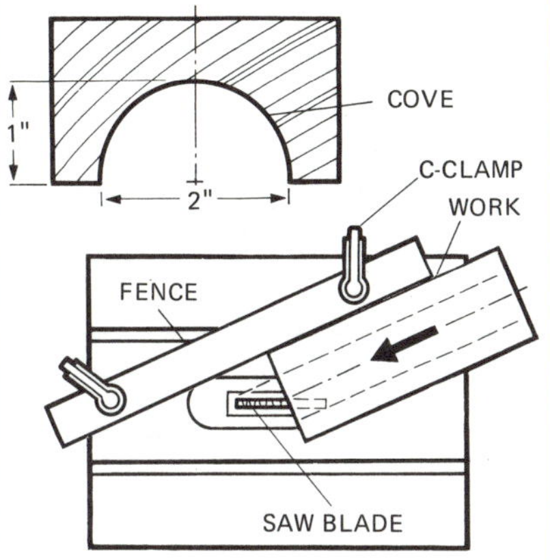

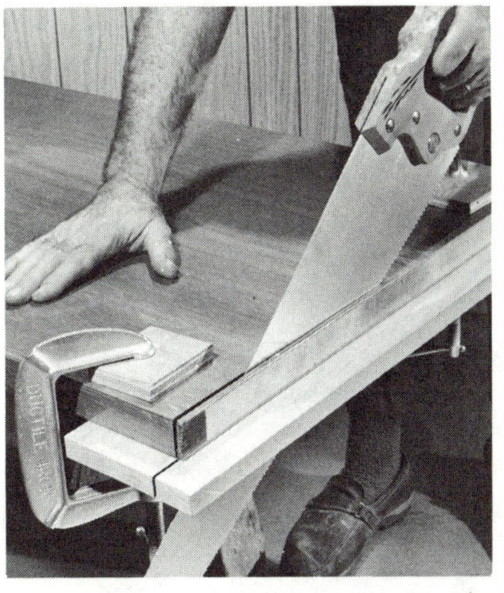

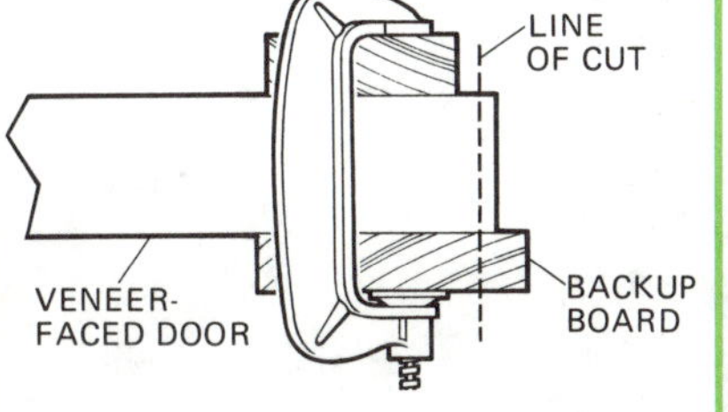

Trim bottom of door with backup

Sawing off a narrow strip from the bottom of a door with a handsaw presents two problems: guiding the saw so it won't run off and keeping it from splintering the opposite side. Both problems are solved by clamping a scrap board to the underside. With the board backing the cut, the saw can't chip or scar the veneer

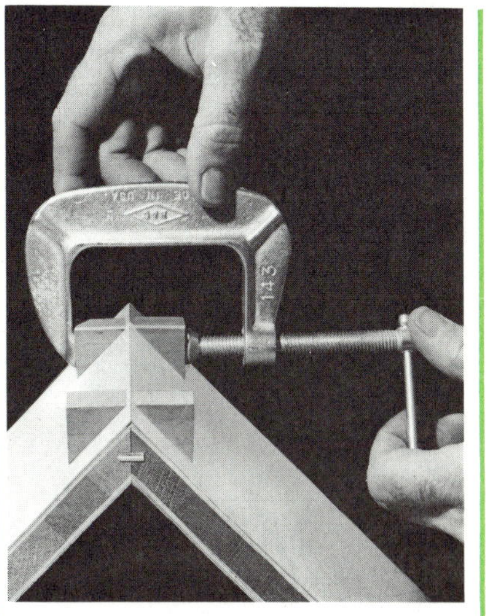

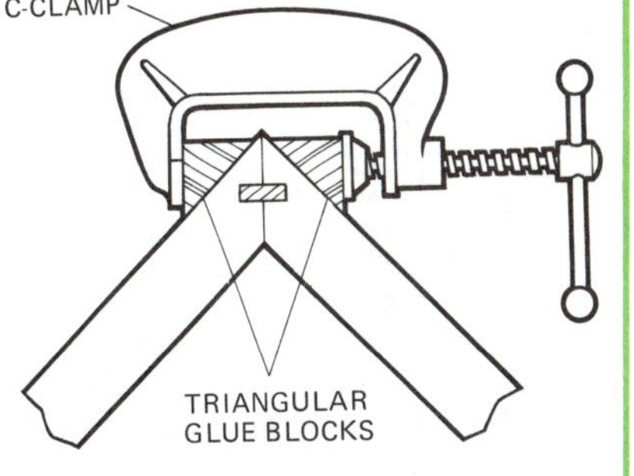

Clamp mitered joints

While there are special "clothespin"-type clamps with swivel barbed jaws for holding mitered joints when gluing, you can make your regular C-clamps do by gluing several triangular clamping ears to each side of the joint. The ears are later chiseled off flush and the surface sanded

Avoid cupping by alternating

When tabletops and other wide panels are built up of random-widths boards, the heart grain of the boards should change direction from board to board and the bar clamps should be placed on alternate sides of the work

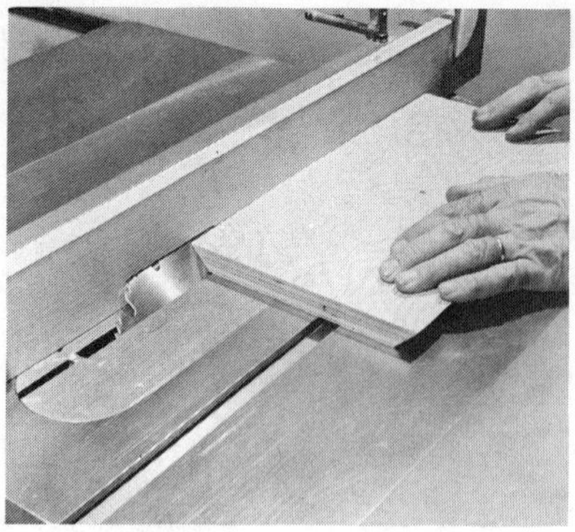

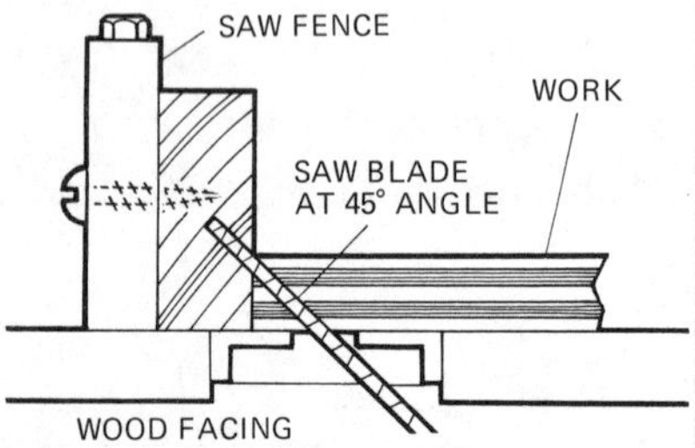

Miter wide boards
How do you rig your bench saw to cut a perfect miter along the edge of a wide board or plywood panel? First you add a wood facing to the rip fence, then with the blade tilted 45° and raised ¾ in., you ease the fence into the rotating blade enough to just bury the tip of the blade in the wood facing. Fence will support miter

Contour legs with a sanding drum
For a perfect fit when doweling legs to a central turning such as the post of a lamp table, use a sanding drum. It works best when both the diameter of the drum and turning are equal. Notch a board to fit around the drum as shown and support it horizontally so its surface is at the very axis of the drum

Two ways to drill a disc
A V-notched board clamped to your drill-press table will uniformly space holes around the circumference of a disc. To bore them in the face, the table is kept horizontal. To bore them in the edge, the table is tilted 90°. The board must be positioned so the V-notch is in line with the bit

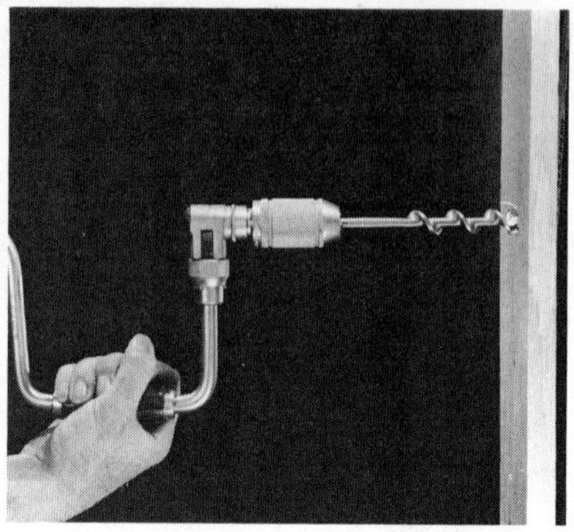

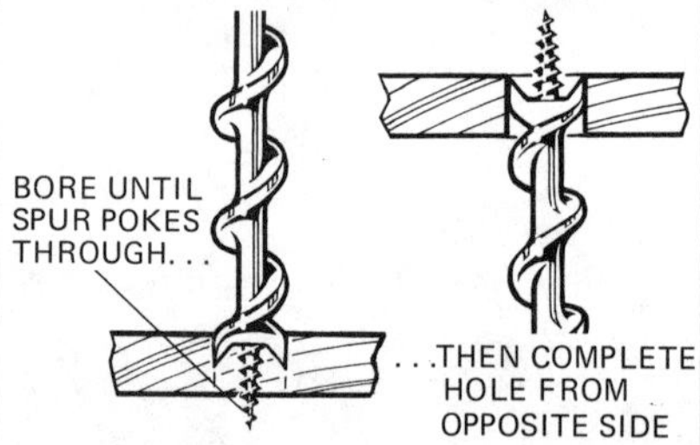

Bore clean-cut holes
Boring a hole from both sides is not always possible but when it is, remember this stunt for producing a clean-cut hole. Start boring from one side until the bit's spur pokes through the other side. Then back out, turn the work around and finish the hole by boring to meet the first. You'll have a clean hole and no splinters

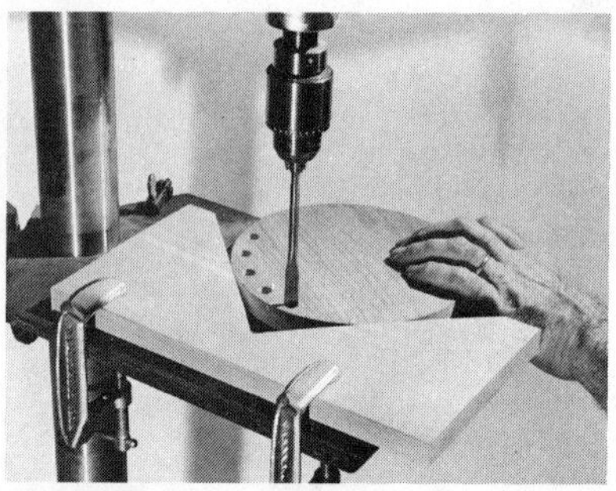

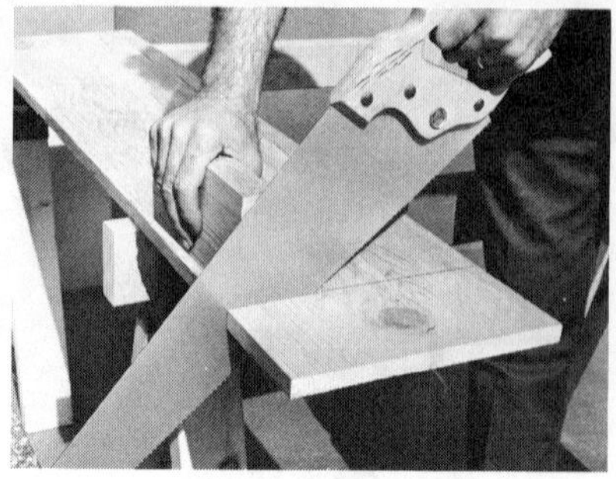

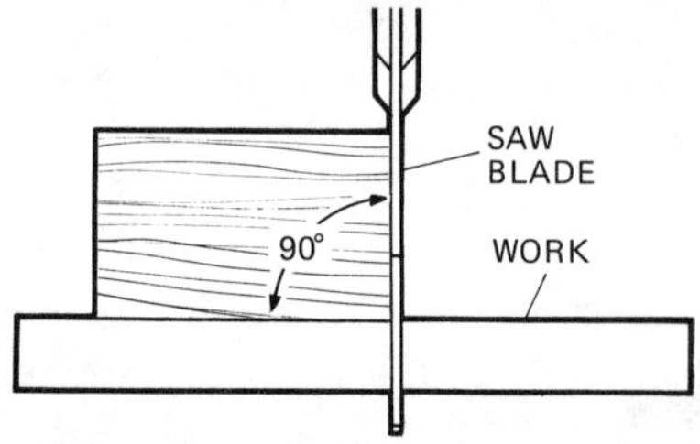

Block keeps handsaw vertical
With practice and a sharp handsaw it's no great feat to follow a line when sawing a wide board. The trick is holding the saw vertically the full length of the cut. When it's important that the cut be 90°, simply hold a square-cut scrap of 2x4 against the saw blade as you continue to saw

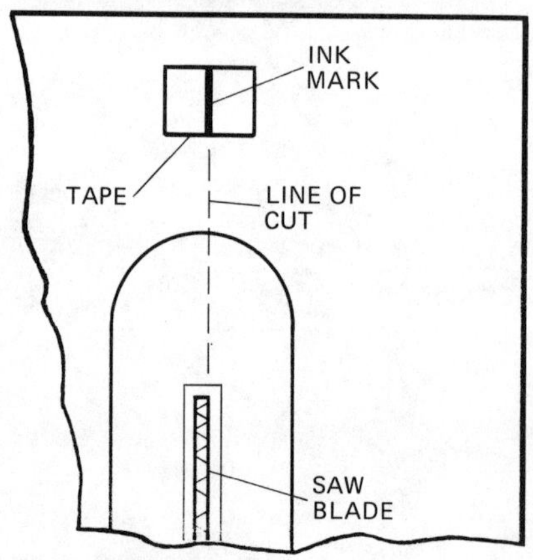

Saw precisely on line
Lining up the mark on the work with the saw blade is easy if you stick a piece of white tape to the saw table and make an ink mark on it directly in line with the inner face of the blade. You'll be right on target when you push the work across the table and into the blade

Removing grout

The grout between our 4 ½-in. shower tiles has become loose and has fallen out in some places. Outside the tub area it has become discolored. I'd like to regrout, but how does the amateur remove the old grout—high speed grinder, muriatic acid, or what?—S. B. Ohrenstein, Burbank, Calif.

You've got your work cut out for you, but loose grout can be removed with a sharp tool such as an ice pick or awl. While applying pressure, repeatedly draw the tool through the joint. Leave any tight grout in place. A putty knife may be helpful in removing any bumpy or rough pieces still clinging to the joint. There are several tile cleaners on the market, since many contain some muriatic acid, wear rubber gloves and protect your eyes with goggles. I have had success with a cleaner and Brillo soap pads. Remove all traces of the pad with soap and water. Since success depends to a large part upon the age and type tile you have, experiment on a tile in an inconspicuous place first.

Camouflaging nail dimples

How do we camouflage the occasional nail dimples that annoyingly appear in the ceiling of our new home?—Sue Hall, Tipton, Iowa

Your problem isn't uncommon. In defense of the spackler, these dimples probably didn't show under daylight conditions, when he finished them. You can purchase ready mixed joint compound (it'll keep for long periods when tightly sealed), and a 4-in. spackle finishing knife. With a small amount of compound on the knife, hold the blade at a 30° angle to the ceiling and draw it firmly over the dimple. The dimple will be filled flush to the adjacent surface. When it's dry, sand patch lightly with fine sandpaper. Touch up with paint.

Applying veneer

I have a chest of drawers that I bought used. The drawers have lost nearly all their veneer due, I suppose, to dampness or flood. I'd like to salvage the piece by placing new veneers on the drawer fronts. But these are curved and I have no way of clamping the veneers in place. Any suggestions for salvaging the chest?—Frank Atherton, Atlanta, Ga.

I'd suggest you use the specially processed, paper-thin wood veneers (1/64-in. thickness). These can be applied with contact cement, which requires no clamping. The veneers come in a variety of common cabinet woods in sheets 8 ft. long and widths of 18, 24 and 36 in. Before laying the veneer, clean the drawer fronts thoroughly, removing all old veneer and glue. Then cut the sheets about ½ in. oversize and coat both sheet and drawer front with cement. Allow to dry tacky, as instructed on the containers, then locate the sheet and roll on by hand as illustrated. Press firmly into contact with a roller. An old wooden rolling pin covered with felt works nicely. When the veneer is firmly bonded in place, trim the excess edges carefully with a sharp utility knife.

Constantine Veneer Glue can be used to glue thicker 1/28-in. veneer without the use of clamps. It is available from Albert Constantine and Son, 2050 Eastchester Rd., Bronx, N.Y. 10461.

Double helping

The previous owner of my home re-sided over the original asbestos shingles and reroofed over the original asphalt roof. Is this good practice?—Kirk Williams, Newburgh, N.Y.

Yes. In fact, it's common to cover existing siding and roofing. Use solid crown molding to fill the gap between the casing face and the new line of shingles. A more expensive way is to extend the casings out to receive the added thickness. Some sidings have their own channel or J-type trim that is nailed to the face of existing trim to receive new siding.

When reroofing, make sure the added load doesn't overstress your roof. Check with your local building department before proceeding. Make sure nails are long enough to penetrate layers of original material. You may need 1¾-in. nails.

Crazed lavatory

In our bathroom, we have a marbleized plastic vanity top. The countertop still looks new, but the lavatory is disfigured, with a network of fine surface cracks, similar to crazing in chinaware. Heavy hand sanding did not remove these cracks. As replacement would be difficult and expensive, is there a special plastic paint or coating I could use to fill these cracks?—Lester L. Myers, Fort Wayne, Ind.

A check with one source that has manufactured these countertops for 13 years brought out the following: You can purchase a clear, casting resin such as 132 Alplex, which is made by Adhesive Products. It's available at hobby stores or plastic supplies.

After fine-sanding the work surface, mix the material and apply it with a brush. Clean the lavatory thoroughly and be sure to follow mixing instructions. A fine sanding preceding a second coat may be required. Wear gloves and goggles, and ventilate the work area while applying.

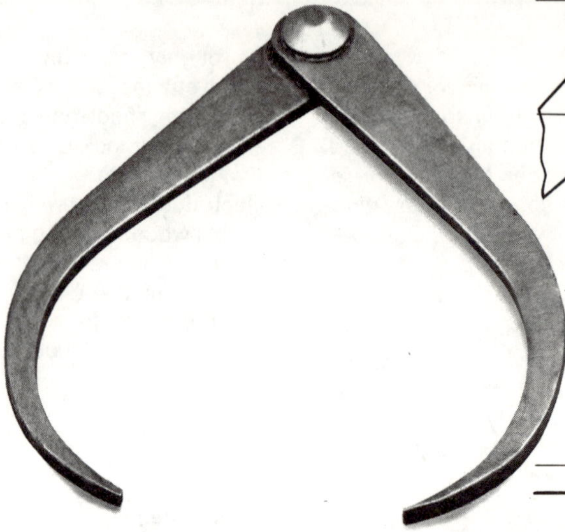

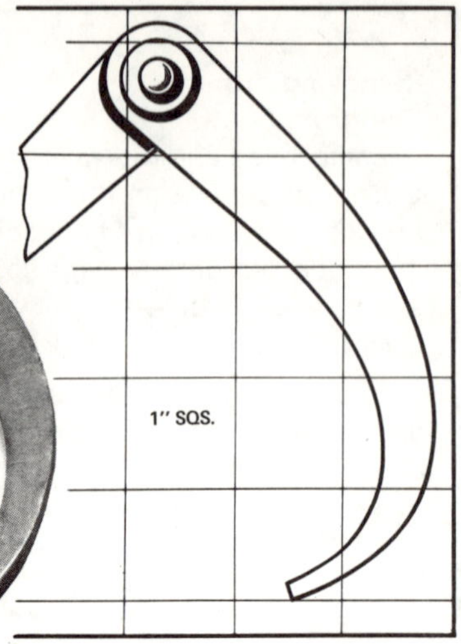

Eight fine tools you can make

By DAVID WARREN

By saving parts of old tools, metal, and scraps of wood you can make these handy tools

FRICTION-FIT CALIPERS ARE FAST-ADJUSTING

If you have a wood lathe and haven't bought a pair of calipers, don't. You can make a dandy 6-in. pair of friction calipers for far less than you can buy them. They're fast adjusting, for you simply pull them open or squeeze them shut. The legs are held with a roundhead rivet and spring washer. Make a pattern following the drawing above on blue $^{3}/_{32}$-in. Starret ground flat stock. Scribe the outline on it and cut out with a metal-cutting blade. Finish the sharp edges with a file. Be sure to use a spring washer under the rivet to provide the necessary friction fit

THERE ARE ANY NUMBER of hand tools and fixtures you can make for little or nothing. The eight shown here will prove extra handy at your drill press, lathe and bench. Among them is a fixture called a bench hook that hooks over a bench to hold small work for sawing, filing and the like. Shown in its simplest form, it can be made without much trouble and with a few boards you probably have around the shop.

Another simple item to make is a V-block which is used to cradle and hold dowels and other turnings when the job calls for drilling a hole through a piece dead-center. You will find it to be very valuable and there should be one near any drill press. Old worn-out bastard mill files make great scraping tools for woodturning when bevel-ground and fitted with a long handle. And you can't beat a pair of friction-type calipers for fast adjusting. It's a tool you can make from a couple of pieces of flat metal and a rivet. These are just some of the homemade tools suggested on these pages.

LATHE CHISELS FROM OLD FILES

You can make a scraping tool for your lathe from an old file. If the file is long, shorten it to about 10 in. Grind it smooth at the tip, then grind a 60° bevel. Hone the bevel but don't remove the wire edge—it helps the scraping action. Fit it with an 11-in. hardwood handle

TWO-FACED SANDER

With ¼-in. cork glued to one side and $^{3}/_{16}$-in. leather to the other, this sanding block keeps sandpaper from clogging and glazing. A 1 x 1½ x 5½-in. wood block fits the hand nicely and is the right size to take a quarter sheet of sandpaper. Use white glue to attach the leather and cork facings. Your hand holds the paper in place when you grip the block for sanding

HANDY BENCH HOOK

For hand work at the bench you can't beat a bench hook for holding work and protecting the bench's top. Generally it is used with a backsaw but you won't be using it just to saw—you'll be filing on it, chiseling and the like. It's nothing more than a flat board with cleats attached to opposite sides and ends so you can flip it over and use both sides. It's easy to replace

SAVE THAT BROKEN SLEDGE HANDLE

When you're swinging a sledge and wind up with a handle in your hand and no sledge, don't toss it away. The broken handle from a sledge, ax or ball bat provides the best kind of hardwood (hickory and ash) for turning new handles for files and beat-up chisels. The handle for a socket chisel is a simple tapered turning, and when fitting a handle to a chisel with a tang, you can size the collar for a drive-fit ferrule cut from thinwall conduit or brass tubing. For the final step, apply a 50/50 solution of shellac and linseed oil to the wood

SHOOTING BOARD PRODUCES SQUARE EDGES

A shooting board is a handy gadget for squaring the edge of a board when you don't have a jointer. The plane is used on its side and is pushed back and forth along a wood fence. The work is placed against a stop and on top of the fence. The plane removes the stock overhanging the fence. Tapered stop fits tapered dado and wedges in place. Lower edge chamfer forms dust groove

YOUR DRILL PRESS SHOULD HAVE A V-BLOCK

V-blocks are needed at the drill press to hold round stock securely and facilitate drilling through the exact center. To make one, cut a 1 x 2 x 6-in. hardwood block and run it through your table saw with the blade tilted 45°. Then run it a second time to form a V-groove. If you lack a table saw, you can mark the V and cut it by hand with a backsaw. Finish the shellac and bore a hole in it to hang by your drill press

SCRATCH STOCK FORMS BEAD BY SCRATCHING SURFACE

When you want to form a small bead along the edge of a table leg or apron, you can do it with a homemade tool called a scratch stock. It's made to fit over the edge of the work and cuts by scraping. All it consists of are two pieces of wood with a blade clamped between. The blade is made from a short piece of hacksaw blade ground to the shape you want. The photo shows the blade pulled out so you can see it. In use, only the tip is exposed in the very corner of the U-shaped block. It makes the neatest beading you ever saw

A SCRAP PIECE OF CARPETING tacked over part of your workbench top offers all sorts of advantages. For one, it acts as a protective pad to prevent finished surfaces from being scratched. Also, the rough texture will keep small parts from rolling off the bench. Finally, it makes an excellent work surface for any glass-cutting jobs in the shop.—*Frank Shore.*

MADE FROM SCRAP stock, this simple jig is designed to guide the drill bit when you drill dowel holes. It allows you to drill in a plane perpendicular to the face of the work. Just cut the filler block sections to form a close-fitting square channel for the drill bit. The rear piece is clamped against the work. To aid in positioning, scribe a reference mark on the front of the rail block, locating it in line with the square guide hole and parallel to the hole's vertical axis.—*F. Louis Rush.*

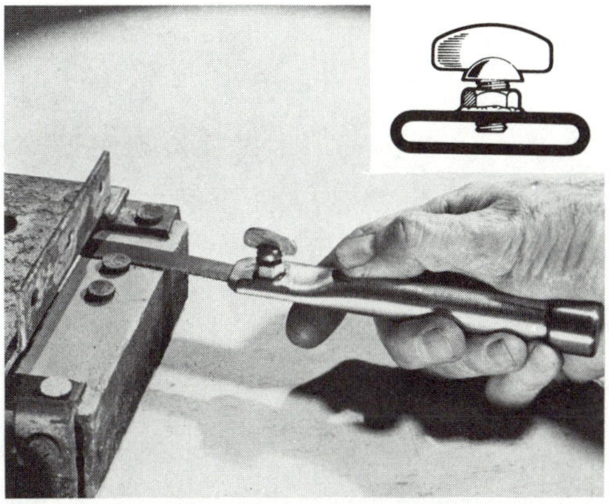

THIS IMPROVISED TOOL is a lifesaver for jobs requiring the use of a hacksaw in tight quarters where the regular handle won't fit. Cut a 6-in. length of ½-in.-dia. tubing and hammer one end almost flat, leaving a slot just wide enough to take the hacksaw blade. Next, drill a 5/16-in. hole through one side of this flattened portion and solder a ¼-in. nut over the hole. Fit a ¼-in. thumbscrew in the nut, then insert the blade to the desired length and use the screw to clamp it securely in the handle.—*W. Herbert Neander.*

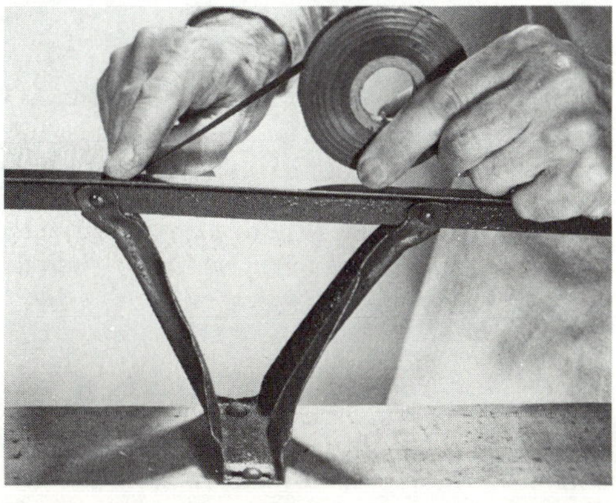

NOTHING SLOWS DOWN a sled like rusty runners, yet it's almost impossible to prevent rust from forming because the exposed bare metal surfaces of the runners are usually damp when the sled is put away. Of course, one precaution you can take is to wipe the runners dry, but this doesn't protect them from moisture in the air. A more efficient idea is to dry the runners, then cover them with two long strips of plastic tape. It's a simple solution, but it works.—*Glen Wilson.*

How to select a modern shotgun

By GARY GILLESPIE

Whether it be for skeet, trap or game, you are faced with a large assortment of guns from which to make a final choice. Here are the basics you should know before you choose a shotgun which is suited to your activities

SEE ALSO
Gun cabinets . . . Gun racks . . . Hunting . . . Marksmanship . . . Muzzleloading . . . Shooting

IN A COUNTRY once described as a "nation of riflemen," the shotgun has become America's most widely used and versatile hunting and target tool. True, the rifle remains king for certain types of long-range accuracy, particularly for big game. But in all-around use, the scattergun now ranks first across fields and forests, trap and skeet ranges. As proof of this popularity, there now exists a wide variety of shotgun models, actions, gauges and prices.

To anyone in the market for the latest in smoothbores, this presents a problem and an opportunity. It is difficult to choose from so many options, but there is also a better chance to find a shotgun particularly suited to your activities.

☐ *Single shot* is usually the lowest priced action, except for expensive trapshooting models. With simple "break-open" design, it is a popular beginner's gun, particularly in "youth" versions with short stocks. Due to its limiting one-shot feature, however, it is a poor long-term choice for serious hunting.

☐ *Pump action* is a feature of America's basic "bread and butter" shotgun. Its rugged dependable action requires little maintenance. For

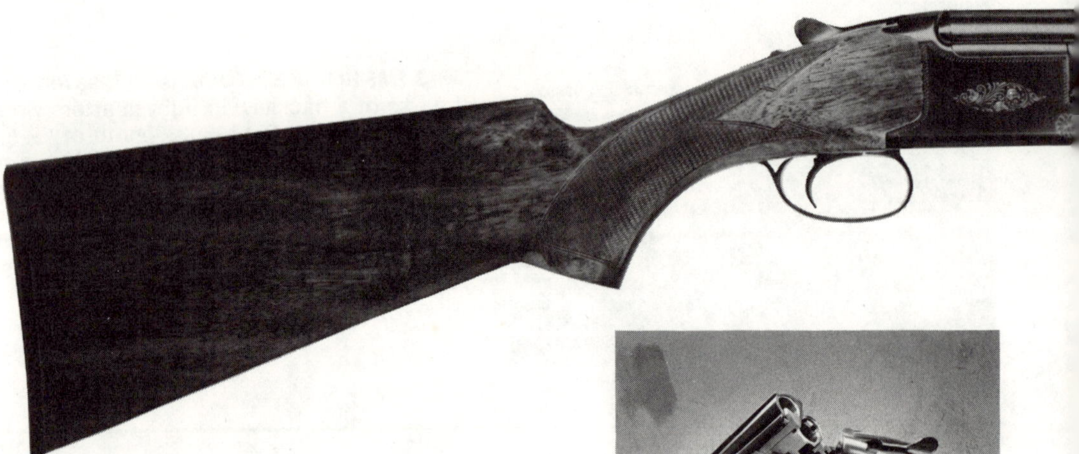

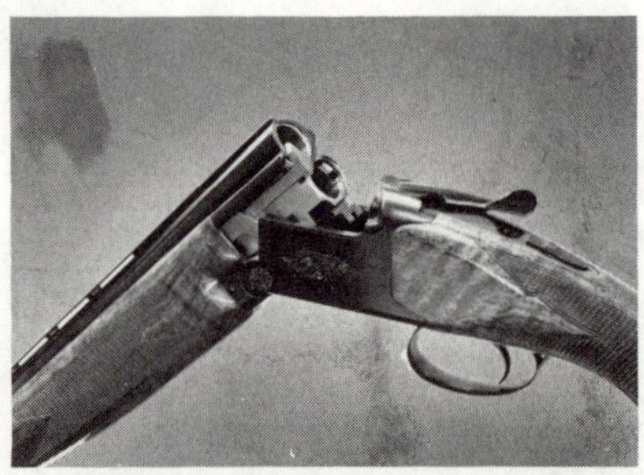

OVER AND UNDERS, like new Browning Liege (above and at top), permit barrels with different chokes on the same gun.

UPLAND GUNNERS prefer a light, fast-handling model, often 20 gauge, for short-range work such as this hunter shooting for quail in the Southwest.

varied types of shooting, look for models permitting interchangeable barrels with different chokes. These can give you, in effect, three shotguns for about 50 percent more than the cost of just one.

☐ *Semiautomatic* is usually called "automatic" or "autoloader." This gun reloads automatically each time you pull the trigger and fire. Automatics are more expensive than pump actions and require more frequent cleaning and maintenance. They are appropriate for all types of hunting and highly versatile when the barrels are interchangeable. They excel for the fast shooting encountered in skeet doubles and such sports as quail and dove hunting. Gas-operated models are lighter in recoil—a worthwhile factor for both youngsters and ladies.

☐ *Bolt-action shotguns* are repeating models that use the familiar rifle-type action. Usually they lack the "feel" and swinging qualities of more common shotgun actions for serious hunting, but can be good, low-priced utility guns for occasional use on garden pests and the like.

☐ *Over-and-under double barrel* models have been growing in popularity recently but generally are the highest priced type of action. Two barrels, positioned one atop the other, permit two chokes on the same gun—open for the first shot and tighter for the second. The over and under is ideal for hunting upland birds such as grouse and pheasant.

☐ *Side-by-side double barrel* has the two barrels positioned horizontally. Advantages are similar to those of over and unders, but these are often lighter and faster handling. For budget buys, look for two-trigger models without automatic ejectors.

☐ *Choke selection* determines the degree of narrowing or constriction at the muzzle or outer end of the barrel. Open chokes such as "skeet" or "improved cylinder" let pellet pattern spread quickly for close shots within 30 yards or less. These open chokes are best for game in close cover. Select intermediate or "modified" choke if your shooting is varied with ranges between 25 and 40 yards. "Full" chokes throw the tightest long-range patterns best for 35 to 50-yard shots when hunting large wary game such as wild turkeys or pass shooting at ducks and geese.

☐ *Gauge designation* tells relative diameter of the barrel. Largest capacity gauges have smallest numbers.

BROWNING LIEGE, with newly popular over-and-under barrels is example of high-quality economy.

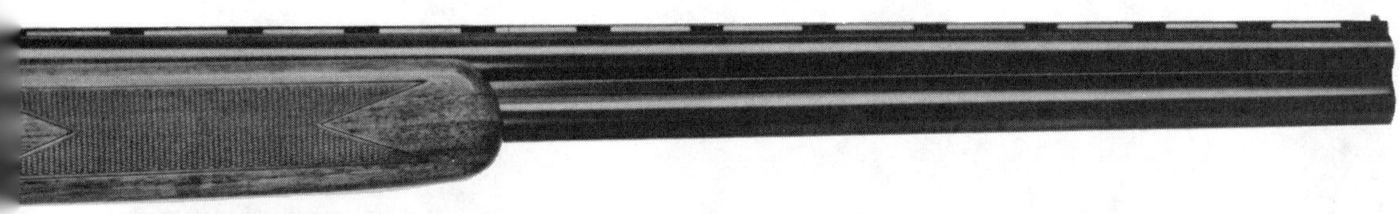

FULLY-EQUIPPED waterfowl hunter can use 20-gauge over decoys; should pass shoot with 12 or 20 magnum.

1. SAVAGE 333, new over and under in 12 or 20 gauge, has ventilated rib, auto ejector and interchangeable barrels. 2. Winchester new single-shot, Model 37A, comes in 12, 16, 20, 28, 410 gauges; has shorter stock for 410, 20. 3. High Standard Supermatic gas-operated autoloaders have 26, 27, 28 or 30-inch barrels. It comes in either 12 or 20 gauge.

4. MOSSBERG MODEL 500 pump comes in 12, 16, 20 gauges. Pederson Custom Guns will feature fitting, import actions. 5. Marlin 120 Magnum 12-gauge pump has 3-inch or standard shells. The trap 120 has a Monte Carlo stock and a 30-inch barrel. 6. Remington's 3200 is a modernized version of the famous Model 32. O/U 12-gauge field, trap and skeet models are available.

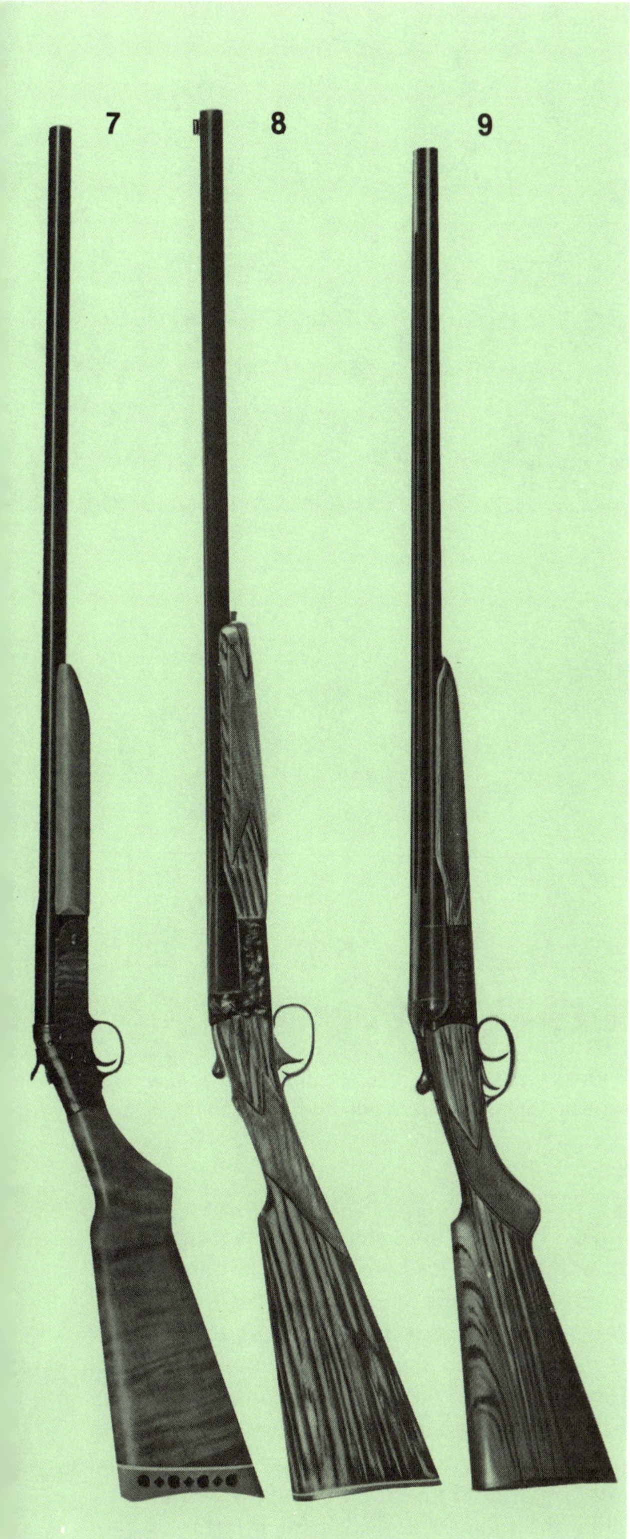

7. HARRINGTON & RICHARDS Model 158 is a single-shot gun that is available in 12, 16, 20 and 410 gauges. 8. Ithaca Gun's new double-barrel Model 280 side-by-side in 12 and 20-gauge has traditional English-style stock. 9. Beretta GR-2 from Garcia is a classic side-by-side double which is available in either 12 or magnum 20-gauge with double triggers.

SEARS EXTENSIVE gun line, all tested by Ted Williams, includes this low-recoil auto. Here Williams is holding the O/U Magnum 12.

10-gauge: Uncommon today. Found only in a few double-barrel shotguns.

12-gauge: The most popular gauge. Appropriate for all target shooting and hunting; best choice for the one-shotgun man who hunts a variety of game.

16-gauge: Declining in use, superseded by heavier loads in some 20-gauge shells.

20-gauge: Good choice for upland game where faster, lighter handling helps. Adequate for ducks over decoys; not for pass shooting. Lighter recoil aids beginners, ladies.

28-gauge: Fast handling with no noticeable recoil, but light shot charge restricts it to experienced gunners hunting small upland birds at short range.

410-gauge: Light shot charge is more likely to cripple than down game. Best reserved for target use or pests of barn-pigeon category. Don't choose 410 for beginners; it's a difficult tool, for experts only.

☐ *Magnum* shotguns in 12 and 20 gauges will take larger shells that open to 3 inches after firing, rather than the standard length of 2¾ inches. Heavier shot charges give greater range.

☐ *Rifled slugs* fit any shotgun, are slightly more accurate in skeet or improved cylinders. Slug barrels with rifle sights are available.

☐ *Selection* should be based on good feel and fit of gun, recommendations of friends, considerable shopping and catalog study. A good dealer can order specific models. Young beginners might start with a 20-gauge pump with shortened stock. For waterfowling, pick 12 or 12 magnum pump or autoloader. Same gun with interchangeable barrels or adjustable choke, or 20-gauge magnum, is a good all-around choice. For short-range upland game, a 20-gauge is suitable, while long range requires 12-gauge or 20-gauge magnum.

And the best buy? An American 12-gauge pump action with interchangeable barrels or adjustable choke probably offers the most for the money.

Build a shuffleboard table

By CARROLL G. HAKENSON

Table shuffleboard can be a fun game for up to four people. When you make the table yourself, complete with inlaid scoring zones and weighted pucks, it adds to your enjoyment

HERE'S A GIFT the whole family can enjoy —a table shuffleboard. The waxed bed is of solid-core birch plywood with the scoring zones inlaid with strips of ⅛ x ⅛-in. walnut. The grooves for the inlays are saw kerfs made on the bench saw.

The 1x3 birch rails have interlocking joints at the corners. To make such joints, you first groove the end rails to the depth shown. Then you cut the ⅛-in. slot and tab with one cut at right angles to the groove. To make the side rails, after cutting a ⅛-in. notch in the end of the rail as shown, you turn the rail over and make a second cut to create a ⅛-in. tab. Finally, a ⅛-in. slot is made to the depth shown. To make the rubber bumpers, insert ⅛" dowels in surgical tubing and cement to the side rails.

The 12 weighted pucks are mass-produced from ⅝-in.-thick wood in the following manner. First the wood is clamped to the drill-press table and a ¾-in. hole is bored completely through the wood. Then, without unclamping the work, the ¾-in. bit is replaced with a hole saw and a 2-in. plug is cut completely through the wood. Next a same-size Formica disc is cut with the hole saw and cemented to the bottom of the puck. Now the outer edge of the puck is smoothed by holding it lightly against a disc sander, after which the top and bottom edges are chamfered slightly by hand with a flat file. Finally, each puck is weighted by filling the center hole with molten lead and capping with a metal chair glide. Each set of three pucks is color-coded by painting the tops.

To make the storage wells, bore 2-in. holes completely through the ¾-in. thickness. Then ⅛-in. tempered hardboard is glued to the underside and 1-in. finger holes are bored in the center of the 2-in. holes.

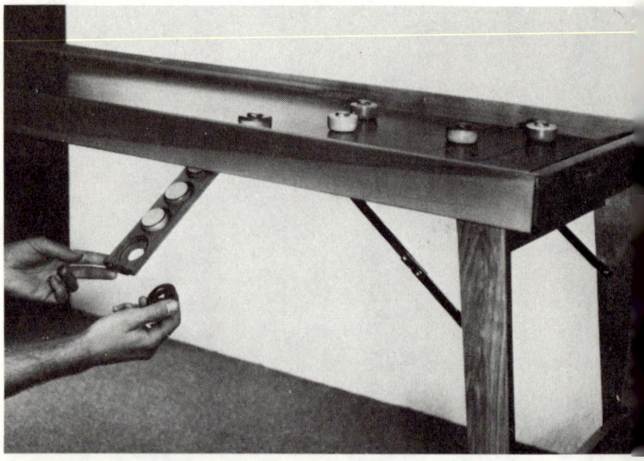

SHUFFLEBOARD weights are stored in the hinged rack beneath table. Each rack will hold six weights.

SEE ALSO
Air games . . . Backgammon tables . . .
Bridge sets . . . Caddies, table tennis . . .
Chess sets . . . Cribbage boards . . .
Family rooms . . . Game tables . . . Pool tables

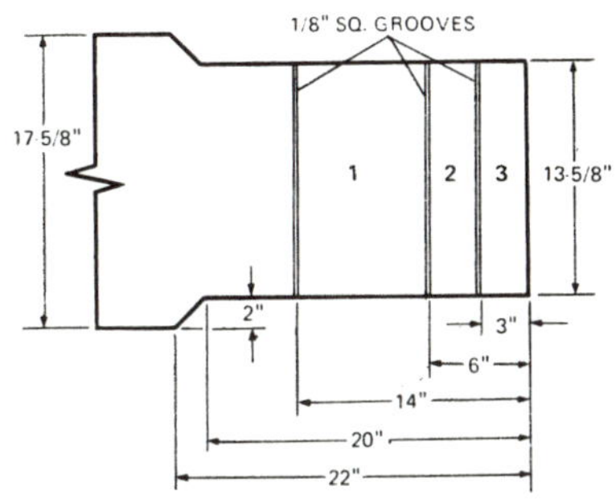

Rules for Shuffleboard

Number of players: Two, three or four.

Object of game is to slide weight down the table, with one rebound off side bumper, and have it land in one of three zones. Nearest zone counts one point, middle zone two points, end zone three points, overhanging weight four points. Score goes to player who has weights ahead of his opponent's. Only weights ahead of the opponent's weights are counted when you're scoring.

Each player has three weights per turn; first player to score 21 wins. Players alternate shots, scorer shoots first on next round.

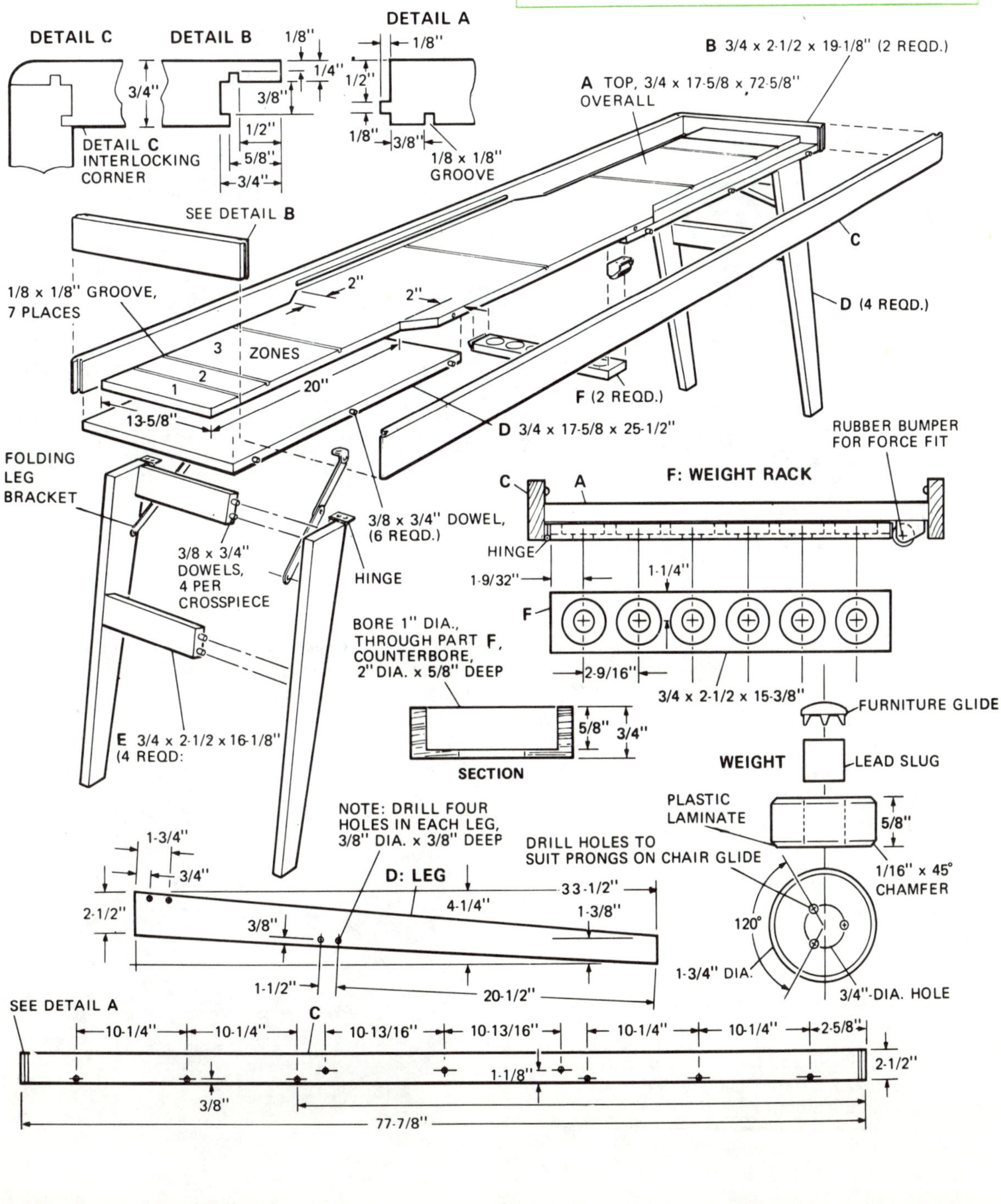

All about siding

By MORT SCHULTZ

■ SINCE THE MATERIAL you use to re-side your home will probably be with you for a long time, take a few minutes to consider all the possibilities. In this article we'll discuss the relative merits—and demerits—of metal sidings (aluminum and steel), vinyl siding, natural wood, and combination wood and synthetic compound (hardwood and plywood) which we will refer to

SEE ALSO

Hardboard . . . House additions . . . Ladders . . . Lumber . . . Nails . . . Remodeling, exterior . . . Scaffolding . . . Sheathing

QUALITY PLYWOOD siding can approximate the look of vertical cedar siding—especially if the horizontal joints between panels are carefully worked into a house's design as visual elements.

as sheet siding. Asbestos is not considered since leading manufacturers have discontinued production because of the health problems associated with it. Masonry siding will also be considered a separate topic.

which is best?

Each siding material has its advantages and disadvantages. The one you choose for your home will probably be selected on the basis of budget, esthetic preference, and/or willingness to put up with certain drawbacks. For example, some homeowners want to avoid painting, no matter what. They shy away from wood and sheet siding and end up paying more money for vinyl or metal. [When speaking about metal siding, we mean aluminum, primarily. However, what is true of aluminum is basically true of steel. Steel siding is stronger than aluminum and offers the advantage of not denting as easily; but it costs 30 to 40 percent more than aluminum and has not been in demand.]

Other homeowners don't think the additional cost is worth the advantages that vinyl and aluminum offer. Furthermore, they want the greater selection of styles and colors afforded by wood and sheet siding.

what about cost?

As matters stand, homeowners have made aluminum the best selling siding material. Over 10 million homes have been sided with aluminum. Cost? A company in my area a few years ago offered to re-side 24x36-ft. ranch houses with 8-in. clapboard aluminum for $3500. The product the company presented sounded like good quality material, being manufactured by Alcan, Revere or Kaiser. Investigation revealed, however, that the material was not outfitted with backer board, which gives siding more insulating value. The addition of backer board adds $1000 to $2000 to the cost of the job, depending on the type and thickness of the backer board. Learn a lesson from this to be sure that you know exactly what you are going to get for the quoted price.

Vinyl is next in line as the best selling siding material, with wood and sheet siding following. The cost of contractor-installed vinyl siding is 20 to 30 percent more than aluminum.

There is no way to pinpoint accurately the cost of wood and sheet siding. Cost varies significantly from type to type, from locale to locale and from week to week because of fluctuating building-product prices. Generally, though, the cost of re-siding a home with wood, plywood or

VINYL SIDINGS come in 8-in. (top photo) and double 4-in. lap panels. They are available in several colors, untextured or with a wood-grain texture. Use of backer board (A) under vinyl or aluminum siding increases their insulative value while reducing noise infiltration. There is a wide variety of styles that range from a rough-sawn shingled look in aluminum (B) to a vinyl embossed with a barn-board-like texture (C).

COST INDEX COMPARISON: WOOD AND SHEET SIDING

Type of Siding	Rating
Hardboard, lap or panel, textured	100
Hardboard, lap or panel, smooth	90
3/8" plywood—cedar and southern pine	93
Superior-grade wood drop siding—horizontal and vertical Douglas fir and southern pine	314
Cedar siding, unseasoned and rough-sawn face—vertical siding with battens	100
Tropical hardwood (shorea), bevel siding	314
Cedar hand-split shakes	141

* Calculated using hardboard textured siding as base of 100.

CEDAR SHINGLES? No, they're actually horizontal strips of hardboard embossed to look like courses of shingles. "Courses" are available in 16-ft. lengths.

hardboard is 25 to 40 percent *less* than re-siding with aluminum.

The chart shown here, prepared by the Weyerhaeuser Co., compares price differences between natural wood, plywood and hardboard. It shows that hardboard and plywood sidings are comparable in cost with lesser-grade solid lumber materials. However, the cost of superior grade solid lumber siding is higher than that of sheet siding.

wood and sheet types

Hardboard siding is composed of wood fibers that are combined with resins and other synthetic compounds. The materials are permanently bonded under heat and pressure into boards or panels that will withstand exposure to the elements.

Siding made of hardboard is grainless. Where finished panels have a wood-grain appearance, the grain has been embossed into the panel. In other words, the grain is simulated. Hardboard siding is available unprimed (least expensive), primed (moderately expensive) and prefinished (most expensive). A suitable quality of such siding is at least 7/16 in. thick. The material comes in two general styles: lap (or clapboard) and panel.

Lap denotes boards that are 16 ft. long and of varying widths (6, 9, 12 in. and so forth), which are installed horizontally. The panel style is available in panels measure 4x8, 4x9 and 4x12 ft. or larger. These panels are nailed to a structure so the long dimension runs vertically. The most readily available size is 4x8 ft., however. Longer sizes may have to be specially ordered.

variety of hardboard siding

Hardboard lap sidings are available several ways:

- Prefinished or primed horizontal clapboard style.
- Unprimed or primed horizontal clapboard style with a simulated rough cedar texture.
- Unprimed simulated wood-shingle siding.
- Primed or unprimed lap siding with a simulated rough-sawn surface.

Similarly, hardboard panel sidings can be bought in the following forms:

- Prefinished or unprimed simulated cypress. Panel edges are shiplapped with ½-in. V-grooves, 8 in. on center, to provide the appearance of individual vertical planks.
- Prestained, primed or unprimed simulated

HARDBOARD panels simulating stone aggregate finish are available.

SIDING: ADVANTAGES AND DISADVANTAGES

	Aluminum	Vinyl	Steel	Hard-board	Ply-wood	Natural Wood (Painted)
No refinishing needed	■	■	■			
Won't split, crack or warp	■	1	■			
Won't blister, peel or flake	■	0	■			
Resists stains	2	2	2, 3			
Won't show scratches	4	■	4			
Won't rot	■	■	■	5		
Resists dents		■	■	■	■	■
Electrically nonconductive	6	■	6	■	■	■
Fire-resistant	■	7	■			
Noiseless	8	■	8	■	■	■
Immune to insects (termites, carpenter ants)	■	■	■			
Comparable ease of installation	Average	Hard	Hardest	Easy	Easiest	Easy

1. Some critics contend that vinyl may crack in extreme cold weather, but others view this as inaccurate.
2. Staining materials usually wash away with rain runoff. If not, a heavy hosing may work. Stubborn stains can usually be eliminated with soap and water or household cleaners.
3. If burred edges are present when siding is installed, rust may form.
4. If scratches aren't treated, corrosion (aluminum) or rust (steel) may form.
5. Not usually.
6. Requires grounding.
7. Polyvinyl chloride products are not combustible, but they will smolder and emit toxic gases when in a fire.
8. Critics contend that a metal siding will amplify the noise of rain and hail. However, the use of backer board will reduce the noise level.

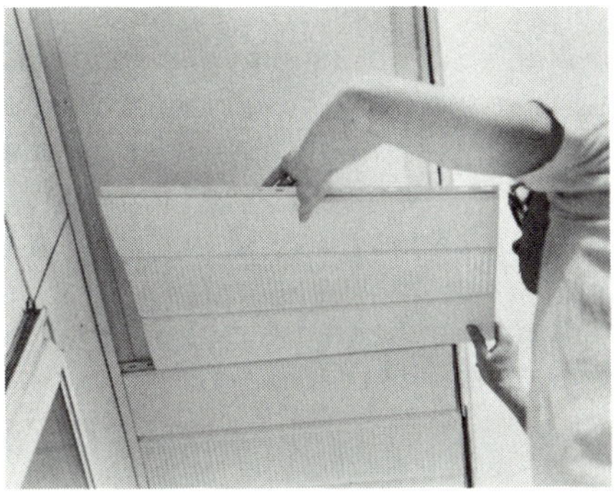

ALUMINUM and vinyl manufacturers provide soffits, fascia and trim.

SIDING: INSULATION (R FACTOR)

Material	Resistance (R)
5/16" plywood	.40
3/8" plywood	.48
1/2" plywood	.64
5/8" plywood	.77
7/16" hardboard	.62
.035" vinyl siding and .024" aluminum siding	.87
.035" vinyl siding and .024" aluminum siding with insulating backing material	2.5-6.0*

* Actual insulating value depends on thickness and makeup of backing material, and construction techniques. For example, more air space, thus greater insulating value, is obtained by nailing to furring strips instead of directly to old siding. Thicker backer boards have higher R values; thus polystyrene backer board offers a greater insulating effect than aluminum reflector foil.

A QUALITY JOB includes foam-board insulation and attention given to details. Jamb extenders should always be used to build a window frame so it will extend beyond the new siding surface. The best way to be sure is to inspect at least three jobs by a reputable contractor before you hire him.

rough-sawn cedar with ¾-in.-wide square-cut grooves on 8-in. centers. Also unprimed board-and-batten panels. Battens are integral (they come attached to panels) on 12-in. centers to reduce installation time.

■ Primed or prefinished smooth or wood-grained panels with grooves on 8-in. centers or battens on 12-in. centers.

■ Prefinished or primed panels having a simulated skip-troweled stucco texture or aggregate stone appearance.

plywood siding

Plywood siding is a construction of wood veneers that are bonded together with exterior-grade adhesives. The surface of plywood is real wood—not simulated. The siding is manufactured from lumber—usually southern pine, fir or cedar—not from wood fibers as in the case of hardboard.

As with hardboard, plywood siding comes in lap and panel styles: unfinished, primed or prefinished. Varieties are numerous, but not as many as hardboard. For example, siding having a shingle or stucco appearance is not available.

High quality solid lumber siding comes available in clapboard panels and shingles. Surface finishes are grained and rough-sawn.

metal and vinyl types

Compared to wood and sheet sidings, metal and vinyl sidings come in a limited number of styles. They are virtually maintenance-free and the colors are fast. Painting or staining is not necessary. This fact alone makes metal and vinyl very popular.

At one time, metal had the advantage of outpacing vinyl in the number of colors it offered consumers. It still does, but the gap has closed. You can select from as many as 9 different colors when choosing vinyl siding and up to 12 colors from one manufacturer of metal siding.

Neither do you have to settle for the traditional smooth 8-in. or double 4-in. lap panels with vinyl siding. The "woodsy" look (simulated, of course) is available. For example, Bird & Son manufacture a solid vinyl siding called Woodside. The 8-in. and double 4-in. lap panels display a wood-grain face in each of the six colors offered.

Aluminum siding, however, does provide greater versatility than vinyl. In aluminum, you can select from the traditional smooth clapboard look (8-in. or double 4-in.) and from panels having a wood-grain appearance, a rough-sawn surface, vertical board-and-batten or vertical walnut look and hand-split shingle appearance.

Test data from Alsco Anaconda and Champion Building Products demonstrates that metal and vinyl with backer board have greater insulating properties than wood and sheet siding. Assuming that new siding will be applied over existing siding, the chart shown is a summary of relative R values. (The R value denotes the efficiency of insulating materials; higher R numbers have greater resistance to passage of heat.)

warranty: more than a number

Champion Building Products offers a three-year warranty. Masonite offers five-year and 15-year warranties, depending upon the product. Hunter Douglas and GAF offer 20-year warranties. Bird & Son, Certain-Teed and Alsco Anaconda offer 40-year warranties.

Length of warranty is important, to be sure, but what the warranty covers is just as important.

Let's consider two typical warranties: those from Bird and GAF. Both companies make vinyl siding. Bird warrants that its vinyl siding panels and accessories (soffits, fascia and rain carrying equipment) are "free from manufacturing defects and won't corrode, blister, peel or flake, won't conduct electricity as to require grounding, and won't deteriorate as a result of salt spray, wind-blown sand or termite activity."

It assumes 100-percent responsibility for the first three years. If defective, the siding will be replaced without charge.

In the ensuing 37 years, if a defect is found with Bird's siding, the company will contribute the following percentage toward repair or replacement cost: First year, 90 percent; second, 80; third, 70 percent; fourth, 60 percent; fifth, 50 percent; sixth, 40 percent; seventh, 30 percent; 8th through 16th, 20 percent; and for the 17th through 37th, 10 percent.

GAF warrants that its vinyl siding panels are free from peeling, flaking, rusting, blistering, corroding "or other conditions" arising from manufacturing defects. It will assume 100 percent of the cost of repair or replacement during the first five years up to a maximum of $150 per 100 sq. ft. From the 6th through the 10th year, the company will assume 50 percent of the cost up to a maximum of $75 per 100 square feet. From the 11th through the 20th year, the amount of responsibility assumed is reduced by 5 percent each year from the 6th through the 10th year. (Note: These figures were in effect when this article was written. Before you purchase any siding ask for a copy of the warranty in writing.)

Bird's warranty can be transferred to someone who buys your home. The GAF warranty is non-transferable.

picking a contractor

Along with consulting the Better Business Bureau and Chamber of Commerce, you should follow these suggestions when seeking a contractor:

1. Ask for and check references. Do this by calling the homeowner. Ask for any problems or delays he may have experienced working with the contractor.

2. Ask the contractor questions based on information contained in installation manuals. You can get the installation manual for the type of siding you are putting on the house by writing to the siding manufacturer. If you are installing aluminum siding, request a manual called *Aluminum Siding Application Manual* from the Architectural Aluminum Manufacturers Assn., 35 East Wacker Drive, Chicago, IL 60601, or from the Aluminum Assn. Inc., 818 Connecticut Ave. N.W., Washington DC 20006. For vinyl siding, write for *Rigid Vinyl Siding Application* to the Society of the Plastics Industry Inc., 355 Lexington Ave., New York, NY 10017.

If I were having vinyl siding installed, some of the questions I would ask a contractor would be:

1. What kind of nail are you going to use? (Answer—Aluminum or another kind of corrosion-resistant nail.)

2. Where will nails be placed? (Answer—Manufacturers provide slots for nails in the siding. Nails will be hidden. Face nailing is not good practice.)

3. How will you make sure that panels are securely tightened? (Answer—I won't. Panels should "float" on nails to allow for expansion and contraction.)

4. How will end joints of adjoining panels be joined? (Answer—They will be overlapped about half length of factory notched cutouts to allow for vinyl's movement as temperature changes.)

5. My home is finished in stucco. How are you going to get siding attached evenly? (Answer—We use furring strips and shim to get an even, nailable base.)

THESE BEFORE-AND-AFTER photos were taken during the first and last weeks of the same month. The old siding (left photo) was cracked and peeling and often needed paint.

By HARRY WICKS

Re-siding: you can do it yourself

LIKE MANY HOMEOWNERS, I simply grew tired of repainting my house every few years. That, plus the fact that I had the unrewarding experience of having paint blister, peel and scale

SEE ALSO

House additions . . . Ladders . . . Lumber . . . Remodeling, exterior . . . Scaffolding . . . Sheathing

text continues on page 2781

WITH ONE SIDE completed, the author and a friend work their way up the front of the house.

MINERAL SIDING can be worked easily with tools most do-it-yourself enthusiasts have at hand. Shingles come in 4-ft. lengths in your choice of nine colors. Scaffolding makes the job far easier and is well worth rental fee. Without it, some siding jobs would become virtually impossible. A close-up view of the totally prefinished siding (left) shows its attractive wood-grain surface and texture.

Why the job was necessary

A STUDY OF the old clapboard siding makes clear why still another paint job held so little appeal. The same sections of the house, shown with the old siding and the new mineral shingles, show how great a difference can be made by new siding. At the time of these photos, the last paint job was only two years old. It had included a thorough scraping, spot priming with aluminum paint, an alkyd prime coat, topped with an alkyd finish coat. Bays between the studs had been vented. But still the paint cracked and blistered. We used quality paint throughout—but it failed. The decision for new siding wasn't difficult to make.

Getting ready for the siding

THE FIRST STEP is to remove all attachments such as shutters (left) and the flower box beneath windows (center). Molding at the soffit-wall joint also comes off. In this instance, workmen replaced that strip of molding with a double layer of wood lath so as to avoid changing the original profile.

re-siding your house, continued

Applying the siding

STAPLING 15-lb. alphalt-saturated felt over the old siding is the first step in installing the new material. Then nail wood lath below the butt edges of the old clapboards wherever you find them needed to provide a solid nailing base. Next, install corner mold at both ends of the wall run (top, right). To install a corner, drive nails through the trim's flanges into clapboard butt edges. Then apply double lath (lower left) to the lowest clapboard. A backing strip goes under each shingle end joint (bottom, center). A long level or chalkline serves to level the panel (bottom, right) and three nails are driven home. You're on your way.

KICK-STRIP UNDERCOURSE, a special plastic shim strip to get an architectural shadowline under shingle butts (far left), sits atop each course. Just press it down firmly around the top of each shingle panel. To ensure staggered joints, start the first course with a full 48-in. panel. Then second and third courses start with half and quarter lengths respectively (near left).

Fitting siding around windows and doors

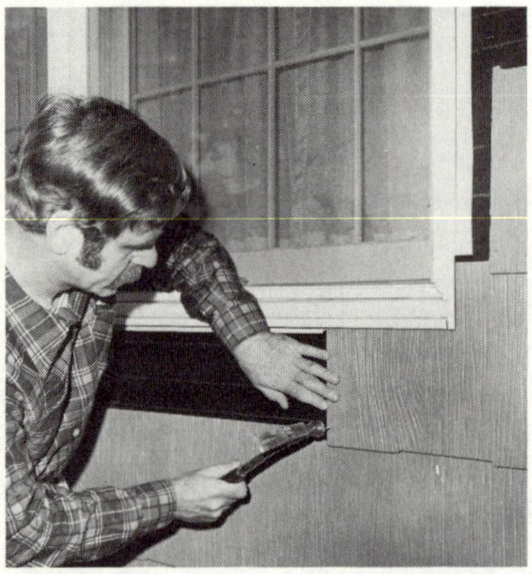

BEFORE SHINGLES go on, install J-channel on all casings around windows and doors (drawing, facing page). When you get to a window, you'll have to cut—and maybe notch—a shingle. Hold it in place and mark it for the cutting operation (left and center photos). Doors, as you'd expect, are treated in the same way (right).

Scribing inside corners

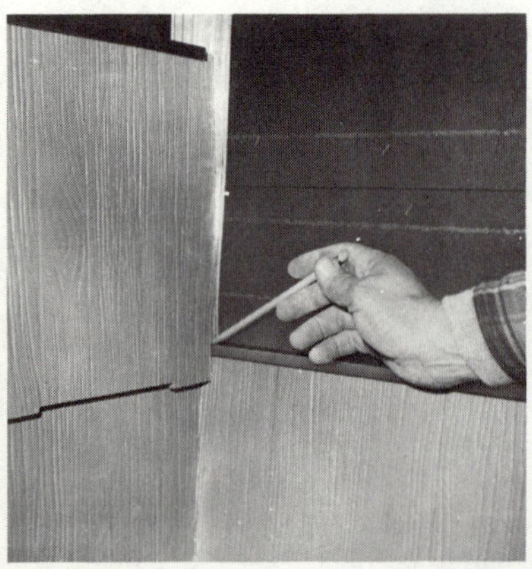

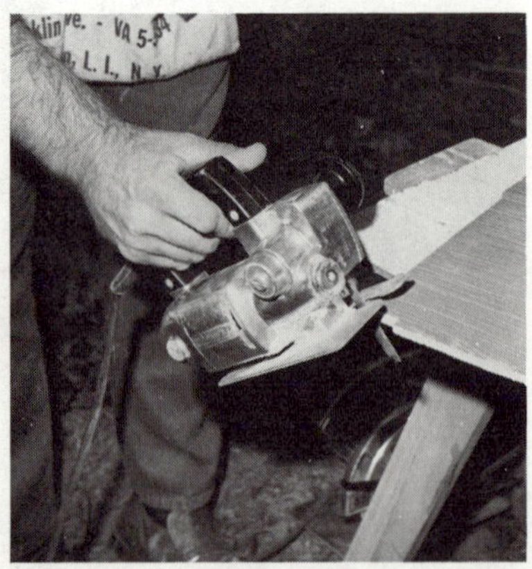

AFTER FELT IS stapled to the existing siding, nail aluminum flashing to inside corners, making a valley for any rainwater seeping into the joint. A corner shingle must be notched for the Kick-Strip it abuts (right). A dust mask would be good to use in cutting shingles; they're generally made of asbestos.

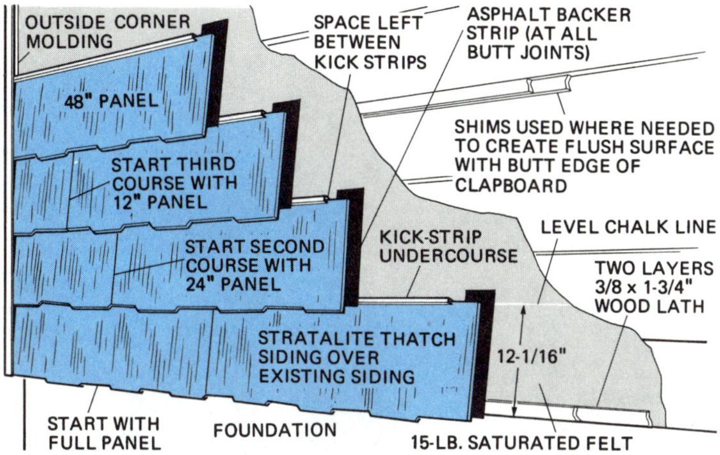

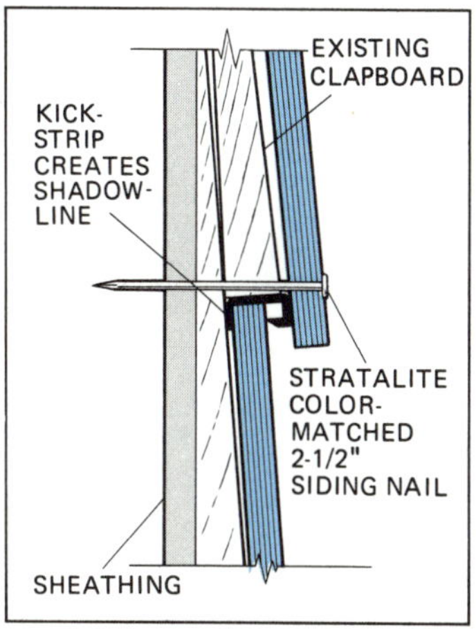

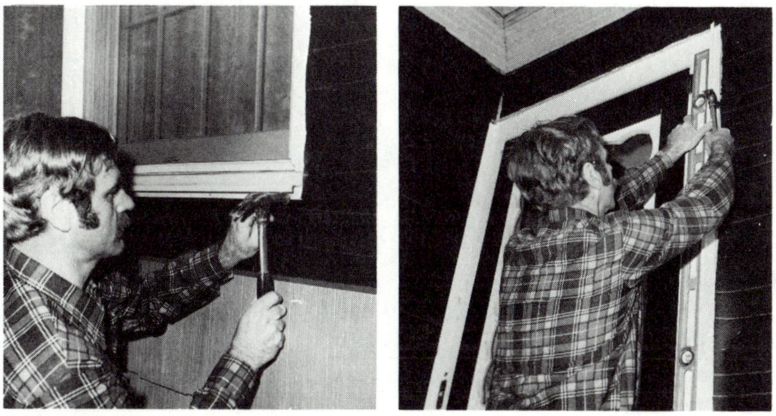

NAIL FIRST J-channel to the sill's underside. Then bobtail the sill ends to accept the vertical channels, which go up next. A spirit level will help the work.

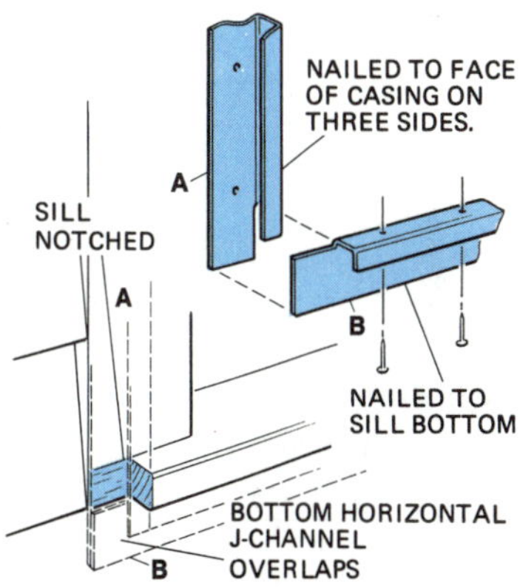

NOTCH all J-channel ends; the horizontal (B) tongue slides into a notch in the vertical piece (A).

re-siding your house continued

A SECOND shingle is held in place and scribed to fit an inside corner.

within two years of painting—despite the hours spent in preparation and painting and the high-quality paint used—meant this was the year for me to re-side rather than repaint.

There were several points to consider when choosing the siding:

First, I wanted my home to present a woodlike appearance that *did not* look factory-made.

Second, due to limited time and equipment, the installation procedure had to be realistically within the range of a do-it-yourselfer.

Working with the materials

TO CUT metal corner moldings and J-channel notches, use a sabre saw with a hacksaw blade.

STRAIGHT CUT on a shingle is made from back. Carbide-tipped blade in a circular saw does best. Use a mask.

re-siding your house, continued

Third, also due to limited time, the siding had to be prefinished.

I briefly entertained the notion to let someone else do it for a change, but price quotes ran from $3000 to $5000, depending on the particular siding the contractor was pushing.

So I decided to do-it-myself with Stratalite Thatch siding S-120 from GAF. This mineral siding, in 1x4-ft. panels and nine colors, is sold in "squares," quantities that cover 100 sq. ft. Color-matched installation nails and Kick-Strip undercourse (which is shown in photos and drawings) are included in the price.

Measure the house for the amount needed. The procedure: Add up the square footage of outside walls and subtract the footage of doors and windows. In my case that came to 20 squares; adding 10 percent to compensate for waste, I ordered 22.

The total cost of my job was $1027. Siding cost $792; scaffold rental was $75; and felt, staples, galvanized nails and wood lath totaled $60. Metal corner trim, J-channel and the like ran about $100. The best contractor bid I'd received for the job was based on lower quality materials. But compared even to that "low" price, I saved close to $2000.

It was well worth the five weekends or so of hustling around.

As these illustrations show, the material is easy to work with, although I'd have been smart to wear a dust mask any time I used a power saw on mineral siding. It's made of asbestos cement and the dust is now recognized as carcinogenic.

The trickiest part is putting J-channel around

The finishing touch

WHEN A SHINGLE must be cut, a thin white line shows up. Matching touch-up paint hides it well.

WHEN cutting a shingle, support it fully on a plywood table. Set the blade barely to clear the work.

A CUT SHINGLE-TOP means the Kick-Strip must be trimmed too. Strips must have a gap to allow for thermal expansion. You needn't cut sections for long runs. Just press them onto the shingles after the course is nailed up.

windows and doors. If a neighbor has recently added aluminum siding, check it closely. It probably went on with a similar system. Remember that the bottom horizontal goes *under* the sill, so sill ends must be sawn off to clear the vertical channels. The drip cap at the top comes off, too; J-channel replaces it. For more information, you can write to Building Products Div., Dept. PM, GAF Corp., 140 West 51st St., New York, NY 10020.

SPECIAL TOUCH-UP paint goes a long way; this little jar was enough to cover all the joints.

THE PAINT matches the shingle finish. Keep it in your nail apron and do joints as you reach them.

How to get started in skin and scuba diving

By DICK JACOBY

SHIPWRECKS lying mysteriously on the ocean bottom. Brilliantly colored damselfish darting through slowly undulating soft corals. The breathtaking configurations of giant sponges.

These are just some of the experiences awaiting the new skin or scuba diver. Every year more than 200,000 people take up sport diving, and you can be one of them, providing you're in good health and you can swim on the surface reasonably well.

There are two kinds of sport diving. Skin diving requires only a face mask, a snorkel and fins, and can be taken up without any formal lessons. Scuba requires a compressed air tank carried on your back. This allows you to dive to greater depths, but it also demands special skills and techniques and therefore should not be attempted without first completing classes.

How old should you be? Diving organizations will teach children as young as eight years old to skin dive. And a child of 12 may be taught to use compressed air scuba equipment if accompanied in the class by an adult. Age 15 is generally the minimum required to take a standard scuba course.

First, you'll need the basic gear: a mask so you can see underwater, a snorkel to breathe through, and a pair of fins. You can buy these things at specialty stores called "dive shops." Some major retailing and sporting goods chains also carry diving equipment.

Remember that fancy doesn't always mean better. Among many varieties of face masks, for example, a simple oval plate of tempered glass that covers your eyes and nose works well for most people. A handy feature is a nose pocket molded into the bottom of the mask's rubber skirt. The pocket makes it easy to hold your nose and "pop your ears" by trying to blow out—an excellent way to prevent your eardrums from being squeezed by water pressure.

SEE ALSO
Inner-tube water sports . . . Sports, water . . . Underwater photography

To check a mask for fit, position it on your face without putting the strap around your head. Now suck in through your nose and let go of the mask. You have a good fit if suction holds the mask in place.

Your snorkel should be of ⅞-inch bore and be made of semi-rigid rubber. Make sure the barrel has no sharp turns or ridges that could hamper air flow. Avoid snorkels with flexible tubes; the air turbulence created by the corrugated rubber makes for difficult breathing.

Start with fins of medium size. You'll want ones that are fairly flexible to prevent cramps in your calves. Also consider whether you plan to dive exclusively in the tropics. Why? Because water temperature will play a part in determining the kind of fins you use. If you expect to dive in water below 75 degrees, you'll probably need a quarter-inch-thick foam rubber body suit to keep warm. The suit includes boots, which is why you will want fins with half-pockets large enough to include thick foam rubber boots. A heavy adjustable strap on each fin stretches around the heel and holds the front of your booted foot in the pocket.

If your diving will be exclusively the warm-water kind you may prefer smaller fins that have full pockets. The smaller fins are easier to use, too, if you are new to diving and your calf muscles aren't built up.

A flotation vest is a good idea when skin diving far from shore. It's a tough bag of rubberized nylon worn around the neck and strapped to the front of your chest. To inflate, you blow into a hose or release carbon dioxide from a disposable cartridge. You deflate by depressing a finger valve.

A weight belt may help you dive 10 or 20 feet while holding your breath, and becomes even more important in scuba diving. Lead weights slip on a two-inch-wide belt of nylon or rubber. The belt has a quick-release buckle so you can drop it in an emergency. You'll need between two and 20 pounds of lead, depending on where you dive, what you wear and your body build.

You can learn to skin dive in any body of quiet water larger than a bathtub. Just stretch out on the surface and you'll experience the thrill of seeing clearly underwater while expending virtually no swimming effort. Breathing is a snap because the tip of your snorkel sticks a few inches above the surface while the other end is held in your mouth. Now kick your feet with long, slow leg movements. Don't use your hands to propel

YOUR FIRST GLIDE through the coral-filled ocean will thrill you with its beauty and a feeling of flying.

WITH A LITTLE practice you can swim right up to a school of French grunt. The secret is to swim very slowly.

you; your fins multiply the surface area of your feet at least five times and thrust you through the water far more efficiently than standard swimming strokes.

It's a good idea to inhale slowly when swimming in choppy water because a teaspoon or two of water may wash into your snorkel. Blast the water out by inhaling gently and then giving a sharp puff.

A short skin-diving course is always useful. You will learn to remove water that leaks into your mask, practice alternative fin kicks and learn how to control your buoyancy so you can float or dive at will. Safety methods are also taught, the most important of which is the habit of always diving with a buddy.

A delightful way to learn skin diving is to combine your lessons with a tropical vacation. Most warm-water resorts employ a staff of experienced divers and instructors who will spend an hour or so in a pool to teach you diving basics. Then they will guide you to shallow coral reefs to test your skills.

Your first sight of a coral reef and its brilliant

THERE'S NOTHING like the exhilaration of an ocean dive. Thousands of Americans take diving vacations each year.

GEARING UP for a dive requires attention to detail. A "wet suit" goes on first when the water is cool.

fish will be one of the most memorable experiences of your life. Amazingly, you are the stranger to be stared at as you rest motionless on the surface or dive briefly the few feet to the coral below. The thought will surely cross your mind: Why not learn scuba diving in order to remain submerged with these beautiful fish?

scuba gear and instruction

"Scuba" actually stands for Self-Contained Underwater Breathing Apparatus. A compressed-air tank is worn on your back and air is fed to your mouth through a regulator. To breathe, you simply inhale and exhale and the demand regulator does the rest.

Scuba gear is virtually failsafe. Still, scuba diving should never be attempted without formal lessons, and since there are several brands of scuba equipment and features to choose from, you'll want the advice of your diving instructor before buying. The instructor can also give you a chance to try several models before you make your final selection.

Scuba diving is classified as a safe sport by the President's Council on Physical Fitness, mainly because such good teaching is available in the U.S. Those who teach scuba must undergo rigorous training, and many don't make the grade. Make sure that the instructor you choose is a member of either the National Association of Skin Diving Schools (NASDS), National Association of Underwater Instructors (NAUI), Professional Association of Diving Instructors (PADI), or the YMCA.

Prices vary, but to give you an idea of cost, a Chicago area dive shop offers a 35-hour course for about $85. It lasts from 9 to 12 weeks and includes 15 hours of pool training, 15 hours of classroom lectures and three training dives in open water.

what happens in a scuba course?

Okay, let's say you've found a certified course that fits your schedule. Here's what it may be like:

A FULL SET of scuba equipment. Clockwise from 12 o'clock: weight belt, buoyancy compensator, boots, dive light, knife, fins, mask and snorkel, dive watch, depth gauge, tank boot, tank and backpack, wet suit top, gloves, pants and hood. Price runs $600 and up, depending on features and sales discount.

YOU SHOULD always dive with a buddy and wear a flotation vest when you use scuba. In this way there will always be someone to help out in any rare emergency.

You'll arrive at your first meeting (well rested, we hope) with three things—writing material, a bathing suit and, ideally, a friend who wants to take the course with you and serve as your diving buddy. After an introductory hour-and-a-half lecture, you and the dozen or so other students will swim several laps of a 25-yard pool, float or tread water for 15 minutes and then swim the width of the pool underwater.

Over the next few weeks you'll learn about aquatic physiology as your instructor explains what happens inside your body when you descend 30 or 40 feet beneath the surface. You also need to know a little physics, and your teacher will show you how a high-pressure air cylinder connected to a deceptively simple set of valves in a regulator makes it possible to breathe underwater for more than an hour.

You'll learn how to prevent pressure-related medical problems such as "ear squeeze." And you'll find out that "rapture of the deep" is actually nitrogen narcosis, in which too much nitrogen pressure causes a diver to become irrational. (To minimize this problem sport divers should not dive deeper than 100 feet.)

Most people have heard of the "bends," or decompression sickness, and your instructor will explain how nitrogen pressure again is the culprit. Most likely he will distribute U.S. Navy diving tables so you can memorize how long you can spend at any given depth before your body absorbs so much nitrogen that it turns into bubbles when you ascend.

You'll learn how to use and maintain your scuba gear, how to take it off and put it on while sitting on the bottom of the pool, and how to get yourself and your buddy out of jams that sometimes, albeit rarely, happen in sport diving.

At the end of, say, 12 weeks you'll be given a written test and a pool test to demonstrate both your knowledge and your diving skills.

at last . . . into the deep

Now comes the real fun: a weekend of supervised diving at a popular location. First, everyone will make a general swimming tour of the area while demonstrating his skin-diving skills. Then, with an instructor, you will scuba dive about 30 feet and show that you can control yourself and your equipment beneath the surface.

Underwater you'll have to remove your regulator from your mouth and then replace it. You'll let water into the mask and then force it out by blowing through your nose. The instructor will probably have you share your regulator with him to simulate giving air to a buddy who needs it. These and other tests will be easy because you will have practiced them many times in the pool.

After a rest and a light lunch, the class will dive again, this time with less supervision. Perhaps you will all expand your skills by navigating a compass course.

Sunday is a free day. Your instructor and assistants will be around to help, but now you and the class will be virtually on your own. After the sun goes down the course will culminate in a graduation dinner. Along with a Certification Card (called a C-Card), the instructor may give each of you a logbook in which to keep track of your diving experiences.

The C-Card is really a license to learn more about diving, and your instructor may tell you about the various advanced courses now available to you.

Your future in diving will expand as exploration of the deeps grows beyond its present infancy. You may even consider becoming a professional diver (in which case you'll find good money and hard work). But whether you dive for sport or career, you'll be joining the vanguard of pioneers who explore that layer of water that covers three-quarters of our planet—the inner space of the future.

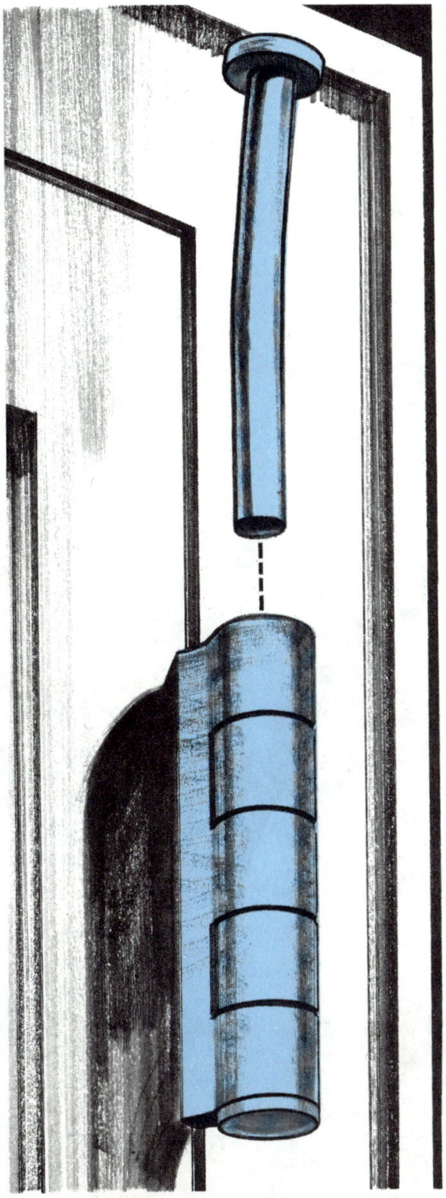

WHEN SETTLING CAUSES your door to swing shut when you want it open or vice versa, remove the hinge pins and bend them slightly with a hammer.

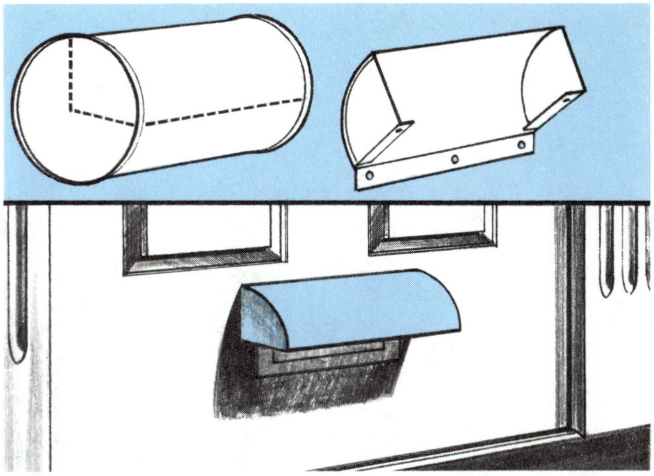

A TIN-CAN AWNING attached over the mail slot in a door will protect letters and magazines stuffed in the slot the from rain. It's made from a 2-lb. coffee can and painted to look like a little awning. Note in the drawing how the edges are bent.

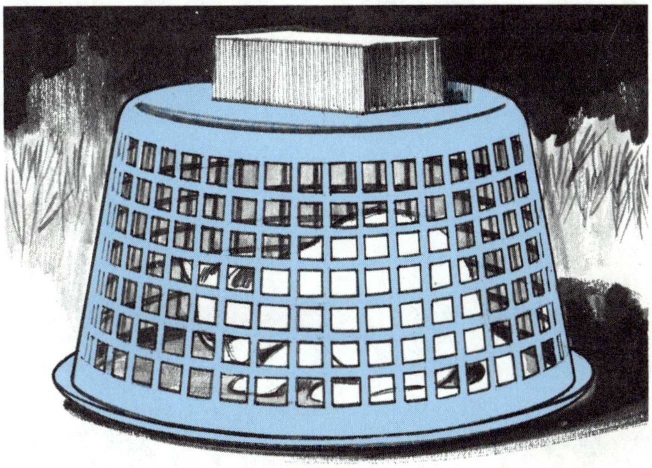

A PLASTIC LAUNDRY BASKET makes a temporary, ventilated cage for a cat that likes to wander off when you put it out. Simply turn the basket upside down over the cat and weight it with a heavy object such as a brick.

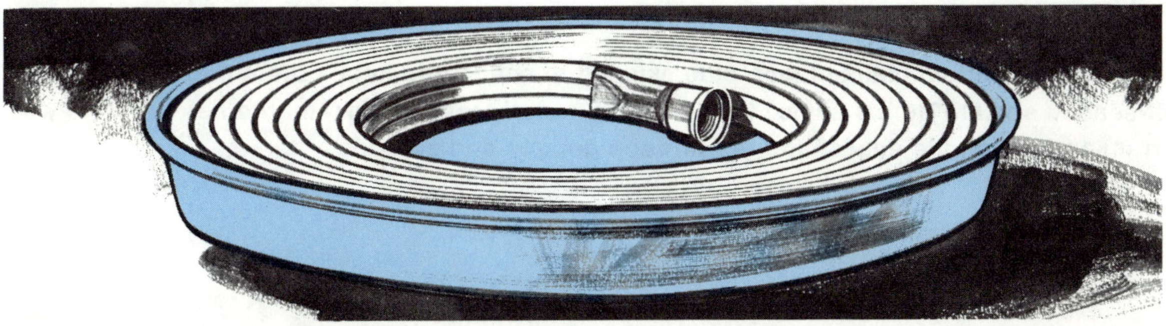

THINK TWICE before tossing away the cover of a beat-up garbage can. It's a perfect holder for a soaker hose and keeps it neatly coiled. Cut off the handle so that the cover lies flat.

How to take care of your skis

Proper bottom maintenance puts skis in top shape and keeps them there during off-season and on. Here's advice from experts, for all types of skis, on the best ways to wax, transport, store, file edges, and repair deep gouges and scrapes

By JACK VAN VLECK

SEE ALSO
Conditioning, physical . . . Exercising . . . Ice skates

■ YOU CAN WHANG UP even the toughest pair of skis, no matter what they're made of and no matter what the salesman says. Even the best equipment, worn by a downhill expert or touring novice skier, is subject to scraping, crossing, bottom gouging, edge dulling and burring. If you believe the "maintenance free" stories you're going to shorten the life of your equipment. And at a steep price tag for some of today's top-design FRP (fiberglass reinforced plastic) "schusslatzen" for instance, you'll be throwing away money if you skip the simple preventive maintenance that keeps skis going in winter and safely stored off season.

"Proper waxing tops your checklist," says Garcia Ski Corp.'s Jeff Garluck. Waxing comes after the edges have been sharpened (since filings can become embedded in paraffin) and can be done hot or cold. Satisfactory cold methods include the old rub-on stick wax technique as well as more modern paste and spray treatments. Cold waxing is easy and convenient, especially for touch-ups on the slopes, and should be done a couple of times during the ski day, often matching wax type to snow conditions.

Hot wax coats, applied by iron-on or paint-on methods, last longer. An iron at medium heat is held, point down, over ski bottoms and wax pressed against it until the wax melts and can be dribbled down one side of the ski, outside the groove, and up the other. Ribbons of wax are ironed out evenly over the entire surface—keep the iron moving so the base won't loosen its bond with the ski. Afterward you'll have to buy your wife a new iron, of course.

To paint on wax, melt it in an old pot and with a ski-width brush dip in and then press out any bubbles against the pot. Paint skis from tail to tip in 18-inch overlapping strokes. After any hot-process application, scrape the cooled coating, tip to tail, to even the finish. A knife or coin can scrape the center grooves. Use plastic or wood to clean edges.

transporting skis safely

Waxing keeps polyethylene bases from wearing down quickly, prevents oxidation, helps turning by avoiding tip-scrape. Tops of skis can use car wax to help guard against road salt when skis are carried on exterior racks. Northland's Jerry Gruggen notes that almost as much minor damage can happen while toting equipment as during actual use. Off the rack, skis should be carried bottom to bottom and strapped together to prevent edge scissoring. Transporting them inside the car is dangerous to skis and riders in case of a sudden stop. When using a public carrier, "Box your gear or use a ski bag," says Blizzard spokesman Frank Moran. Wrap newspapers between skis to avoid marring waxes' bases. Bagged in canvas, burlap or plastic on a roof rack, skis are protected from flying stones, ice and road salt.

Store skis vertically in wood racks at ski areas and at home so snow can drain off and no one will trip over them. When finished for a weekend—or season—wipe skis dry, wax tops and bottoms lightly and coat edges with light oil or Vaseline. Modern skis don't need to be blocked in the

SHARPEN SIDE EDGE with flat No. 10, removing rough spots, nicks. Result should be even edge that forms 90° angle between bottom edging surface and side.

TIP EDGING of ski should not be sharp. Starting even with front end of center groove, round edging forward toward "shovel" tip to prevent tip-tripping.

DEEP GOUGES require more than waxing to fill and repair. First use knife or other sharp tool to dig out any loose foreign matter before starting repair.

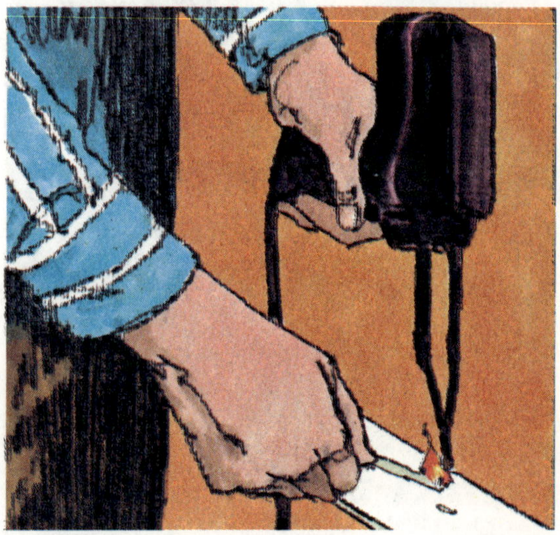

FOR BEST BOND, a clean soldering iron is used to heat base around gouge edges. Molten repair-stick "spaghetti" is dripped in. Extinguish burning drops.

middle to maintain camber, but should be stored away from temperature extremes. Strap together and suspend from cellar beams or closet hooks. Wall racks from ski stores are good. Rest ski tails on wood blocks rather than concrete floors.

Edges and bases take the worst beating. After each trip, knock off edge burrs with emery paper or a file. Run your fingernail crossways over the edges and bottom. If it sticks against an edge, you have the start of a "railing" problem—bottom wear has exposed the inside steel edge corners. To remedy this and other edge faults yourself, get a No. 10 flat crosscut mill bastard file. Then clamp your skis, one at a time, base up in a vise.

Lay the file flat on the base and angled about 45° in the direction the ski is pointing. Keep weight on your thumbs at the middle of the file and push easily in long strokes down the length of the ski. Don't shift pressure to file ends or press hard. You're working for a flat-edge surface flush with the base. If the base is worn too far, you'll have to build it up with layers of wax.

Next, clamp the ski with one edge up. File the ski edge flat down the ski length to get a 90°-angle edge flat on the base and the side. At the front, from a point parallel to the groove end, bevel the

SHAVE OFF excess polyethylene with knife or metal scraper to bring fill down to ski level. Use repair sticks without soldering iron for field patch.

IRON-ON WAX METHOD uses wax held against iron at medium setting. Drips from iron are dribbled on surfaces each side of groove, ironed out smooth.

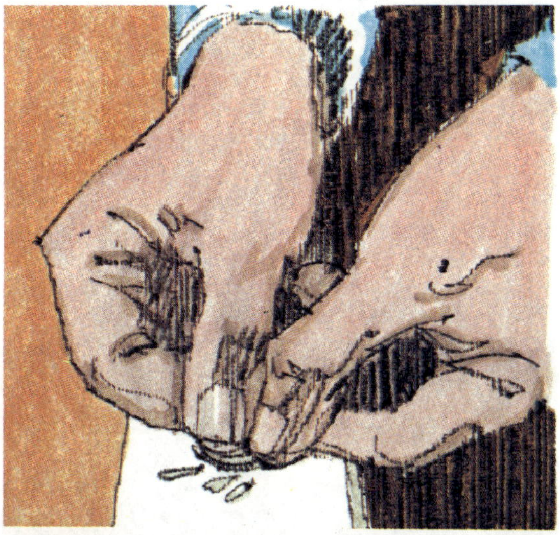

CENTER GROOVE is scraped out and smoothed with coin or knife. Wax runs in during ironing. Keep hot iron moving over bottom during smoothing of wax.

PEEL WAX from edges with plastic or wood scraper to guard against scratches. Full surfaces of the ski are then leveled with metal scraper for even coat.

edging as far as it runs up the "shovel" (tip).

Deep gouges and scrapes caused by "fast grass and rock garden" conditions need special attention since moisture can work into holes and start delamination. Kofix or P-Tex candles (often called spaghetti) are the answer, and come in colors to match your ski bottoms. Clean base with a rag and benzine or a brass pot cleaner (never use steel wool). Heat damaged area with a clean soldering iron. Split repair candle (for smaller drips), light and drip melted polyethylene into gouge until it's higher than base layer. Smooth cooled material with knife or gadget like Stanley Pocket Surform. Very gently sand patched area with fine sandpaper, rewax as usual.

Today's fancy top ski surfaces can be scratched, "but that won't affect performance," says Ron Guisick of Hart Skis. "The melamine (finish coat) can chip but good skis have plastic or metal strips running along the outside edges to prevent excessive damage if skis cross during a run." Scratches can be sanded and waxed.

Your warranty may require professional repair for major damage like delamination or edge separation. But most modern skis can last a number of seasons with minimum—but regular—basic maintenance.

Trim the fat from your slide shows

By LEN HILTS

Stop boring your friends and relatives with hours and hours of dull slide presentations. Learn how to trim redundant slides from your presentations

A SLIDE SORTER with a built-in light to assist in editing your slide shows is a must if you intend to get rid of unwanted shots. A magnifying glass helps in spotting photos which are out of focus.

■ WHEN YOU BRING OUT your slide projector after dinner, does everyone suddenly remember previous engagements and make for the nearest exit? If they do, you aren't alone. Too many avid slide shooters have bored audiences for so many years that the home slide show has developed a bad reputation.

What makes a slide show boring? It isn't the quality of the slides, as a rule, but it is the *quantity* of them. Most slide shows present far too many pictures—often running to half a dozen different views of the same scene—and they kill the audience interest by sheer weight.

Therefore, the first rule in preparing an interesting slide show is: *Trim out the fat.* Line up the slides from your trip during your editorial session and remove those that are duplicates or near duplicates. For example, one or two shots of the Eifel Tower are sufficient; you don't need six views of it; you don't even need two views unless they are very different in nature.

While you are editing out the duplicates, also get rid of shots that are out of focus, tilted, or that otherwise aren't good pictures. Don't throw any of these slides away. Just put them into a storage tray. You may be able to use the duplicates or salvage some of the poor shots later. They just don't belong in your presentation to the public.

After you have eliminated the poor and duplicate shots, arrange the remaining slides as you intend to show them. For a trip, chronological order is the usual way, but sometimes you can be clever by arranging flashbacks or other devices to heighten the viewer's interest.

Place the slides, arranged as you want them, into a tray and project them for yourself—but this time, be extremely critical. Edit so that the

SEE ALSO
Bird photography . . . Boat photography . . . Candid photography . . . Night photography . . . Outdoor photography . . . Photography . . . Projector stands . . . Theaters, home

show has pace—seems to move right along—and has a high interest level. Ruthlessly take out slides that slow down the pace, even though you think they are marvelous pictures. The saddest line of narration comes when you say to your audience, "This slide doesn't really belong here, but I wanted you to see. . . ." You can hardly hear your voice over the noise of the audience yawning when this happens.

The best tool for preparing a slide show is a slide sorter of the type shown on page 2796. You can display several dozen slides at one time on the white plastic front of the sorter, and see each clearly because of the light mounted behind the front.

As you edit, examine each slide through a fairly powerful magnifying glass. You can spot those that are out of focus or poorly composed without going to the trouble of putting them through your slide projector.

Taking the bad slides out of your show is easy. The tough part comes when you begin to remove the good ones. As one film editor told me, "That takes character." You have a dozen shots, all beautiful, of the same scene and you are proud of them—but when editing you must remember that your slide show is not a salon display of fine photography.

Naturally, you save all the shots you take out of your show. Use them in other slide shows; give them to friends; show them at the next camera club meeting.

The second problem you run into while editing is the not-so-good shot which can't be left out of the show because it leaves a hole in the narrative. Everyone has pictures like this. Perhaps the camera was tilted or the subject is off to one side of the frame; or maybe you were too far away for the shot. Whatever the problem, you often can save pictures like this by cropping or reframing them.

To do this kind of work, you need a couple of pieces of equipment: a small press for mounting slides and a cutter for cutting individual pictures from a roll of film. You also need some empty slide frames. You can get all of these for an expenditure of less than $40.

One word of advice before you start working with slides: Always wear editing gloves. Kodak and others make very inexpensive white gloves (a couple of bucks will buy half a dozen pairs) which you can purchase at all photo stores. You should use these gloves even when just sorting your slides; if you don't, you are sure to get fingerprints all over the film surfaces. These

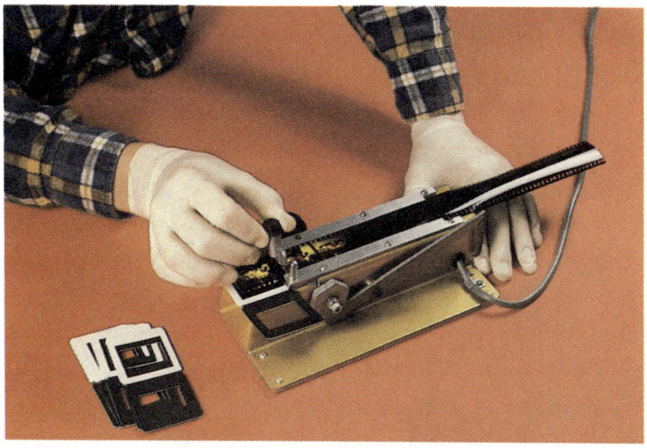

WHEN MOUNTING your slides, use white gloves to keep from fingerprinting the film. A cutter makes it easy to cut a roll of film into frames.

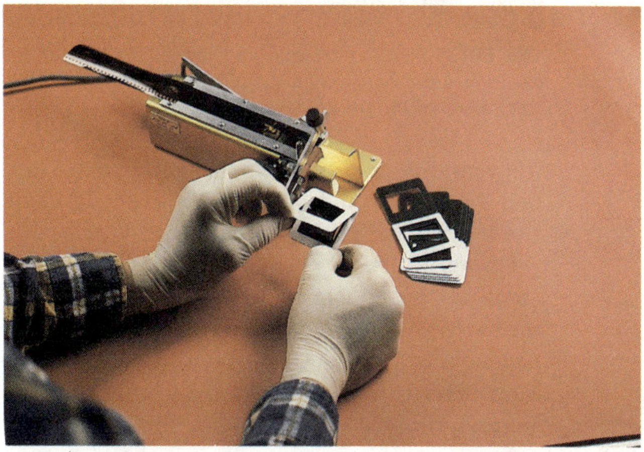

THE CUT PHOTO is placed in a new slide mount, the mount is folded over the film, and then the mount is sealed by heat and pressure.

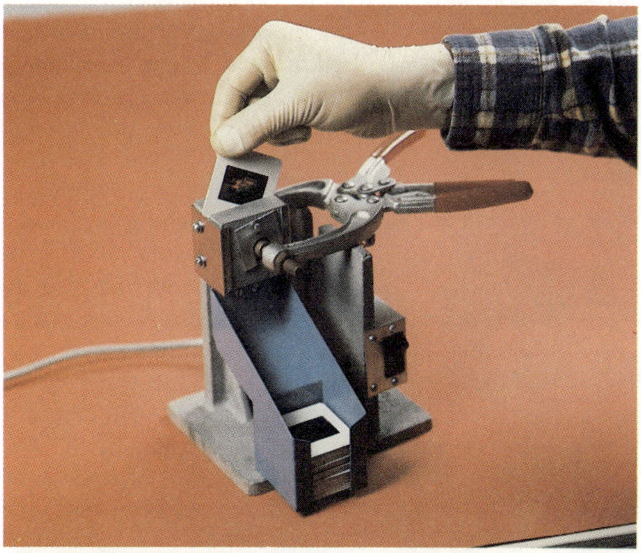

THE SLIDE MOUNTER is a small unit which applies heat and pressure to the edges of a mount to seal in the film. Sealing a slide takes only a minute.

THE FIRST STEP in cropping a slide is to cut small cardboard pieces from an extra slide mount. The cardboard of the mount is the right thickness.

PLACE THE CARDBOARD pieces on the slide to crop out unwanted areas of the picture, then secure them in place with strips of opaque tape.

fingerprints are almost impossible to wipe off, and your skin oil will cause an eventual deterioration of the image.

Cropping. You shot a speeding boat and somehow it ended up way over on the left side of the picture. The boat and its wake make a fine picture, but there is a lot of empty water to the right. You can heighten the picture interest by simply cropping out the empty water.

For most cropping, you don't need to remove the film from the slide mount. You can cut small cardboard inserts from an extra slide mount, slip them into place on the slide being cropped, and secure them with a bit of plastic tape. The best tape to use is the kind which is opaque (black plastic electrical tape works fine for me). The pictures on this page show how this work is done.

Cropping in this fashion is a fine solution for a very common problem—the outdoor picture with too much sky in it. Unless there are some remarkable cloud formations which add to the picture interest, too much sky can reduce picture interest. Use a cardboard strip to block out part of the sky.

Using simple cardboard forms, you can crop one or both sides, top and bottom. Each time, you produce a projected picture of a different shape, which in itself adds a dimension to your slide show.

You can also cut special masks out of cardboard and insert them into your slides. By masking, you can make the shape of the projected picture different—oval, round, a double oval that looks like you are peering through binoculars at the picture, heart-shaped, etc.

To make such a mask, first cut a cardboard insert to fill the slide frame completely. Then draw the shape you want on the insert and use a sharp knife (Exacto, for example) to cut it out. Now place the mask over the film in the slide frame and tape it in place.

Once in a while, you can take a number of shots of the same subject and make an interesting display by cropping. If you have half a dozen shots of an approaching speed boat, for example,

WHEN CUTTING A PHOTO, use an extremely sharp knife or razor blade. Also use a steel rule as a guide to assure that the cut will be straight.

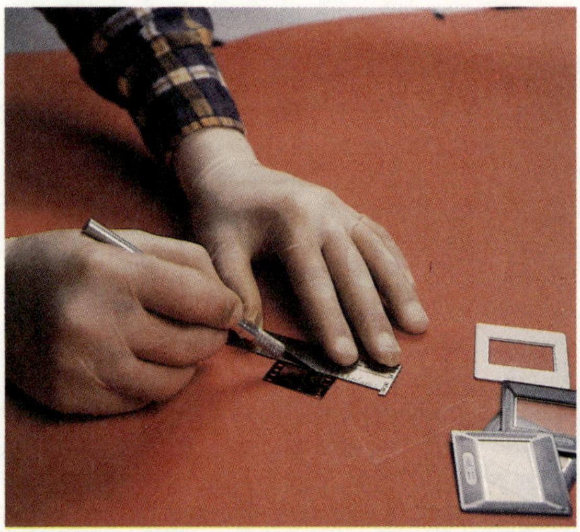

you can arrange these in sequence, with the first shot showing the boat some distance away and the final shot showing it close up. By cropping in tight on the first shot, so the projected picture is quite small, and then making each succeeding picture a little larger, you can enhance the feeling of the boat's approach.

Double and triple pictures. Suppose, in your show, you have shots of San Francisco's Trans-America Building and Chicago's John Hancock Building. You'd like to show them side by side for dramatic effect. You can do this by mounting both pictures in the same frame, making a double picture.

To begin with, of course, both shots must be tall and narrow so they'll fit in the same frame. Remove both pictures from their original mounts and then carefully plan where you will cut them. Remember that if you goof in the cutting, you will ruin the pictures. I lay the pictures over an empty slide mount, which enables me to see where the cut must be made and assures me that I have left enough film around the edges to fit into the mount.

When cutting the film, use a steel-edged ruler to guide your knife so you make a perfectly straight cut. Usually, you'll have to cut something from each side of each film to make them fit into the mount.

It is possible to mount the two pieces of cut film side by side in a new slide mount, but a far easier and better way is to purchase some glass slide mounts (or binders). You can obtain them in any photo shop that carries a complete line of supplies.

While you are buying these, also pick up a roll of very narrow opaque tape, the kind used by artists and persons making layouts for printers. Photo stores sometimes stock this tape, and all art supply stores have it.

Now lay the two pieces of cut film on one side of the glass mounts, positioned as you want them in the final picture. Place a strip of the thin tape between them to act as a divider. Lay the second half of the glass mount over the first one. If you have done the job right, you now have a double picture of your two buildings, divided by a very thin black line. If you have cut your film with care and laid the black tape down correctly, no light will project around the edges of the pictures and you will have a very interesting comparative composition.

You can use the same technique to make three-part pictures, too. You can have pictures side by side, top and bottom, or cut diagonally. To be on the safe side, get some practice by cutting a couple of discarded slides first. Then carefully work on your better slides. You'll have fun with this technique.

The final editing. When you have eliminated all the dull and duplicative slides, and cropped and remade those which could be improved, you are ready for the final editing of your show. Here there is one rule to follow: Keep the story moving. Each slide must give the viewer a sense of progress and of anticipation.

After you've shown an evening or two of slides, edited as we have described, you'll find people asking to see your shows—rather than suddenly remembering other engagements.

PLACE THE CUT film pieces on a glass slide, positioning them so they will show properly. Then use thin black tape to divide the pictures.

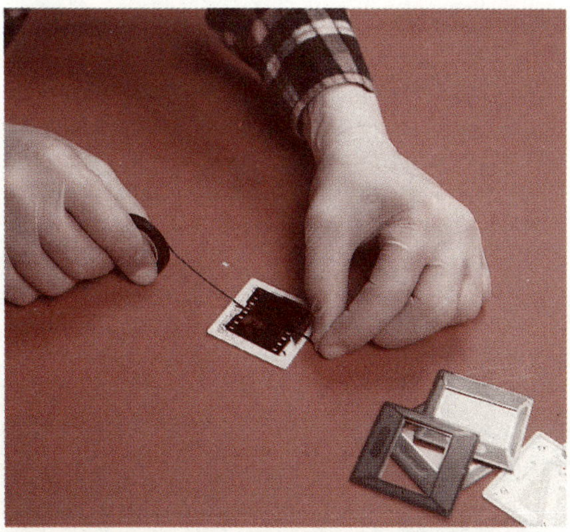

WITH THE FILM in place, put a second glass slide cover over the first, and insert the resulting sandwich into a metal slide binder.

Let the outdoors in with sliding glass doors

By HARRY WICKS

If the view outside your home has visual appeal, sliding glass doors will bring it all inside

SEE ALSO

Doors . . . Locks, door . . . Patios . . . Remodeling, exterior . . . Storm doors and windows

THIS WEEKEND HOME (below) began traditionally: a door flanked by double-hung windows. It looked pleasant, but see above and on the facing page how a transparent wall enhanced its livability inside and out.

■ THE PROBLEM FOCUSED on an attractive weekend retreat at the eastern tip of Long Island. This summer home and vacation hideout was its owner's delight, but it didn't give the indoors much of the outdoor beauty so precious to refugees from New York's urban pressures.

"What can I do to modernize the place?" he asked. "What kind of change will let me enjoy it more?" Wayne Leckey, *Popular Mechanics'* Home and Shop Editor, offered a suggestion: Make a wall of the kitchen-dining area all-glass to let in the great view. The suggestion was an appealing one and the owner went to work.

The good-looking results, from both inside and out, are obvious in the photos on these pages. The front porch has been transformed from a simple walkway leading to the front door to a small patio for lounging. The sliding glass doors not only give a great view of the countryside but brighten up the kitchen-dining area by letting in more sunlight. The increased exposure also gives better air circulation.

The important point, when laying out a job such as this, is to insure that the installation matches the architecture of the home. The job is not difficult. As shown in the existing and new structural drawings on the next page, it consists basically of opening the wall and installing studs and header to suit the doors you buy. It pays to make an accurate scale drawing of the existing structure before you start. Then decide how big the sliding doors are that you wish to add. By laying out the new framing on tracing paper placed over the existing framing you will have an accurate picture of the raw materials you need.

Be sure the framing you install meets the minimum requirements of the Federal Housing Administration. If the area you intend to glass-in is longer than that shown here, be sure to check

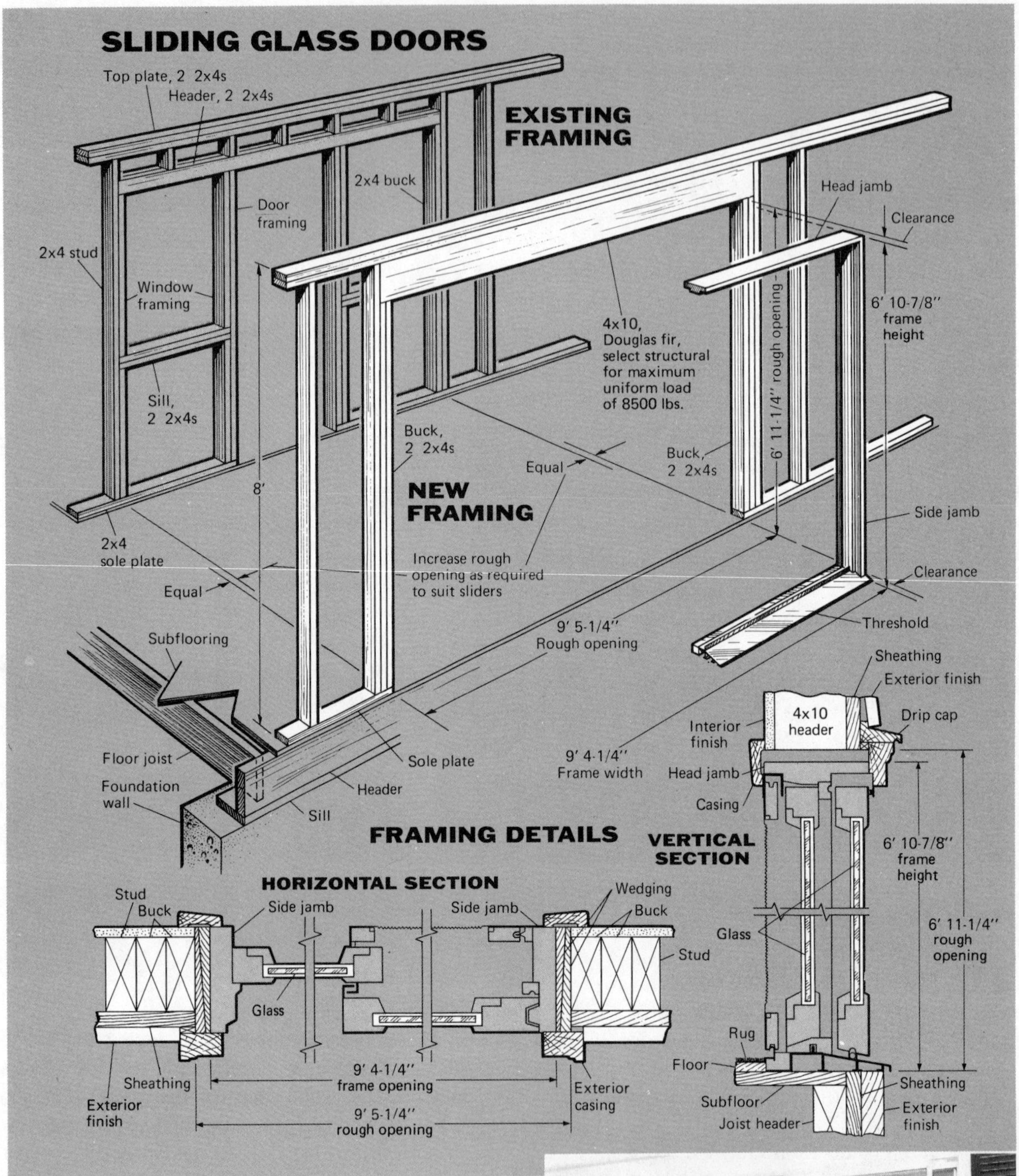

with the building department in your area to make certain that structural members meet the local code requirements.

When you are certain you have all the dimensions and materials correct, start by removing the existing framing. The new framing is constructed of 2 x 4s with the bucks on the end being doubled 2 x 4s for added strength. The top of the new framing is a 4 x 10 piece of Douglas fir. With the new framing in place, the door jamb is fitted into the opening and anchored securely.

'Eggs' hold small parts

By WYATT YOUSAY

Here's a workshop shelf to hold nuts, bolts and assorted odds and ends in the best possible containers (no kidding)—discarded panty-hose shells

SEE ALSO
Fasteners . . . Shelves . . . Storage ideas

■ MANY THROWAWAY containers have been put to use in the home and workshop to hold a variety of things. Baby-food jars have made great holders for screws, nails and the like. Modified bleach bottles have served a multitude of uses from grain scoops to paintbrush holders to funnels. Still another container which lends itself to holding things is the egg-shape one in which L'eggs panty hose are sold. It consists of a two-part white plastic shell. The half shells provide perfect little cups for brads, screws, nails, you name it, when supported by a shelf. Being conical in shape, they make it easy to pick out the very last brad, and the upper half of the shells can serve as covers.

A row of holes 5 in. on centers is made in a scrap of plywood with a circle cutter chucked in a drill press; then the plywood is glued in a groove run in a scrap of clamshell door casing.

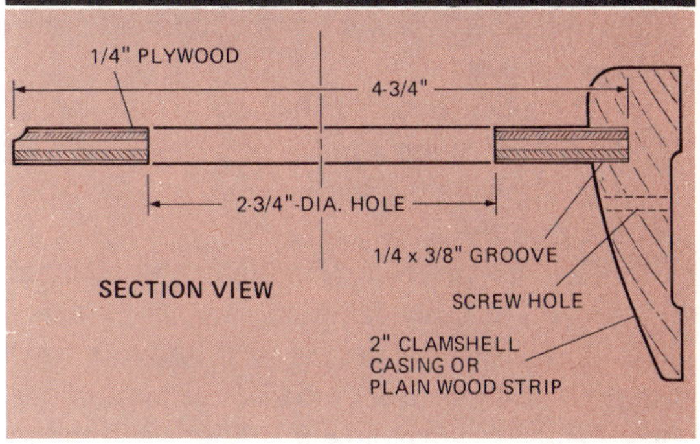

Easy-to-build snack table

By FRANK H. DAY

■ THIS BEAUTIFUL snack table folds perfectly flat and only 1¾-in. thick for compact storage. It is made of redwood with a tortoise-shell laminate top, but pine or hardwood and a different style laminate can be used. Along with the plans opposite, here are some additional hints to help you along:

1. The pivot blocks (D) must be attached to the underside of the top (G) with screws and glue prior to applying the plastic laminate. Be sure to countersink the screws.

2. Cut the laminate (H) slightly smaller than the top (G). Apply laminate contact cement to both surfaces to be joined and allow it to dry until it's no longer tacky. Since the laminate will be difficult to move once it is bonded to the top, use kraft paper slipsheets to keep the surfaces apart until they are aligned. Assure a good bond by rapping laminate surface with a hammer on a softwood block.

3. The binding strips can be mitered at the corners, but the joint shown in the plans is less likely to splinter and is also good looking. Attach the binding to G with glue and brads.

4. Since folding tables generally take a beating, be sure all joints are tight. A brad driven through the top of the leg and dowel (E) will help keep this joint from pulling apart. Similarly, a drop of white glue on the tip of the screw that passes through the fixed legs and into pivot block (D) will help prevent it from backing out with use.

5. The aluminum guides (I) must be identical in length and formed so that the swinging legs of the table will slide easily.

Accurate forming of the guides is greatly simplified by the use of jig shown in the plans. Make trial bends on a short piece of aluminum to check for clearance before screwing block (N) to jig permanently.

Then take a short measured length of aluminum strip, say 8-in. long, and form the two ends. Measure the finished length. The difference between the two lengths is the distance that must be added to the length of aluminum strip from which the finished guide will be formed.

6. Finishing the tables is a matter of individual taste. If a hardwood has been used, a rubbed finish with Danish or tung oil topped off with polished hard wax gives a handsome effect.

The aluminum guides can be covered with brass-colored spray lacquer to match brass screws, or with a color that will harmonize with the wood.

All the brads should be set and holes filled with matching wood putty. Use of a hollow-ground saw blade on all cuts will produce surfaces that require only fine sanding.

MAKE TRIAL BENDS on jig before screwing on the block (N); use clamps to secure temporarily.

SEE ALSO

**Bridge tables . . . Butler's tables . . .
Family rooms . . . Finishes, wood . . .
Nesting tables . . . Occasional tables . . .
Party tables . . . Serving carts . . . Trays, folding . . .
Wood finishes**

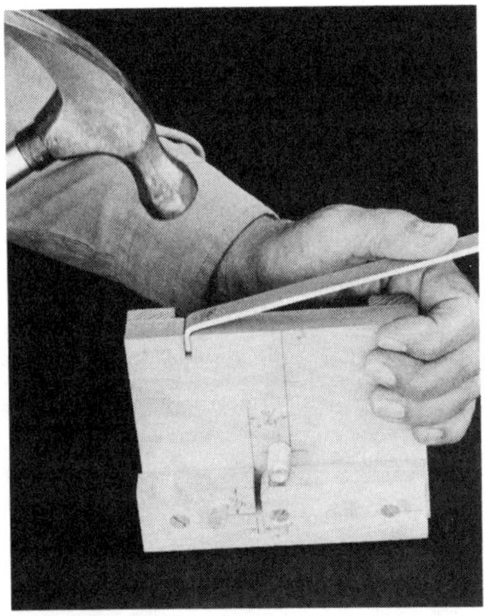

USE EDGE slot to make first bend in guide. Strike strip close to bend.

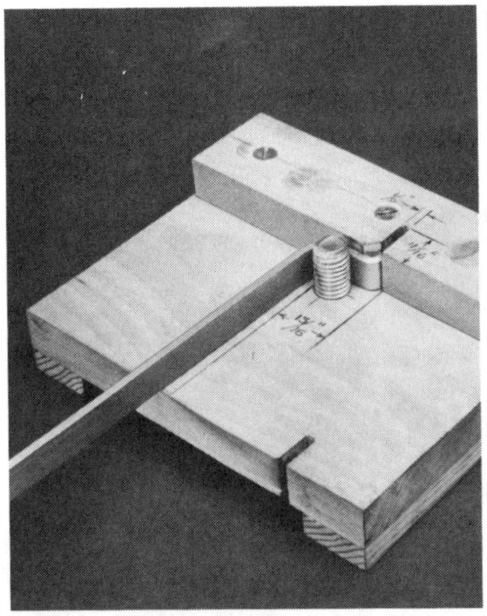

INSERT BENT end in slot on N and force strip around bolt threads.

MATERIALS LIST—FOLDING TABLE

Key	No.	Size and description (use)
A	4	¾ × 1⅛ × 28¼" redwood (leg)
B	1	¾ × 1⅛ × 14⅛" or to fit redwood (brace)
C	1	½" dia. × 15⅞" or to fit dowel (stop)
D	2	¾ × 1³⁄₁₆ × 2¾" redwood (pivot block)
E	2	⁷⁄₁₆ × ½ × 20" redwood (edging)
F	2	⁷⁄₁₆ × ½ × 15½" redwood (edging)
G	1	⅜ × 15½ × 19½" plywood or particle board (top)
H	1	¹⁄₃₂ × 15½ × 19½" plastic laminate
I	2	⅛ × ½ × 18" cut to suit aluminum (guide)
J	2	1½" No. 10 fh brass screw
K	11	1¼" No. 10 fh brass screw
L	4	½" No. 10 pan head screw
M	1	¾ × 5 × 6" hardwood (bending jig)
N	1	¾ × 1½ × 6" hardwood (bending jig)
O	2	½ × ¾ × 6" hardwood (bending jig)
P	1	½" dia. × 1½" hex bolt (bending jig)

Misc. ¾" brads, glue, and laminate contact cement as you require.

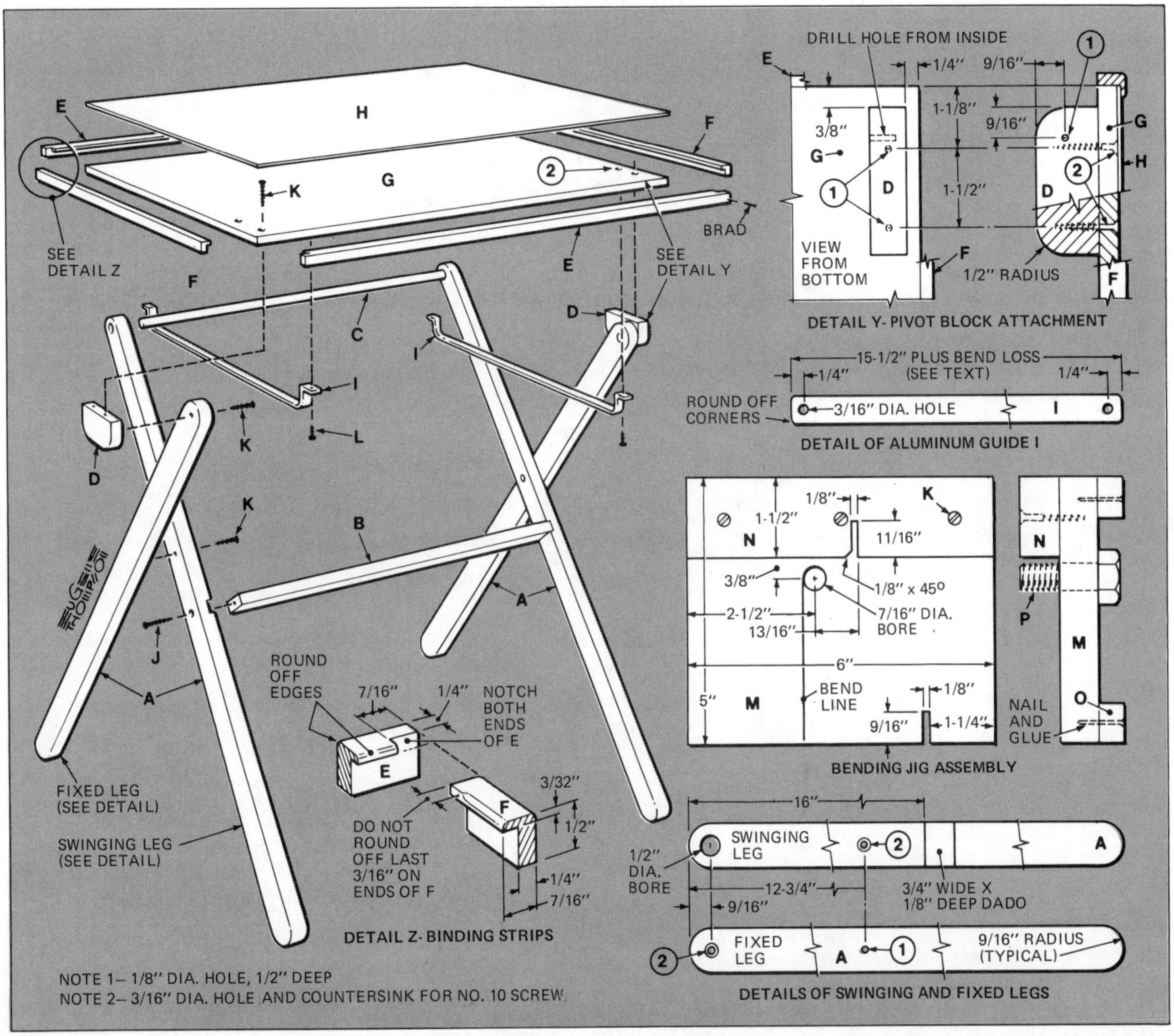

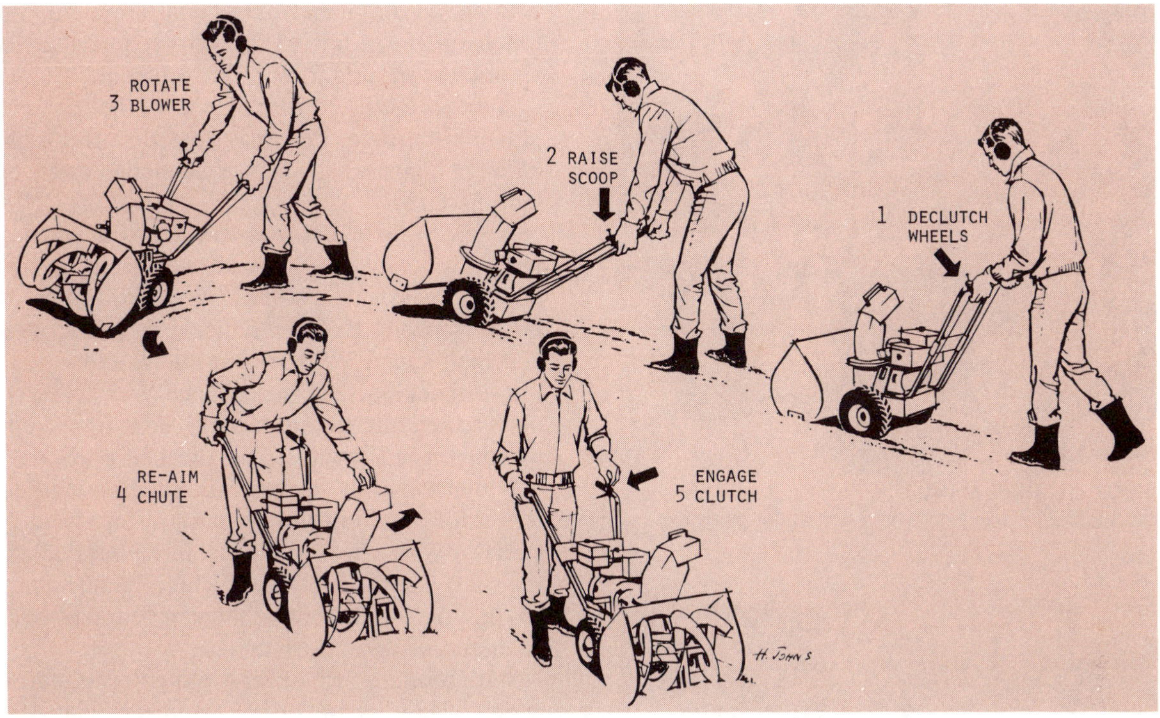

The right way to run a snowblower

■ THE TACTICS of farm or street plowing just don't work when you're clearing your property with a snowblower. You have to consider many more things.

First is the snow-removal area itself—a conventional walk, side drive close by the house, two-car garage ramp or a long, exposed drive are typical. Other factors are:

Type of surface. A smooth, hard surface is easiest; just set the blower height low. Crushed rock and gravel take a higher setting; rocks and pebbles thrown far and wide create a safety hazard.

Grades, slopes. A level-running speed may suddenly become too fast for a steep downgrade. A runaway snowblower pursued by a frantic householder isn't funny.

Targets to avoid. A neighbor's picture window, windshield, children and dogs are vulnerable to hard-flung stones or ice.

Property or machine damage. Stones along flowerbeds, buried survey stakes, shrubs, flowers and ditches should be cased and marked before starting. It's easy to tear up both blower and obstacle.

Wind direction. If you have a smooth, more-or-less even depth of snow, try starting the cut so the wind will cross your path at an angle, thus blowing snow to right or left. If a building is a factor, make a first cut close to it and cast the snow away.

Two mistakes often beset the beginner. First, he has seen television ads of blowers throwing snow 40 ft. or more, so he turns the chute discharge high. This rooster tail may be impressive, but it's seldom necessary or practical. Sooner or later it will lash back and leave you gasping. There's a chance that the blower will pick up something you didn't know was there and fling it into a target you don't want to hit.

The second mistake is assuming that unless the snow is thrown far away it will be handled a second time, doubling the work. A few trials

SEE ALSO

Asphalt driveways . . . Engines, small . . . Mowers . . . Snow-melting systems . . . Snowplows . . . Tractor lifts . . . Tractor trailers

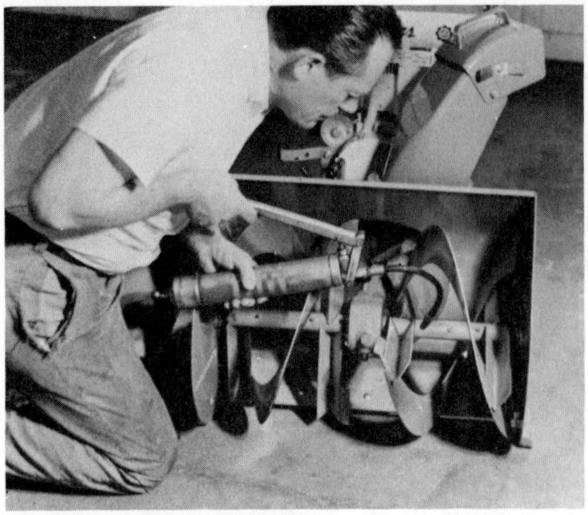

CHECK OWNER'S MANUAL for lube points. This unit was accidently delivered with a dry, auger gearbox.

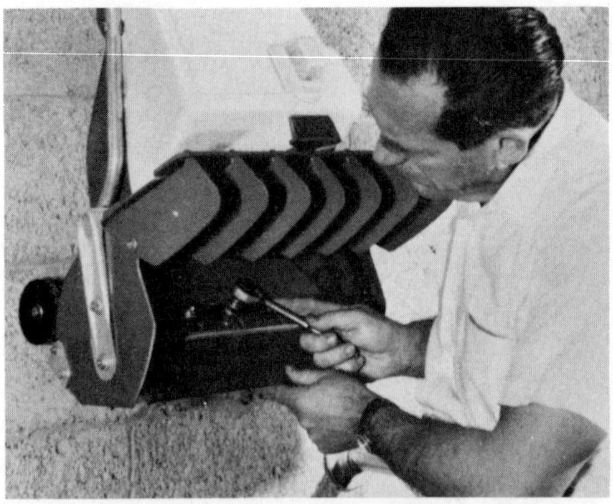

PLASTIC PADDLES on lightweight blower are easily replaced. Be sure to check for the proper clearance.

with the chute aimed down will convince you this isn't true. Chewed-up snow redeposited in an uncleaned area just isn't a problem.

Another tactical error is based on the farmer's plowing method. You may feel that the most efficient approach is to make a constant circle or loop pattern.

It's better to make a pass close to your starting point, reverse the blower and back up for another pass; then repeat until you have a cleaned area that allows a nice easy turnaround and realignment for the next cut. Some time is lost in backing, but the cleaned area lets you reverse and turn the chute at the same time without throwing snow over the cleaned portion.

Sometimes this forward-and-reverse method is best for the whole job—especially on a bitterly cold day with a high wind. Just turn your back to the wind and keep it there. Generally, however, it's practical to do this for three or four passes at each end of your work area.

With room to turn at each end you just start a series of loop passes at the windward side and work towards the downwind finish point.

Learning how to turn a blower around properly takes practice. One good method is to declutch the hand clutch just as you come to the end of the loop. This disconnects the power from the drive wheels. At the same time, bear down on the hand grips and elevate the scoop a few inches so the auger doesn't start picking up snow until you're headed into your new pass.

Always turn so your body goes into any side or quartering wind. Turning the other way places

WOODEN SHIMS give adequate adjustment when the blower is to be used on a smooth, even surface.

SPRAY WAX applied to the inside of chute and discharge area will prevent snow from sticking to the metal.

the chute discharge between you and the wind.

On a straight walk or drive, usually you start to the windward and work to the lee with up-and-down passes. If working quarters are tight, such as a driveway between two houses, it is often practical to discharge the snow into a central windrow by working from both sides. This narrow heap of snow can then be cleaned up by starting at the garage and working toward the street with chute discharging straight ahead. A street plow throws it on your drive, so you might as well throw some back.

Hardened drifts, always tough to clear, are formed by heavy snow and howling winds. Often they are preceded by rain so that lower layers are soaked and well glued to the surface. When followed by below-zero weather, the drifts become almost solid and lower snow layers are rock hard. The usual snow blower doesn't have the weight and ripping power of a commercial plow to get under this type of drift. Instead, it rides up over the drift and trims a little off the top. A number of techniques can help:

- Remove the little skids on the snow scoop to get the sharp scoop edge down into the snow as much as possible.
- Place a sack of sand or salt on the scoop to hold it down.
- Put chains on blower drive wheels.
- As the auger bites into the hard, deep snow, declutch drive wheels so the blower can digest and clear the material. This lets all the engine power feed the blower and doesn't crowd the machine faster than it can work. By clutching and declutching with a rhythmic pattern, the blower will dig in and back off in a series of bucking actions, like the rocking of a stuck car.
- Break up the worst areas with a shovel jammed downward at intervals or use a small paddle-type blower to chop up the hard spots, then clear with the big machine. Amazingly, these lightweights will tear into snow the big augers can't touch. Small machines, gas or electric-powered, can be scooted all over like a vacuum cleaner or picked up in a two-hand grip like a shovel. They will clean steps and tough spots easily.

Regard the paddles as expendable. Made of a tough, durable plastic, they will take all sorts of arm-jarring beatings and come up smiling. Replace them after the season to be ready for next year.

If you don't already have a snowblower, check the kind of snow-removal problem you have before you buy. No blower is ideal for all jobs. Often a small paddle-wheel type and a larger auger model may do the work faster and easier than a single blower. Here are other considerations:

Slopes and grades. Dragging a heavy blower back uphill is dangerous. If you have a slope, be sure to buy a machine with power reverse. If the area is small, a superlight job without reverse is good.

Steps, porches and patios. A big auger job is practically useless for cleaning small areas or a series of steps. A light gas or electric paddle-wheeler can be handled like a shovel.

LOW DISCHARGE is less dramatic than high rooster tail, but it is a more practical setting for the chute.

LIGHTWEIGHT paddle-type blower is best for steps and small areas. It can also break up large drifts.

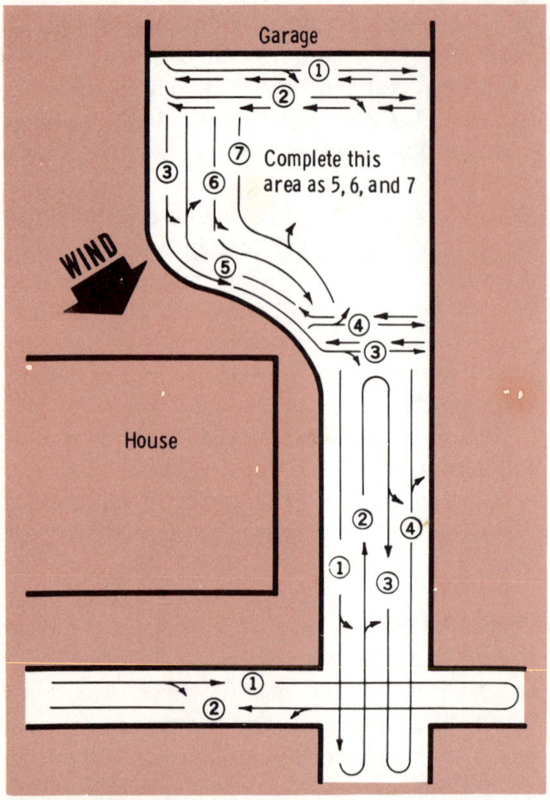

WIND DIRECTION is one of the most important factors to consider when planning your attack. Here are two methods of handling a more-or-less typical layout that demonstrate how the pattern is varied to suit the wind.

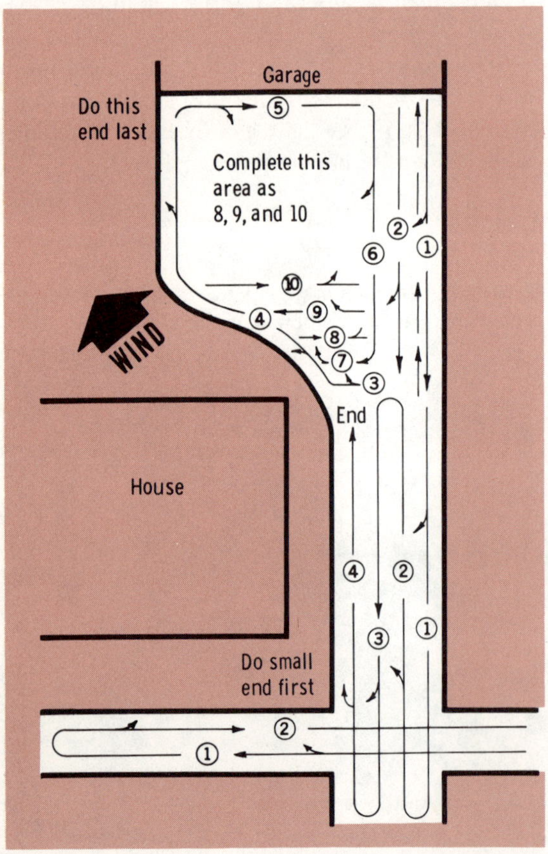

Long runs. Clearing long drives and walks can get tedious, especially when snow cover is moderate, unless the blower has three or four forward speeds. A good one travels at a peppy walk. Fixed-speed types will merely prolong your exposure.

Storage. If you can wheel the blower into a garage or shed, size and weight are no problem. If you'll store it in a basement or elevated porch, think light.

Special uses. Maybe you want to take your blower to a hunting cabin or carry it in your car's trunk in case you get stuck.

Snowblower design and construction is not quite so standardized as that of automobiles. With a new blower, give yourself an hour of unhurried study to read the instructions and examine the guts of your machine. Search out the lubrication points, and if you don't have the grease guns, oil cans and lubricants, spend a bit to set up for quick servicing during the heavy-use season. Time spent now and an occasional lubrication and chain and belt adjustment will save hours of future trouble.

Before you take your new blower out for a trial spin, keep these points in mind:

Panic stop. Know the quickest and safest way to cut the engine in case you should run into an unexpected obstacle.

Blower declutch. With a dog-clutch drive to the blower you can tear things up by trying to engage a dead blower shaft with a spinning, main-drive shaft. Your instructions will give the proper sequence. You can also play hob with your blower by driving it into a garage or storage shed with the auger spinning.

Fuel shutoff. Some engines have none; others have a manual shutoff valve and a few have carburetor drains that dump a trickle of gas when stopping. Leaking gas in a closed, heated garage can spell danger. If you have a gas valve, get in the habit of closing it.

When spring finally arrives, take an hour or so to prepare your snow blower for summer:

- Get rid of all old gas in tank and carburetor. Run it dry, if necessary.
- Drain the oil; replace it with fresh.
- Grease and oil all bearings, chains.
- Replace the vee belts if they look worn.
- Replace the sparkplug.
- Oil the control linkages and Bowden wire cables.

Finally, if it was a hard season, have your repair agency look over the clutch and drive train before next fall's rush.

Install a snow-melting system

Stretch an electric cable out on your roof or embed a cable or hot fluid system in your sidewalk and you will do away with the drudgery of snow removal, prevent accidents and eliminate snow damage to your home

By PENELOPE ANGELL

■ HOW MANY TIMES have you grumbled to yourself about there "being a better way" as you headed outdoors, shovel in hand, to clean the walks? There *is* a better way. Snowmelting systems can be installed to keep ice and snow from accumulating on your roof and to clear your driveways and sidewalks.

Three types of snow-melting systems are available for home use: 1. Electric heating cable can be installed on your roof to eliminate snow dams on the overhang. 2. An electric heating cable system can be embedded in driveways and sidewalks. 3. A hydronic pipe system in which a heated mixture of antifreeze solution or hot oil

YOU CAN INSTALL heating cables on your roof with clips fastened under the shingles. About 2½ ft. of wire are needed per linear foot of roof. For installation in gutter or downspout, a straight run is sufficient. Install it before the snow starts falling.

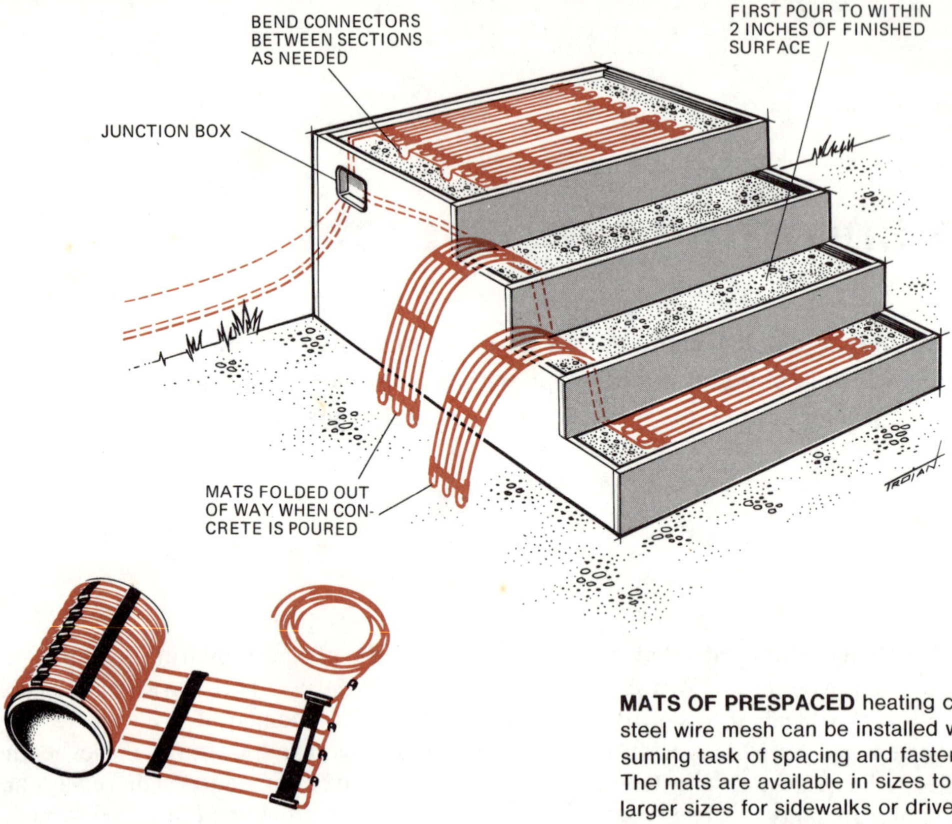

MATS OF PRESPACED heating cable embedded in steel wire mesh can be installed without the time-consuming task of spacing and fastening down each cable. The mats are available in sizes to fit a stair step, or in larger sizes for sidewalks or driveways from 1½ by 4½ ft. to 3 by 30 ft. Mats can be shaped to fit around odd-shaped obstacles.

circulates through the pipes to melt the snow can also be embedded in the pavement.

Heating cables can help prevent damage to the roof gutters and interior walls of your home. They melt the snow, eliminating heavy snow and ice accumulation on roof overhangs and stopping ice dams from forming in gutters and downspouts.

Ice and snow accumulations tend to develop particularly on homes with large roof overhangs that are not warmed by heat from the building interior. Snow dams are formed when sunshine and heat rising from the heated building partially melt ice and snow on the upper part of the roof. The slush runs down to the old gutter or unheated roof overhang where it again turns to ice and continues to collect. Beneath this buildup, water rises under the shingle tabs, spills over the back shingle edges and can drain through the layers of stapled felt paper, down the rafters, and onto interior ceilings and walls.

The cable that prevents these ice dams is an insulated wire that heats to melt the snow when electrical current flows through it. Available in varying lengths from 5 to over 160 feet, it can cost from 50 cents per foot for the short lengths to 25 cents per foot for the long ones. The cable and kits that include clips for fastening it to the shingles are available at hardware stores and electrical supply houses. Each length of cable is equipped with a cold lead wire, several feet long. It plugs into a waterproof outlet box, usually located near the eave. The cable operates on normal house current of 120 volts and consumes electricity at a rate of 6 to 16 watts per foot.

You should install the cable in a zigzag pattern along the roof edge. In this pattern about 2½ feet of wire are needed per linear foot of roof. For installation in gutter and downspout a straight run of wire is used. Where eaves don't overhang the house, you may only need cable in the gutter and downspout to melt the snow. If heating cables are used on either roof overhang or gutter, the downspout must also be heated to carry away the water from the melted snow and ice. A heated length of wire is dropped inside the downspout to the bottom (even if it is underground), using weights if necessary. All gutters and downspouts should be grounded to a driven ground rod.

The best way to provide electric current to the cable is to locate waterproof outlets on the exterior walls of your home fed by a No. 12 gauge or other heavy wire. Cables can't be shortened or spliced. Each length must be plugged in separately.

To turn on the system easily, a switch should be located inside the house. A pilot light that shines when the system is on is recommended to remind you to turn off the system when it's not needed.

heating cables in pavement

Melting snow and ice on driveways and sidewalks is easily done by means of heating cables embedded in the cement or asphalt. These cables are available either already prespaced in mats, or in individual lengths which can be laid down at spaced intervals.

Mats can be cut to follow contours or to curve around objects. However, care must be taken that the heater wire is not damaged in the process.

Cables are covered with plastic insulation which permits them to be buried directly into concrete or asphalt. Cold lead wires are attached to the heating cable. These lead wires must be long enough to reach a dry location for terminating.

Snow-melting systems are designed for average conditions. This means that during heavy downfalls the snow will accumulate slightly. You can minimize installation and operation cost by using two 18-inch-wide heat strips for the wheel tracks of your car, rather than a system to melt snow off the entire driveway. A mat 18 inches by 4½ feet costs approximately $30 without installation at the time this was written. Cost of two 18-inch-wide by 30-foot-long mats for a 30-foot driveway would be about $165. Cost of individual cables would be less.

You can install heating mats and lay individual cable yourself. A licensed electrician can wire and connect the units to the household electric supply. A reputable supplier of heating equipment can usually give adequate advice on the capacity needed for your situation and the method of connection. Manufacturers can also give helpful information.

The spacing of individual heating cables depends on the watts-per-square-foot required, which varies with the average number of hours and inches of snowfall per year in each area. Cable is usually rated at 10 watts per square foot. There are many variables involved in the cost of operation. Yearly operating cost in Chicago, for example, for a 30-foot-long driveway with 18-inch-wide mats for car tires, using a system consuming 40 watts per square foot would be about $26 at the time this was written.

When you install the cable, a lead wire must terminate at a junction box. The junction boxes can be placed in the slab where the cable is laid, or brought out to a main supply point. If boxes are exposed to weather they must be of the outdoor waterproof type as specified by the National Electric Code.

Wires can be laid when new cement or asphalt drives are built. To wire an existing asphalt drive, a cable-asphalt sandwich can be built.

hot fluid melting systems

An alternative to the electric cable method of melting snow from driveways and sidewalks, particularly for large homes and commerical use, is the hydronic pipe snow-melting system. Pipes are embedded in the pavement through which heated anti-freeze or oil circulates to melt snow.

The Hydronics Institute, 35 Russo Place, Berkeley Heights, NJ 07992, publishes a booklet containing information and procedure on installing a home hydronic system called *Snow Melting Calculation and Installation Guide for Residences* (No. S-40).

A standard system uses ¾-inch pipe on 12-inch centers buried within concrete, or on 9-inch centers in asphalt. These pipes are in S-shaped coils that can be connected by means of a supply and return main to a heat exchanger which is attached to the house heating boiler or auxiliary boiler.

Components needed for the system include a gas or oil-fired boiler, heat exchanger, heater pump, expansion tank, gauges, valves and controls, the pipe that circulates the liquid and the liquid. A boiler needed to melt snow on a 500-square-foot area would take up less space than a washing machine in your basement. Flexible polyolefin and rigid copper tube or wrought-iron pipes are among those used in the system. A thermostat is also suggested for heat control.

Some manufacturers provide a package arrangement including design, engineering, materials, labor, on-site inspection and a guarantee for installing the system. This package is the most trouble-free but also the most expensive. A homeowner who is handy could purchase needed materials and do his own installation for much less. However, it would be wise to employ a specialist for welding work if rigid pipe is used.

House too vapor-tight?
When we built our electrically-heated house, we made certain we had a vapor barrier installed under the dry wall in all walls and ceilings. In the winter, with the thermostat set in the mid sixties, the humidity level hovers around 60–65 percent. The dehumidifier doesn't seem to work well under these conditions. Even our Thermopane windows sweat, and we're now seeing signs of mildew. What should we do?—Richard Castor, Bedford, N.Y.

I assume your house has electrically-heated warm air, and as such, is too tight for the same air to be constantly recirculated. Fresh, cooler air must be introduced into your plenum, and provision made for eliminating the excess. Duct systems with automatic dampers can be installed. Such a system will alleviate your high winter humidity quickly.

Since I've outlined only the basics, a licensed mechanical engineer or heating contractor should be consulted for system design and layout.

White spots in the attic
Should roof vents be left open in winter? I have three vents and usually keep them closed in winter. But now I notice a white spotting on rafters and roof boards.—L. R. Osgood, Scranton, Pa.

Chances are the white spots are caused by condensation—a sure sign of inadequate ventilation. It is essential to leave ventilators open all year round. In winter, when warm, humid air rises and enters the attic, it contacts the cold roof and deposits its moisture. This condensed water can ultimately rot the wood. Louvers, placed at gable ends, vent the attic without undue heat loss. The size of the area that the louvers take up should be equal to 1/300th of the attic floor area.

Radiant heat cracks?
We love our electric radiant heat with cables buried in the ceiling plaster. However, in the summer, with the heat off, ugly cracks appear in the ceiling. When the heat is on, the cracks close tight. We've filled, taped and painted the ceiling to no avail. Would vinyl wall covering stick to this hot surface? No one seems to be able to supply an answer. Covering the ceiling of a 24-ft.-sq. room would be a bit expensive for experimentation.—William Schier, Three Oaks, Mich.

You've picked on the most comfortable type of heating, so I don't doubt you love it. Your cracks sound more like stress cracks caused by overspanned joists or improper bridging, even though they may follow cable layout patterns. I've spoken to Proko Industries, one of the largest suppliers of this type of heat. Although they haven't experienced cracks due to heat in their installations, they do stock a self-adhering tape that's applied over the cracks and a special heavy, pliable paint to cover the tape. The combination may work in your case.

I would shy away from the vinyl wall covering. If the vinyl is applied in the winter, there's a strong chance of the cracks opening and causing it to tear. If it's applied in the summer, closing cracks may crimp the vinyl.

Caulking quandary
Asbestos shingle siding extends over the foundation walls of my house by about 2 in. There appears to be another layer of shingles between the siding and the foundation. Can I caulk the gap between the inner layer and the foundation wall, or will I create condensation and moisture problems? Which type of caulking would you recommend?—Joseph Lynch, Yonkers, N.Y.

By all means, caulk. The area you mention is as important to the air tightness of your home's exterior "skin" as window and door trim. If the gap is too wide, you may want to prefill it with oakum, which is manufactured for this purpose. However, make certain the asbestos shingles still project at least ¼ in. below the caulking, so rain that drips off the shingles doesn't follow the caulking to the foundation wall. Although more expensive, use a caulking with a silicone base. Follow the manufacturer's instructions, and be sure to wear gloves when applying.

Talking floors
To avoid the cost of hardwood flooring 10 years ago, we carpeted directly over our plywood subfloor. Our floors now squeak constantly. Short of removing the carpeting, how can we correct this?—L.L. Jones, Royal Oak, Mich.

If your squeaking is widespread, the only solution is to roll back the carpet and underlying pad. Use 8d common nails every 6 in. along the edges of the plywood sheets, and every 12 in. on center in each panel's field.

Isolated squeaks can sometimes be eliminated by driving and setting 10d finishing nails through the carpet and underlying pad into the joist.

The joist location can usually be found from the ceiling below and transferred to the floor through careful measurement from a common reference point, like a wall or partition.

METRIC CONVERSION

Conversion factors can be carried so far they become impractical. In cases below where an entry is exact it is followed by an asterisk (*). Where considerable rounding off has taken place, the entry is followed by a + or a - sign.

CUSTOMARY TO METRIC

Linear Measure

inches	millimeters
1/16	1.5875*
1/8	3.2
3/16	4.8
1/4	6.35*
5/16	7.9
3/8	9.5
7/16	11.1
1/2	12.7*
9/16	14.3
5/8	15.9
11/16	17.5
3/4	19.05*
13/16	20.6
7/8	22.2
15/16	23.8
1	25.4*

inches	centimeters
1	2.54*
2	5.1
3	7.6
4	10.2
5	12.7*
6	15.2
7	17.8
8	20.3
9	22.9
10	25.4*
11	27.9
12	30.5

feet	centimeters	meters
1	30.48*	.3048*
2	61	.61
3	91	.91
4	122	1.22
5	152	1.52
6	183	1.83
7	213	2.13
8	244	2.44
9	274	2.74
10	305	3.05
50	1524*	15.24*
100	3048*	30.48*

1 yard =
.9144* meters
1 rod =
5.0292* meters
1 mile =
1.6 kilometers
1 nautical mile =
1.852* kilometers

Fluid Measure

(Milliliters [ml] and cubic centimeters [cc or cu cm] are equivalent, but it is customary to use milliliters for liquids.)

1 cu in = 16.39 ml
1 fl oz = 29.6 ml
1 cup = 237 ml
1 pint = 473 ml
1 quart = 946 ml
= .946 liters
1 gallon = 3785 ml
= 3.785 liters
Formula (exact):
fluid ounces × 29.573 529 562 5* = milliliters

Weights

ounces	grams
1	28.3
2	56.7
3	85
4	113
5	142
6	170
7	198
8	227
9	255
10	283
11	312
12	340
13	369
14	397
15	425
16	454

Formula (exact):
ounces × 28.349 523 125* = grams

pounds	kilograms
1	.45
2	.9
3	1.4
4	1.8
5	2.3
6	2.7
7	3.2
8	3.6
9	4.1
10	4.5

1 short ton (2000 lbs) =
907 kilograms (kg)
Formula (exact):
pounds × .453 592 37* = kilograms

Volume

1 cu in = 16.39 cubic centimeters (cc)
1 cu ft = 28 316.7 cc
1 bushel = 35 239.1 cc
1 peck = 8 809.8 cc

Area

1 sq in = 6.45 sq cm
1 sq ft = 929 sq cm
= .093 sq meters
1 sq yd = .84 sq meters
1 acre = 4 046.9 sq meters
= .404 7 hectares
1 sq mile = 2 589 988 sq meters
= 259 hectares
= 2.589 9 sq kilometers

Kitchen Measure

1 teaspoon = 4.93 milliliters (ml)
1 Tablespoon = 14.79 milliliters (ml)

Miscellaneous

1 British thermal unit (Btu) (mean)
= 1 055.9 joules
1 calorie (mean) = 4.19 joules
1 horsepower = 745.7 watts
= .75 kilowatts
caliber (diameter of a firearm's bore in hundredths of an inch)
= .254 millimeters (mm)
1 atmosphere pressure = 101 325* pascals (newtons per sq meter)
1 pound per square inch (psi) = 6 895 pascals
1 pound per square foot = 47.9 pascals
1 knot = 1.85 kilometers per hour
25 miles per hour = 40.2 kilometers per hour
50 miles per hour = 80.5 kilometers per hour
75 miles per hour = 120.7 kilometers per hour